A LONG DREAM OF HOME

Praise for the Book

A Long Dream of Home is poignant, passionate and beautifully told. It fills a crucial gap in the Kashmir discourse – the story of Pandits forced into exile - and these deeply personal essays are essential reading for anyone who wants to understand the turmoil of Jammu and Kashmir.

– **Barkha Dutt,** *Journalist and Author*

A Long Dream of Home reminds us of one of postcolonial India's most unregarded tragedies: the genocidal persecution and expulsion of a religious minority from its homeland, while the State and the country looked on. Through the testimony of victims and the memoirs of survivors, Siddhartha Gigoo and Varad Sharma present the harrowing experience of the Kashmiri Pandits since 1990, the portrait of a community that has suffered both exile and an indifference to their anguish. The story of the expulsion of the Pandits is one of the many interlocking narratives about contemporary Kashmir. Unfortunately, it has not received the empathetic attention it merits. Siddhartha Gigoo and Varad Sharma remind us that the true principle at stake is that, in a state that aspires to be a liberal democracy, the interests of any minority community must be safeguarded against the pressures exerted by any majority community, no matter what the specific ethnic or religious identity of these communities. The tragedy of the Kashmiri Pandits is that they have been misleadingly presented as members of an imagined majority, while actually leading the lives of an imperiled minority.

– **Ranjit Hoskote,** *Poet and Cultural Theorist*

A Long Dream of Home belongs on the same shelf as Manto and Levi, for it is a book forged from quivering hands, frayed nerves, and broken hearts; and yet the pen that delivers it is remarkably steady. The prose is laconic; each word has its own density. *A Long Dream of Home* is a necessary book. It is a book that must be read and re-read.

– **Anand Rangnathan,** *Author and Columnist*

Siddhartha Gigoo and Varad Sharma have compiled emotional reflections of Kashmiri Pandits who suffered, making this book a community's call for attention to its plight.

– **Lt. Gen. (Retd.) Syed Ata Hasnain,**
Former GOC (XV Corps and XXI Corps), Indian Army

A LONG DREAM OF HOME

The persecution, exodus and exile of Kashmiri Pandits

Edited by

Siddhartha Gigoo
Varad Sharma

BLOOMSBURY
NEW DELHI • LONDON • OXFORD • NEW YORK • SYDNEY

BLOOMSBURY INDIA
Bloomsbury Publishing India Pvt. Ltd
Second Floor, LSC Building No. 4, DDA Complex, Pocket C – 6 & 7,
Vasant Kunj New Delhi 110070

BLOOMSBURY, BLOOMSBURY INDIA and the Diana logo are trademarks of Bloomsbury Publishing Plc

First published in India 2015
This edition published 2018

ISBN 978 93 87146 06 8

2 4 6 8 10 9 7 5 3 1

Printed and bound in India by Replika Press Pvt. Ltd.

To find out more about our authors and books visit www.bloomsbury.com and sign up for our newsletters

For Omkar Nath Gigoo, Uma Shori Gigoo, Pushkar Nath Dhar, Pushpa Dhar, Prabhawati Sharma, Prem Nath Sharma, Mohini Pandita and Niranjan Nath Pandita.

In memory of the countless Pandits who perished in exile hoping to return to their homeland, Kashmir.

Imagine living in a strange dark city for twenty years.
– Carol Ann Duffy, *Foreign*

When I look ahead I only look back, when I stare at the paper
I only see the past.
– Imre Kertesz, *Kaddish for an Unborn Child*

And the last remnants memory destroys.
– W G Sebald, *The Immigrants*

Contents

Preface to the Second Edition

The first edition of this book came out in December 2015. Since then very little has happened as far as the displaced Kashmiri Pandits' return to their homeland, Kashmir, is concerned, but much has happened in Kashmir. The situation there has worsened. Kashmir's timeline of the past two years continues to be scarred with bloody events. The summers of 2016 and 2017 were the bloodiest. The voices of Islamist fundamentalists and separatists seeking Kashmir's secession from India have grown louder. While the displaced Pandits' longing for 'home' has deepened, the hope in their hearts has started to tremble, given the unabated proliferation of terrorism and the terrorists' call for jihad in Kashmir.

In July 2016, in Haal (Pulwama), Vessu (Kulgam) and Nutnasu (Kupwara) a series of disturbing incidents took place at the transit camps set up for the Pandit youths employed under the Prime Minister's Return, Relief and Rehabilitation Package 2008. The Pandits living in these transit camps were threatened and attacked by raging mobs of Muslims. Over 1,600 Pandit employees along with their families lived in these camps at the time. Once again, the clamour for the ouster of Pandits from Kashmir was heard and felt by the people living inside the camps. The incidents shattered Kashmiri Pandits worldwide, particularly those who had taken up government employment in Kashmir. They had hoped to be eventually rehabilitated along with their families despite the socio-political uncertainties. On 31 August 2016, Islamists burnt down four residential quarters of Pandits in Nutnasu, Kupwara. Fearing for their lives, almost all Pandits who were living in the camps fled Kashmir once again. The attacks on them proved that they were unwelcome in their own land. The messages conveyed that Kashmir was for Muslims only and that Pandits would not be spared if they tried to reclaim their homeland.

A young author, who has contributed an essay to this book, was in one of the transit camps at the time of the attack. He was to join a job in a government department. He recalls the night of terror: 'My worst fears have come true,' he writes in his diary. 'Terrorism has intensified. Stone-pelters and terrorists are attacking our camp. They are asking us to leave Kashmir. What kind of a homecoming has the government thrust on us? Once again, we're being forced to leave our homeland. We're the twice-displaced people. I will return to Jammu now, and do something else.' The fear of being attacked in Kashmir still looms in his heart. He wishes to remain unnamed because the fear persists. Many youngsters, who spent their early years in squalid camps in Jammu, were given jobs in Kashmir, and then were forced to leave Kashmir once again and return to the camps. He, too, dangles between two 'homes'—a long-lost home in Kashmir and the one in Jammu where, after the exodus in 1990, he spent his exiled childhood. His has been a life of strange departures and arrivals.

A woman, whose relatives were massacred by militants in Wandhama in 1998, lives in a camp at Buta Nagar in Jammu. She suffers alone, carrying the burden of the martyrdom of her relatives. In 2016, Sagar Pandita lost his mother, Fancy Pandita. Fancy was 42 years old. She, too, lived in the camp at Buta Nagar in Jammu.

On 19 January 2017, the government of Jammu and Kashmir adopted a resolution calling for the return and rehabilitation of Pandits. Within hours, the Kashmiri separatists warned the government against having separate colonies for Pandits. For days, the separatists held protests and gave statements against the Pandits' rehabilitation in Kashmir.

On 24 July 2017, the Supreme Court of India dismissed a public interest litigation that sought a fair and independent investigation into the killings of Kashmiri Pandits that took place during 1990s and early 2000. 'We decline to entertain this petition under Article 32 of the Constitution of India, for the simple reason that the instances referred to in the present petition pertain to the year 1989-90, and more than 27 years have passed by since then. No fruitful purpose would emerge, as evidence is unlikely to be available at this late juncture,' said the Apex Court. The killers still roam free.

On 17 July 2017, Jai Kishan Sharma (Varad Sharma's father) lost his battle to cancer. He was 64. A Sanskritist and scholar of Kashmir Shaivism, he dreamt of returning to his village, Akura, in Kashmir. Like many others who died pining for their homeland, his dream, too, remained unfulfilled. Before passing away, he wrote about his village. His memoir, *The River of My Lost Village*, appears in this edition of the book.

Over the last 27 years, an entire generation of Pandits was wiped out in camps. In a few years, we will be left with nothing but residue. This residue will cast a long shadow over the history of Kashmir.

Pandits dream of the land where they wish to return and resettle once again and rebuild their homes and temples that were destroyed by those who banished them in 1990. They dream of sowing new seeds of settlement, leading happy lives and dying in peace.

The challenges before us as a community are manifold. How do we keep the exile consciousness alive? How do we pass on the story of our persecution and exodus to successive generations? More importantly, how do we sing the songs of our homeland in unison like the Jews have done for centuries?

The losses Pandits have been made to incur are unimaginable. Yet, there have been gains. Our sufferings during the past 27 years have led to an immeasurable understanding of human morality and existence. And, like Imre Kertész says, if we preserve this wealth, it will enrich the consciousness of future generations of Pandits who will have nothing but an inherited memory to rely upon for an understanding of their ancestry and age-old history.

This year, India celebrated her 70th year of Independence. The young celebrated with gaiety and fanfare, while those who witnessed the horrors of the Partition in 1947 commemorated silently. Kashmir continues to be a place where its original inhabitants—the Pandits—are neither welcome nor allowed to re-settle. India's stature as an emerging global superpower means little to the displaced Pandits who are still made to live and die far from their homeland.

Undeterred by adversities, the displaced Kashmiri Pandits continue to be resilient and resurgent. The fight for justice will not end. It's the dream of home that keeps the Pandits alive.

We find solace in the words of the Kashmiri Pandit poet, Dina Nath 'Nadim':

mye chham aash pagahich
pagah sholi duniyah
(I have hope for tomorrow,
The world will glisten tomorrow.)

Siddhartha Gigoo and Varad Sharma
December 2017
New Delhi and Jammu

Preface to the First Edition

Over the centuries, the Hindus of Kashmir (known by the exonym 'Pandits') have faced persecution by successive Muslim rulers. From 1389 to 1413, Sultan Sikandar 'Butshikan' (destroyer of idols), descendant of Shah Mir, founder of the Shah Miri dynasty of Kashmir, unleashed a reign of terror, imposing jizya (poll tax), ravaging ancient temples and forcibly converting Pandits to Islam. He established Sikandarpora on the ruins of the temples which he razed to the ground. To escape religious conversion, thousands of Pandits fled to Kishtwar and Bhadarwah in Jammu region. Those who didn't leave or refused to be converted to Islam were burned alive at a place near Rainawari in Srinagar. Even today, the place is known as Bhatta Mazar (the graveyard of the Pandits). From 1413 to 1420, Butshikan's eldest son, Noor Khan (who assumed the title Sultan Ali Shah) continued his father's policy of intolerance towards Pandits. Noor Khan's brother, Zain-ul-Abidin (Budshah), succeeded to the throne in 1420. Pandit Shri Bhat, a physician who cured the king of a disease, influenced him to turn sympathetic towards Pandits. Zain-ul-Abidin abolished the jizya and allowed the Pandits to rebuild their temples. Pandits flourished under his rule which lasted fifty years. Thereafter, the Chak and the Mughal dynasties took over. The repression continued during their rules especially during Aurangzeb's reign from 1658 to 1707.

The period from 1753 to 1819 was another dark period in the history of Kashmir. During this time, Afghans under Ahmad Shah Durrani ruled Kashmir and persecuted Pandits by reintroducing jizya and forcing them to embrace Islam. The Afghan rulers made oppression of Pandits their political policy. In 1819, Mirza Pandit Dhar and Pandit Birbal Dhar, who were revenue collectors under the zealot Afghan governor Azim Khan, secretly persuaded Maharaja Ranjit Singh of Lahore to annex Kashmir to bring an end to the Afghan rule. Maharaja Ranjit Singh's forces under Diwan Chand, Gulab Singh of Jammu and Hari Singh Nalwa defeated the last Afghan governor Jabbar Khan. From 1819 to 1947, Kashmir was under the Sikh and Dogra regimes.

In October 1947, during Maharaja Hari Singh's rule, tribal militias from Pakistan's North-West Frontier Province, supported by the Pakistani army, invaded Kashmir, killing hundreds of Hindus. To save Kashmir from Pakistani aggression and an imminent occupation, Maharaja Hari Singh signed the Instrument of Accession with India on 26 October 1947, paving the way for the Indian Army to enter Kashmir to defeat the invaders.

With the eruption of Pakistan-sponsored armed insurgency in Kashmir in 1989, Pandits became soft targets for the militant outfits who wanted to wipe out the 'Indian element' and liberate Kashmir from India. Many Pandits were on the hit lists of several militant groups. The night of 19 January 1990 was one of terror for Pandits. Kashmir resonated with anti-India and anti-Pandit slogans. Mass protests and violent clashes between militants/ protestors and security forces crippled the state administration. The law and order situation collapsed.

In April 1990, Hizb-ul Mujahideen, a militant outfit gave the Pandits an ultimatum to leave Kashmir in 36 hours or face dire consequences. Suspicion, betrayal and mistrust divided the Muslims and the Pandits. Both the communities stood divided on religious and ideological lines. Militants kidnapped and killed several ordinary and prominent Kashmiri Pandits. This created so much panic and fear among the Pandit families that they started leaving their homes in Kashmir. Some, who didn't want to leave, sent their children away and lingered on in their homes for some time, hoping that the turmoil would end. Some of the Pandits managed to carry a few belongings while most left empty-handed in terror, unable to pack even their necessary household possessions. The security forces including the police were unable to provide protection to the minority community. The authorities in the state and the centre made no effort to prevent the atrocities committed against the Pandits. Targeted kidnappings and killings, rapes and massacres of Pandits who lingered on became a routine affair. The massacre of Pandits by militants in Sangrampora, Budgam in March 1997, Gool in June 1997, Wandhama near Ganderbal in January 1998 and Nadimarg, Pulwama in March 2003, made it clear that Pandits were not safe in their own land.

By the end of 1990, about half a million Pandits had left their homes in Kashmir. The displaced people sought refuge in Jammu and adjoining districts. Thousands found shelter in temples, sheds, barns, canvas tents and schools. Many others took rooms on rent. The role played by the people of Jammu was commendable at those critical times. The displaced, jobless Pandits, many of them agriculturists, lived on the meagre dole given to them by the government. They suffered in 'migrant camps' and private rented accommodations in Jammu and nearby districts. The camp-dwellers lived in deplorable conditions in canvas tents and ramshackle one-room tenements that lacked even basic civic amenities. In these cramped spaces there was neither privacy nor security and safety. It was a life of degradation, deprivation and indignity. Year after year, the exiles struggled, nurturing hope and battling a deep sense of alienation and desolation. Thousands perished due to diseases, mental sicknesses, heat strokes, sunstrokes, hostile climatic conditions and accidents.

During the nineties, Kashmir passed through its darkest years of conflict and political upheaval in contemporary history. The popular uprising of the Muslims of Kashmir against the Indian state was met with force by the security forces. Hartals, 'civil curfews', mass protests, stone-pelting, bomb blasts, encounters, strikes, violent clashes between the militants and the security forces, army crackdowns and detentions, became a way of life in Kashmir. Army and paramilitary forces launched full-scale operations to curb militancy. Thousands of Kashmiri Muslims—young and old—lost their lives. Kashmir became one of the most militarised zones in the world and a very dangerous place to live and visit. The cycle of protests and violence continues even now. There is no political solution in sight to restore peace, stability and normalcy in Kashmir.

The exodus of Kashmiri Pandits remains one of the darkest chapters in the history of contemporary India. 1990 (when the exodus started) is a watershed year in the history of Kashmiri Pandits. The year 2015 marked the 25th year of their exile. While many Kashmiri Pandits are settled in different parts of India and some other countries, several thousands are still languishing in the township for the displaced at Jagti near Nagrota and in other camps in the Jammu province of the J&K state. They continue to live as refugees in their own country, still unsure about where they belong. Constantly plagued by a sense of humiliation and displacement, their long-cherished desire for a peaceful return is still unfulfilled. Even today they oscillate between despair and hope, and pray for normalcy to return to Kashmir.

In the current political scenario Pandits are a forgotten entity. The young and the middle-aged visit Kashmir as tourists and pilgrims now. About two thousand youths have been given non-transferable jobs in government departments in Kashmir. They live in rented and transit accommodations in their own land because there are no homes to go back to anymore. They can't take their families there. Thousands of houses abandoned by the Pandits lie in a dilapidated condition. Hundreds of temples in Kashmir have been destroyed.

Kashmir, ravaged by two-and-a-half decades of terrorism, militancy and counter-insurgency, continues to be a flashpoint between India and Pakistan. The displaced and homeless Pandits, who are the original inhabitants of Kashmir, find themselves caught in a vortex. There hasn't been much progress on their return to and rehabilitation in Kashmir. Their demand for truth, reconciliation and justice has remained unheard for years.

This book marks the end of twenty-five long years of silence of a community whose predicaments, ordeals and valid demands have not only been forgotten by the nation, but also not even addressed adequately by successive governments. The stories of the struggles and plights of Kashmiri Pandit exiles have remained untold. The old are fading away, taking away with them the untold stories—stories of who they were, what they faced, what they lost, how they struggled and what remains now. Those who were born and brought up in exile are struggling to understand their own identities and the history of their elders. It is this burden of history that they will have to carry for the rest of their lives.

The writers of the memoirs in this anthology belong to three generations—the old and the middle-aged who were born and brought up in Kashmir, and forced to leave while they were in their forties, fifties and sixties; those who got displaced in their teens; and those who were born in migrant camps in exile. The young generation of Pandits born and brought up in exile is living off an inherited memory.

This book is divided into four sections. *Part I: Nights of Terror* features narratives about what Pandits witnessed and faced in Kashmir from 1989 to 1991. *Part II: Summers of Exile* features memoirs about how the displaced Pandits struggled to survive during the past two and a half decades in exile. *Part III: Days of Parting* features memoirs about the horrific events and circumstances leading to the mass exodus of Pandits from Kashmir. The writings in *Part IV: Seasons of Longing* reveal the longing and desire of the Pandits to return to their homes in Kashmir.

Indu Bushan Zutshi's *She was killed because she was an informant; no harm will come to you* is an account of the persecution of a Pandit family in Anantnag in the spring of 1990 after militants had kidnapped and murdered a nurse, his neighbour, working at the Sher-i-Kashmir Institute of Medical Sciences in Soura, Srinagar. In *One day Kashmir will become part of Pakistan. What will you do that day?* Pradeep Kaul writes how several global events shaped, fuelled and reinforced the anti-India and anti-Hindu sentiment of Kashmiri Muslims and paved the way for militancy and the expulsion of Pandits. In *It is for your own good to leave*, Kundan Lal Chowdhury talks about his life from 1989 to 1990 and the militants' directive to Pandits to leave Kashmir. In *If we're killed, the gold buried in the earth under that apple tree belongs to you*, Ashok Pandit reveals that his brother was one of the seventeen Pandits whose names were on the hit list of a militant group in their village in Handwara, Kashmir. In *Ya Allah, they have killed them; pour some water into their mouths*, Adarsh Ajit describes how his friendship with Muslim friends turned bitter owing to their differences in political ideology and religious belief. He also writes about the killings of his friends and some officers of the Indian Air Force by 'mujahids'. In *When the time in the clocks was made to go back by half an hour*, Bushan Lal Saraf narrates an account of the days when the time in the clocks and watches in Kashmir was made to go back by half an hour to synchronize with the Pakistan Standard Time. He also recounts how militants killed prominent people including a Communist leader and an engineer. Susheel Pajnu, in *Mata Roop Bhawani will protect us*, writes about his skirmishes with militants and sheds light on what it means to be the only Pandit family living in downtown Srinagar. He hints at the price they have paid for living there. In *Nights of Terror,* Meenakshi Raina recalls living through several nights of terror in their house in Srinagar in January 1990, and reveals the ordeals of her father during his tenure at Doordarshan Kendra in Kashmir. In *Summers of Exile,* Sushant Dhar paints a haunting picture of the horrors of camp life. In *My House of Stone*, Neeru Kaul talks about the transformation she undergoes upon visiting her old house in Kashmir after twenty-two years. In *Season of Ashes,* Siddhartha Gigoo recollects the last days of his grandfather who died of Alzheimer's in exile and his grandmother who died when her family took her to Kashmir to visit their ancestral house in Srinagar. In *From Home to Camp,* Santosh Kumar Sani reveals that his family, after being threatened by militants, left their home in Pattan, Baramulla and lived in a camp at Purkhoo. Sani also describes the conditions in which the displaced Pandits live at the largest settlement for the Kashmiri Pandit exiles in Jagti, Nagrota. BL Zutshi, in *Camp Schools and Colleges for the Displaced Students*, writes about the struggle of the displaced school and college lecturers to establish camp schools and colleges for the displaced students in the Jammu province in the early 1990s. In *Life in the Camp,* Pyari Dhar, Sagar Pandita and Vishali Dhar share their experiences of living in a migrant camp for twenty years. In *Days of Parting,* Arvind Gigoo recounts the societal and political changes in downtown Srinagar before and during the turbulent period, paints a disturbing picture of his struggles in exile and sums up with two open letters addressed to Kashmiri Muslims and Pandits. In his account, Pran Kishore describes the conditions in which he and his production team shot the television serial *Gul Gulshan Gulfam* in Srinagar despite threats from militants in 1989. In *Dear brother, our part in this story is over,* Tej N Dhar describes how he was forced to leave Kashmir because he was on the 'radar' of militant groups. In *The Fatal Seconds*, PL Waguzari narrates how Ratnipora, an idyllic village, where only twenty Pandit families lived, became infested with Islamic fundamentalists in 1989. Waguzari also describes the killing of his friend and neighbour. In *My Home! My Home!* Maharaj Krishen Koul Naqaib describes the people's attitude that became the cause of his family's migration. Rattan Lal Shant's *Roses Shed Fragrance* is an account of the twelve days he and his wife spent holed up in fear, isolation and gloom in their own home in Srinagar because they were not welcome in Kashmir after a brief stay in

Delhi. Shant also recounts the horror of escaping three attempts on his life. Kashi Nath Pandita's *Merge, Leave or Perish* starts with an account of the murder of the Kashmiri Pandit leader, Tika Lal Taploo, and describes the events which led to the exodus of Pandits. In *The Knights of Shiva*, Rajesh Dhar narrates how some people misbehaved with three Pandit girls when they were about to leave Kashmir. Namrata Wakhloo's *The Pomegranate Tree* is an account of her parents who sent their relatives away to Jammu in 1990, but refused to leave their home in Srinagar despite threats from militants. *The Day I Became a Tourist in My Own Home* is Minakshi Watts' tribute to her homeland, Kashmir, where she went after twenty-three years as a tourist. In *Seasons of Longing*, Prithvi Nath Kabu narrates an account of the days when Pakistani raiders entered Kashmir in 1947 and raided their village in Baramulla. He also talks about his life in exile after the killing of his son by militants in Gool. Varad Sharma in *The Inheritance of Memory* describes the conditions in which his family migrated from Kashmir, and explores how an inherited memory has become his only connection with Kashmir where he can't return. In *Why I Established Radio Sharda*, Ramesh Hangloo talks about how, after leaving Kashmir, he started a community radio service for the Pandit exiles so that their bonds with Kashmiri Pandit culture could remain alive. Badri Raina in *Remembering the Unforgettable: Kashmir as She Made Me* traces his own journey from his early childhood to youth in Kashmir, and captures his experiences during his repeated visits there. In *An Imaginary Identity*, Nikhil Koul recollects his earliest memories of his family's exodus from Kashmir and his own growing up in exile. He also describes how the memory of past events lives in the consciousness of the younger generation of Pandits.

We thank the authors for writing these memoirs. We're immensely indebted to Arvind Gigoo for his support, and to Himanjali Sankar and Rajeev Beri at Bloomsbury India for their belief. Without their encouragement and assistance, little would have been possible.

Siddhartha Gigoo
Varad Sharma
December 2015

PART I

NIGHTS OF TERROR

'Loot, plunder, arson, mayhem, murder, exodus: these words recurred day after day, and a phrase from another part of the world that had flown many thousands of miles to find a new home in Kashmir.

"Ethnic cleansing."

"Kill one, scare ten. Kill one, scare ten."

Hindu community houses, temples, private homes and whole neighbourhoods were being destroyed…

Kill one, scare ten, the Muslim mobs chanted, and ten were, indeed, scared.'

– Salman Rushdie, *Shalimar the Clown*

1

She was killed because she was an informant; no harm will come to you

Indu Bushan Zutshi

It was 20 April 1990, and the sun was shining that day. People were in the process of emerging out of the harsh winter that had just ended and preparing for springtime. Normally such times were most suited for going out on picnics, but curfew and the widespread infiltration of militants and terrorists from across the border with Pakistan into the Kashmir valley prevented people from making such forays.

Anantnag was under curfew. On some days when the violence was unmanageable for the police, shoot-on-sight orders were given. People's movements were totally restricted to their homes. One morning in April, as I looked out of the window of my room, I saw a vegetable vendor, who lived nearby, returning from the main road with a cart full of unsold vegetables. He was forced to return because curfew had been imposed. He was visibly annoyed and was belching invectives. His immediate neighbour, Gulama, politely advised him to keep quiet. The hapless vendor retorted, 'How shall I feed my family when I am not allowed to go to work? It is curfew day today. This movement will hurt the poor people like us. We will die of starvation. God should save us now.'

Because of curfew, offices, schools, colleges and business establishments shut down indefinitely. In the afternoon I heard somebody weeping and wailing outside in the street. The screams punctured the deafening silence in the neighbourhood. Some neighbours stepped out of their houses and assembled in the narrow street to find out what was going on. All of us came out into the street, and saw our neighbour, Shambu Nath Bhat, a teacher by profession, weeping hysterically and inconsolably. 'They have killed her. They have killed Sarla. They have murdered my daughter,' he sobbed uncontrollably. One of his relatives, Prithvi Nath, along with a police officer who had brought the news to him, was trying to pacify him and asking him to go back to his house. This father of the slain girl could not be consoled or comforted, and continued crying and weeping. The police official informed us that Sarla Bhat had been killed in Srinagar.

It had been a Pandit-majority mohalla, but at that time, counting Shambu Nath's, only three Pandit families lived there. All other Pandit families had fled their houses in the mohalla because of death threats issued by the militants in our area, and the social distrust that had started manifesting itself in various forms, with a section of Muslim youths taunting the Pandit minority and spreading venom against them. The war cries and the frenzied religious slogans in the mass rallies and protests, which often were violent, had started unnerving the minorities. The clashes between the protestors and the security forces used to turn violent with stone-pelting and crossfire. In this frenzied atmosphere, the terrifying news of the murder of our neighbour's daughter was a shock to all three Pandit families in the mohalla. Our Muslim neighbours came out of their homes to console the bereaved family. They expressed their anger and disapproval of the senseless killing of an unmarried girl. Sarla Bhat was working as a nurse at Sher-i-Kashmir Institute of Medical Sciences in Soura, Srinagar. She had been going to work even during the peak of militancy in Srinagar.

Somehow, we dragged Shambu Nath back to his house. Inside the house, his wife and younger son sat huddled in shock and grief. There was a lot of commotion. The neighbours were trying to comfort the parents of the slain girl. Shambu Nath's son was seething with anger and outrage, yet his agitation was overcome by the grief that had befallen the family.

The Muslim police officer who had come to convey the news seemed to be a pious and God-fearing man. Through him we came to know that Sarla Bhat, working as a staff nurse at the Sher-i-Kashmir Institute of

Medical Sciences in Soura, had been abducted from her hostel on April 15. On the morning of April 19, her mutilated dead body was found in the downtown area of Srinagar. A hand-written note was attached to her body, describing her as a police informant. Sarla Bhat had remained in the custody of terrorists for four days. The Police officer further informed us that her body would be sent from Srinagar to Khannabal police station from where the police personnel would bring it to be handed over to her parents in our locality in Anantnag.

In his state of sorrow, Shambu Nath asked us to convey the news to his uncle, Sham Lal Bhat, who lived about two kilometers away in an adjacent mohalla. There weren't any telephones in the neighbourhood, and going out during curfew was risky and impossible, yet my brother and another Pandit neighbour volunteered to meet the commander of the Border Security Force deployed in our area to seek his help in the matter. They went to the concerned commander and told him about the incident. The Commander, a Punjabi officer, listened patiently and provided a vehicle. The two volunteers were taken to Sham Lal Bhat's house. Later, the vehicle brought all of them back to Shambu Nath's house.

This going and coming took nearly two hours. By the time Shambu Nath's uncle's family reached his place, a very strange incident had occurred. We noticed that all our Muslim neighbours, who had been part of the gathering and who were equally aggrieved by the death of an innocent girl, had disappeared. This alarmed us. The terror-stricken Pandits present there became doubtful and suspicious. Shambu Nath's family was left alone to grieve. None of our Muslim neighbours were in sight. Leave this out? It has just been mentioned that the Muslim neighbours had disappeared and Shambu Nath and his family were grieving alone. We sensed that the sudden disappearance of our neighbours was a signal that we should not expect any help or support from them in case the militants came to terrorise us. Shambu Nath felt that even he would not be spared.

Sham Lal Bhat's arrival provided the much-needed consolation to the three Pandit families living in the mohalla. In his presence we felt relieved. He was an elderly man who was regarded as a guide in such critical, desperate and life-threatening situations. Thereafter, we waited for Sarla Bhat's body. The long and lacerating wait for the body ended at ten in the night when a police vehicle brought the body. We were horrified to see the body when it was handed over to Shambu Nath. It was bullet-ridden and covered with blood. There were torture marks all over the body. It became clear to us that she had been violated and sexually assaulted before being killed.

Sarla Bhat was in her mid-twenties. Her tormentors and killers had put an end to her dreams and life. The police took away the clothes she was wearing and handed over the body to Shambu Nath after obtaining a receipt from him.

The ensuing night was nothing but a nightmare for all of us. We placed Sarla Bhat's cold body on the floor. The skin was a mess. Her parents and relatives spent the night crying. The rest of us sat in a corner thinking of ways to do the cremation in the prevailing conditions. We didn't know how to arrange firewood and other necessary items for cremation. We wanted the funerary rituals and the last rites to be carried out without any problems. Everything was shut because of the curfew. We had seen the apathetic attitude of our Muslim neighbours.

Later, we came to know that our Muslim neighbours in the mohalla had been instructed by the local militants not to offer any help to us. The grip of terror was so strong that not even one from the majority community came forward to help. Everyone stayed away. After careful deliberation, we decided to go to another mohalla nearby where only one Pandit family lived. We made it to Dwarka Nath's house in the dead of night and sought his support in arranging timber from a temple compound in Nagbal. Dwarka Nath owned a cart. He assured us that he would bring the timber the next morning. He met the BSF personnel on duty, and reached our mohalla at dawn on 21 April with a cart full of timber.

Then we started preparing for cremation. There was no priest to perform the rites, no flowers or incense, no other material normally used during the last rites. We feared for ourselves. It was not safe to take the body to the cremation ground because the entire locality was infested with militants who had warned the local Muslims against helping us. So we decided to cremate Sarla Bhat on the bank of a rivulet near our mohalla. We gave her a last bath. We cleaned the blood on her body. We didn't have any flowers to place on the body. Shambu Nath caressed the body of his daughter for the last time. He cried as he placed a shawl on her. We placed the body on a wooden plank to be taken away for cremation. Eight of us carried the body on our shoulders to the spot which we had identified for cremation. As we were rushing through the rites, two youths came to the spot and instructed us to stop the cremation and go back to our houses. These youths told us that Sarla Bhat was a police informer and the militants didn't want anyone to cremate her. All of us felt unnerved, and did not know what to do. We pleaded and begged. After some time, the youths left. Perhaps they sensed our misery and distress and became sympathetic. We rushed through the last rites and cremated Sarla Bhat in barely an hour. Performing all the rituals was not possible.

To escape being noticed, we took a different route consisting of narrow and dingy lanes to go back to our mohalla. None of us wanted to be identified as the ones who cremated Sarla Bhat.

Upon returning to my house, I collected some food and took it to the bereaved family. The women told me that some neighbours had come to the house and advised them not to go to Shambu Nath's house.

The next day, I avoided going to Shambu Nath's house, even though I wanted to. The advice from my neighbours kept me from going there. On April 22, the curfew was lifted. I went to my office, and on my way there I met Sham Lal. He inquired about Shambu Nath's family. I told him that I had been advised by the neighbours not to meet Shambu Nath. Sham Lal told me that Shambu Nath and his family had left Kashmir quietly. I was surprised to hear this. 'When, how?' I asked. He held my arm and took me aside. 'A grenade was hurled at his house last night, and later the police escorted his entire family to Khannabal from where they boarded a bus to Jammu. Luckily, the grenade didn't explode.'

After Shambu Nath's departure, the last two Pandit families in our mohalla lost all hope. They feared that they would be killed. On April 30, I stepped out of my house along with Dwarka Nath Bakshi of the other Pandit family of our mohalla to purchase some eatables. Both of us were depressed and sad. We thought that the end was near. At the bazaar we met Gulam Hassan, our neighbour. He expressed his condolence and sorrow at the death of Sarla Bhat, but at the same time accused her of being a police informant and an agent. 'She was killed because she was an informant,' he said. We did not react to his preposterous and vile assertions, and he went on to inform us that twenty more mukhbirs (informants) were to be handed the same fate by the freedom fighters. 'Don't worry. No harm will come to you. You're safe here,' he went on.

On May 4 1990, the last two Pandit families (Dwarka Nath's and mine) in our mohalla left. We went to Jammu and joined Shambu Nath and his family.

2

One day Kashmir will become part of Pakistan. What will you do that day?

Pradeep Kaul (Khudballi)

Pandits have been the original inhabitants of Kashmir. Ours is a chronicled history of 5000 years. Having been forced out of Kashmir in 1990 because of the armed insurgency, we are now nothing but a non-entity. If one were to sum up our history over the last 25 years, it would be this: We were persecuted and hounded out of our homes by the majority community, which wanted Kashmir to merge with Pakistan.

My earliest memories take me to the mid-sixties of the last century. The year was 1964. Pandit Jawaharlal Nehru had died on 27 May. I was five years old. There was an animated conversation in our family. The faces of my grandfather, father and uncles wore a sad look. A huge procession took place in which thousands of Pandits were crying loud, *Kotu gav soony Jawaharlal?* (Where has our Jawaharlal gone?) I accompanied my grandfather to join the procession. His large fleshy hand clasped mine. People were crying but soon something untoward happened and the procession was stopped by a huge mob that came from the opposite direction. There was mayhem at the far end of the road. We heard noises and slogans and people started dispersing. My grandfather lifted me, and starting walking briskly. When we reached home, the elders said that some locals hurled stones at the mourners in the procession. Some days later the ashes of Pandit Jawaharlal Nehru were brought in a cavalcade and taken by road to Shadipur where they were to be immersed. I was with my grandfather and saw a fleet of buses passing by. The elders were still apprehensive of stone-pelting.

My father's office was in Gowkadal. He worked as a clerk in the Electrical department. Brave and learned, but crippled by polio, he walked with the help of crutches. One day he returned home and told us about a stone-pelting incident near his office. Gowkadal was a place where unrest brewed all the time.

Exactly three years after Nehru's death, in 1967, the Pandit community launched a strong agitation because a seventeen-year-old Pandit girl, Parmeshwari Handoo, had been forcibly married to a Muslim with the tacit connivance of some Muslims and the police. Pandits protested for weeks, but nothing happened. After the marriage, Parmeshwari was not allowed to see her mother who was a poor woman. Parmeshwari's father had died earlier. The police did nothing to investigate the matter despite a complaint lodged by the girl's mother. She believed that her daughter had been abducted and coerced into marrying a Muslim. During one of the protests, the police opened fire on the Pandit protesters in which many were injured. Some were taken to jail.

My elders would take me to the Sheetalnath temple complex. This place was of immense cultural significance for us because several Kashmiri Pandit reformist movements originated there. It was at this place where our newspaper *The Martand* was launched. Therefore, Sheetalnath became the main venue of the protest demonstration. As kids, we were assigned the responsibility of offering water to the protesters and bystanders. By the time this historic agitation came to an end, houses of several Pandits near Sheetalnath had been vandalized and burnt. Many Pandits were threatened, and some were even beaten up by mobsters belonging to the majority community. The failure of this great agitation was a setback for the Pandits. The fear of an overwhelming and domineering majority started haunting us.

The following year, our father got my younger brother and me admitted in DAV School, Magarmal Bagh, which was a posh locality in South-eastern Srinagar. We were elated that we could join the school. Our classes had a good mix of students—Pandits, Dogras, Hindus, Sikhs and Muslims. After a month or so I began to feel a strange unrest in the school. Hindu and Muslim boys did not mix well. A strange divide lurked between us. I became friends with some Muslim boys who had a cricket team of their own. Being an avid cricket buff I saw this as an opportunity to play cricket. But the sense of unrest became deeper as I came to know them more. One day, in August of 1969, their faces were lit with enthusiasm. The whole group of seven Muslim boys was happy and exchanged greetings. When I inquired about the reason for their sudden jubilation they said they were celebrating because an Arab woman, Leila Khalid, had hijacked an airplane. I was surprised. How could the 'heroics' of an Arab hijacker who had nothing to do with these Muslim boys make them happy? At home, my father and I listened to the BBC on the radio. A TWA Boeing flight 840 from Rome to Athens was hijacked midway to Damascus. The hijackers were from the Popular Front of PLA and one of them was Leila Khalid. Seeing the behaviour of my Muslim friends, it became clear to me that Hindu and Muslim communities were strikingly different from each other and nurtured opposing ideological and nationalistic affiliations. I was overcome with a strange sense of alienation, since my friends were the majority. This sense of alienation grew more and more with time. The events that unfolded in the times to come put all my doubts to rest.

In August 1969 my Muslim classmates came to school in an agitated state of mind. They talked about the Al Aqsa mosque. I saw expressions of hatred and anger on their faces, and this time their ire was directed at me too. Later that evening, I learned that on 21 August 1969, an Austrian man, Denis Michel Rohan had set the pulpit of Al Aqsa mosque in East Jerusalem on fire. Riots broke out in the Kashmir valley. Muslims took out violent demonstrations. A few lives were lost. Many were injured. Pandits were also targeted and their houses were subjected to heavy stone pelting, especially those located on the streets. Such events which took place elsewhere always spelled trouble for us—the minorities. We were made to suffer as though we had committed some crime. The Muslims of Kashmir directed their anger and hate at us and made us their victims. Did Pandits play a role in the incident of Al Aqsa? Clearly not! Then why were we targeted and ridiculed? This question haunted me. I became fearful in my own native place.

At home, a strange incident worried me. A sole Muslim family lived in our neighbourhood. They were milk vendors who reared cows and sold milk at a local shop. In the evenings they played their radio at a loud volume and listened only to the news broadcasts from Muzafarabad in Pakistan Occupied Kashmir. During the conversations with us, they glorified Pakistan and lamented that Kashmir was not part of it. 'One day Kashmir will become part of Pakistan,' the milk vendor would say to us. 'And that day is not far. We will all be Pakistanis. What will you do that day, Panditji?'

My grandfather had purchased a piece of land in Ladhoo, a village about 20 kilometers from Srinagar city. He had planted apple and almond trees on it. The orchard was a lovely sight. Soon a house was constructed there and we started to visit the house on weekends and stay there for a few days. Such visits became a regular event, which gave us a feel of rural life. There were a few army battalions in the vicinity near Khrew, an adjoining village. The soldiers would undertake a regular mapping or recce of the area. But when the women of the village saw them they would run for cover and shower nasty expletives on them. Some women who cut grass in our orchard called the soldiers 'Jangi' (a derogatory term for a soldier). The influential people who ran shops and owned orchards in the village were clearly anti-India. They would tell us the same thing. 'Kashmir will go to Pakistan. We will drive you out. Your place is in India. You must leave.'

We were enjoying our winter holidays when, on 30 January 1971, an Indian Airlines Fokker Friendship plane named 'Ganga' was hijacked to Lahore. The hijackers were Hashim Qureshi and his cousin Ashraff Butt. The sole Muslim house in our neighbourhood was abuzz with enthusiasm. Pride swelled in their hearts for at least Kashmiris had avenged the many wrongs done to them by the Indian Government and its stooges in Kashmir. My father told us about his heated arguments with his Muslim colleagues. The worst followed. The passengers of the plane were released and sent to India but the plane was not released. On 1 February 1971, the plane was blown up. As 'Ganga' went up in flames, a new geo-polity came to the fore in the subcontinent. India, in response, banned all Pakistani over-flights to Dacca or other places in what was then East Pakistan. The ban continued till the liberation of Bangladesh. When schools opened, my Muslim friends started teasing me over the 'Ganga' episode. I protested knowing fully well that they were in many ways different from me—in thoughts and deeds. In November 1971, four

Pakistani Sabre Jets intruded into Indian air space in the Eastern sector. IAF pilots in their Gnats fighter planes chased and shot three of them. This incident paved the way for a war between India and Pakistan. On 3 December Pakistani planes bombed many Indian airfields. The war between India and Pakistan in 1971 solidified the anti-India sentiment of the majority of Muslims in Kashmir. Schools were closed but my father narrated to us his ugly skirmishes with his Muslim friends in the office. Pakistan was defeated and it lost a big chunk in area and population which became Bangladesh.

In the summer of 1972, my grandfather told my father and my uncles about the second Land to Tillers Act, a law passed by the state assembly. The law, as per their view, was not in the interests of Kashmiri Pandits, and snatched from them whatever remnants of land were left with them as a result of sweeping land reforms under Sheikh Mohammad Abdullah in 1950 in which land was granted to tillers without any compensation to the owners. This law was yet another ploy to marginalize the Pandits from the social milieu of Kashmir. With loss of land, the Pandits' only source of sustenance was the government service. It became increasingly difficult for Pandit students to secure admission to technical colleges. There was corruption in the government departments, and Pandits were denied jobs in the government sector. Merit was given no priority. We witnessed protest demonstrations that turned violent when Women's College was named Jawarharlal Nehru College of Women. Intolerance to anything Indian, even to Jawaharlal Nehru, was vehement and extreme. When Lal Ded Hospital's name was proposed to be changed to Lalla Arifa Hospital, the Pandits strongly opposed it and carried out protests. The proposal was shelved.

After much struggle, I joined the Agriculture department in 1984. My salary was fixed on a consolidated basis. Our head office was at Sopore. It was my first brush with this town famous for apple orchards. As I entered the town its outlandish air was telling me something else. When I met my colleagues who hailed from Sopore and its surroundings they behaved differently. A few women recruits who had visited Pakistan spoke proudly about the trip to Mamlikat-i-Khudadad (God's own country). Posters of several several Muslim leaders adorned the walls of the shops and walls. Yassir Arafat, Gaddafi, Ayatollah Khomeini and Maqbool Butt stared at me through these posters, and fortified a sense of 'otherness' in me. In 1985, I got posted to Sumbal, a new place for me. Here, too, the same sentiments were visible but in a muted way. At Sumbal, the division between Shias and Sunnis was noticeable. The different localities they lived in made this division more palpable. One day a new batch of employees joined us. Two were Pandits but ten were Muslims. Among this batch a few persons were staunchly anti-India. I had heated arguments with them in the office. Two among the batch were rabidly anti-India and had visited Pakistan recently. They glorified the progress made by Pakistan and showered generous praises over the Shahri-e-Pakistan, the modern motorway built between Rawalpindi and Islamabad.

Jamat-i-Islami chief, Ali Shah Geelani, would give fiery anti-India speeches in Sopore. In many of these speeches he advocated Kashmir's merger with Pakistan.

All of a sudden many Muslims were visiting Pakistan and gloating over its progress and advancement. New stakeholders of the dark forces started emerging on the political and religious front, and this time, for a change, the ominous storm brewed in South Kashmir. A moulvi, Qazi Nissar, emerged as the new fundamentalist voice. His fiery lectures instigated the masses to revolt against traditions. He defied the authority of the government and led protests with a strong anti-India tone. Pandits for him were agents of India who, at best, were to be tolerated as chaff or, at worst, thrown out. Open sale of beef was encouraged. The Pandits had not seen such huge carcasses hanging from the butcher shops earlier. The very sight was revolting. These carcasses were now hanging all over. To escape this ignominy thrust upon us we found ways to escape their nauseating sight by making lengthy detours through side alleys and bylanes to escape these butcher's shops. The common Kashmiri had now found a new metaphor for 'freedom' in these dangling beef chunks.

The winter of 1985 was tenuous. But storms were already gathering by February. One day the pent-up hate of the majority community found expression in a communal frenzy which had not been seen earlier. Many temples and shrines in the Anantnag district of South Kashmir were torched. The mayhem was so profound, and hate so widespread, that the idols in these beautiful, quaint temples were smashed beyond recognition. Some of the idols were pieces of art, and part of our collective heritage. These temples were spread over many villages in serene places, overlooking natural springs and sacred groves. Our greatest festival Shivratri was approaching. The sudden and violent attack on our symbols of culture and faith made us sink to the depths of despair. Several Pandit men and women were injured, and many killed, in the communal riots. The Muslims of south Kashmir were full of hate for the Pandits. My friends and I visited these ravaged villages. Pandits were greatly dejected and were unable to understand the cause of this communal frenzy. They said their own villagers too joined the violent mobs. When we asked them, they had the same standard answer: 'We did not do it; some villagers from other villages came in mobs and we could do nothing.'

One day while on a walk I went to a nearby field to urinate. Four or five Muslims gathered around me. Thinking that I had urinated in the field, they abused me saying that there was a mosque nearby. A verbal spat got underway but soon they retreated, not before impressing upon me that I was an infidel, and had no place in Kashmir. In 1989 hartals, protests, shutdowns became a regular feature. A cricket match between India and West Indies became a slanging match between the Pandits and Muslims. As the one-day match started in Srinagar's Sher-e-Kashmir cricket stadium, Indian players were mocked. Bottles and metal pieces were hurled at them. The West Indian team was perplexed to see such sentiments in a place which they thought was Indian. India lost the match and an unprecedented festivity erupted in the city. The arch enemy of Kashmiris had been laid low. The enemy of their enemy—West Indies—was now their friend. We were at the stadium but the scale of hate demonstrated against my own country by my fellow Kashmiris was fiery and intense.

Come September and a leader of Pandits, a man of great nobility and stature, a man of peace and humanism held in esteem by Pandits and Muslims, was shot dead. Tika Lal Taploo's assassination unnerved us all. Thereafter, a series of assassinations of other prominent Pandits followed. The end of 1989 signalled the snapping of a slender thread that tied us to our Kashmir. Another towering social activist, a man of peace and a sagacious scholar, Prem Nath Bhat, was killed by militants in Anantnag. For us this was a clear sign that we were the enemy and becoming the victims of militancy. On the night of 19 January 1990, as we lay fretfully in our beds, loudspeakers from the mosques exploded with announcements and slogans. It happened with clockwork precision all over the city. Slogans of Kashmir's merger with Pakistan bellowed all over. The announcements made it clear that the Pandits should leave Kashmir or face the consequences. I was posted in Uri, a border town just a few miles from Pakistan Occupied Kashmir. At that time, I was staying with my maternal uncle who was posted as an engineer in the Mohra power project plant. He would tell me about the strange and hideous behaviour of his Muslim seniors and other staff. Many among the employees knew me and we often got into animated discussions regarding the 'imminent merger of Kashmir with Pakistan'.

On 2 February 1990, I received the tragic news of the killing of Satish Tickoo, my brother-in-law. Some militants had killed him in cold blood. My wife went into a state of shock. The whole family was shattered and devastated. As I reached my in-laws' house, Satish had already been cremated. On the day we collected his ashes, curfew had been imposed in Kashmir. Somehow, we managed to reach the cremation ground, but the killers and their sympathisers hounded us. My age-long association with Kashmir was now under threat. I held Satish's ashes in my hand one last time and, in a few days, bid adieu to Kashmir. I knew there was no way my family and I could linger on. We were ordered to leave. Had we stayed longer, all of us would have been killed. We chose not to perish at the hands of the majority community who wanted to rid Kashmir of the 'Hindu infidels', the name given to Kashmiri Pandits, the original inhabitants of Kashmir, whose history goes back 5000 years. The plan was simple. The danger to our lives and peaceful existence was clear and present. They wanted to erase the age-old history of Kashmir and write a new one. They wanted to destroy the symbols of Pandit heritage and tradition. They were successful. Temples and houses were torched. The names of several places were changed to indicate that Kashmir was an Islamic state. Kashmir was fast becoming a place where Muslims would soon be the only dwellers, and Islam the only religion. Nobody else was welcome.

3

It is for your own good to leave

Kundan Lal Chowdhury

August 1989

Usha, my younger sister, has come to visit us from the USA, first time after our father's demise following a year-long engagement with his battle with cancer. She desires to spend some time with us, especially our grieving mother.

For several years I had been planning a trip to the famous Gangabal Lake. This seemed a good time to combine the hiking expedition with the post-funeral rites of our departed father on the shores of the sacred lake, twelve thousand feet above the sea.

On the first lap of the pilgrimage, we stayed for a night at the rest house in Prang, a pretty little hamlet on the banks of the Sindh. Here, the river spreads wide across the valley for some distance in a shimmering transparent sheet on her vast stone bed with the brown and rainbow trout darting across.

After dinner, we came out for a stroll in the lovely lawns of the rest house to gaze at the stars and listen to the music of the river. What we saw was unsettling. A bunch of young boys were performing drills not unlike military exercises. It was about ten pm. I had never witnessed such activity during my earlier visits to my favourite holiday haunt. At this hour, these boys should have been doing their homework or getting ready to sleep.

They turned to look at us but the instructor gave us a severe look and shouted them back into the workout. We cut short our stroll and returned inside.

I felt uneasy; sleep was fretful and hard to come by. Was this the evidence of what we had been hearing about young boys from the city and villages being inducted into Jihad? During the past two years there had been reports of boys firing in the air at different places in downtown Srinagar that were dismissed as mere fun games. But subsequent events seemed to fortify our fears that they were rehearsals of ominous militant operations. The two simultaneous explosions on 1 August 1987 in Srinagar Club and Central Telegraph Office were no accidents. A militant organization, Jammu and Kashmir Liberation Front (JKLF), had claimed responsibility. Yet any allusion to terrorism was being downplayed for quite some time by the government, even in the face of other undeniable signs of its eruption. Random firings and blasts had become an everyday phenomenon. On 27 October 1988 different parts of Srinagar had been engulfed in a series of explosions and gunfire. The murder on 9 December of Pandit Kashi Nath, the high priest of Vicharnag, a sacred spring temple of Kashmiri Pandits, had gone unnoticed. In January 1989 the police had claimed a major success with the smashing of 'some gangs' and capture of a few terrorists with Kalashnikovs. Later, in April, during my father's funeral, Gulam Mohammad, his Muslim clerk from downtown, had presaged terrible times. 'Bullets will fly from every house in every direction,' he said, his green eyes lighting up. We laughed it off even as we had been feeling, for quite some time, a strange viciousness around, people talking in hushed tones, looking at you with suspicion, their discourse tinged with bitterness, sarcasm and even hostility.

Soon after, in June, a militant group, Hizb-e-Islam, had slapped a dress code on women, threatening them with dire consequences if seen moving about without the traditional Muslim veil. There was talk of 'revolution' breaking out, of young boys having disappeared from villages, absent from their schools for weeks and months, of busloads carrying jihadi aspirants from Chattabal to Uri and other border areas, from where they crossed over to Pakistan Occupied Kashmir (POK) to the training camps. And yet, no parent or teacher reported the disappearances, and none in authority seemed to know or notice!

Now, unknown to the world outside, the training in armed combat was going on at Prang. The beautiful lawns of a pretty tourist place had turned into a training ground for budding terrorists.

Next morning, during the arduous climb up the Buthsher range on the way to Gangabal, I quizzed the porters who accompanied us. They confirmed that a massive campaign of indoctrination was going on in the village mosques and madrassas and a whole generation of young boys was being recruited into militancy. 'Some have volunteered, others are being lured with incentives, yet others through coercion,' they said. 'The schools are almost empty save the small, the weak and the only children of their parents. If a family has two or more sons, they have to donate at least one of them for the Tehreek, the freedom movement.'

Our pilgrimage to Gangabal was a nightmare. The journey was plagued with incessant rain, hail and windstorm, as if echoing the bad times that have fallen upon the beautiful vale. It is with great difficulty that we escaped unscathed, albeit worn out by the experience and troubled by what we had witnessed in the lawns of the Prang rest house and what the porters told us.

September—November 1989

On 14 September 1989, unidentified militants gunned down Tika Lal Taploo just outside his home as he was leaving for the law courts. He was a lawyer, a leading Kashmiri Pandit politician and a courageous crusader for the rights of his community. His funeral procession, attended by thousands of his supporters, was heavily stoned. On 4 November, Justice Neel Kanth Ganjoo was shot dead by militants on the road near Amirakadal. A note stuck on his body warned of death to anyone who dared to remove the body from the road or come near it. Some years earlier, Justice Ganjoo had passed a death sentence on Maqbool Bhat who was one of the founders of the militant organization, Jammu and Kashmir Liberation Front, and who had been convicted of the murder of an intelligence officer.

The two assassinations sent shock waves across the Pandit community. But the militant organisations explained this killing as a political murder, a punishment for the 'crimes' committed by the Indian state against the Kashmiris. A spate of indiscriminate abductions, tortures, rapes and murders of the Kashmiri Pandits ensued. The victims were ordinary innocent civilians—men, women, and children, who had nothing to do with any political ideology or organization. Their only fault was that they were Pandits.

December 1989

The past two months have seen the terrorists in full charge since the governing machinery has made its customary move to the winter capital in Jammu along with the bureaucrats, politicians, legislators and ministers. The valley has fallen in the iron grip of mushrooming militant organizations. Their diktats are flying from all directions and bringing about drastic changes in the social-cultural-administrative milieu of the valley. Cinema owners have been forced to close down, kiosks selling alcoholic drinks have been banned, clubs have shut down, beauty parlours and boutiques have disappeared. There is a breakdown of law and order. Every house, neighbourhood, village and town is agog with an eerie enthusiasm and expectation. Chants of tehreek rend the air: 'Azadi has become the mantra, Islam the idea, Pakistan the utopia.'

There has been an increased number of bomb blasts as the abductions and killings of Pandits go on. By now more than thirty Kashmiri Pandits have been gunned down. There is an all-pervasive sense of fear and insecurity in the community. They are like frightened chicken in a cage in the butcher's shop. The murderers kill with impunity. What remains of the administration in the valley is too defunct to take any action.

The Pandits endure the pogrom. The outside world remains silent. The Pandits have no options, and nowhere to turn to except the very people who have ordered their decimation. That is why, the other day the president of a prominent socio-cultural organization of Pandits sent a candid public appeal to JKLF through an open letter invoking Kashmiriyat, the much-touted Kashmiri spirit of amity and tolerance: 'We desire to live in peace and harmony with our Muslim brethren. We have nothing against your tehreek. Please spare my community and stop the killings.'

The reply came forthwith through a stinging note strung to the dead body of his deputy that had been thrown by the riverside during the night. It read, 'We presume you got the answer, Mr President.' That has forced him to declare his community unsafe. He has asked Pandits to exercise their own judgment and discretion since the whole community is persona non grata in Kashmir and there is no one to protect the Pandits.

By and large, the State Government Muslim employees from the valley are not unsympathetic to the motivation behind terrorism or the means adopted by its perpetrators. In flagrant violation of service rules, some of them are aiding and abetting terrorism—working as moles, passing vital security, logistical and related information to the militants and their mentors. Others, including several policemen, have even enlisted as jihadi volunteers and crossed over to POK while still being on the payrolls of the government.

The regional print media, under the directive and dictates of the numerous militant outfits, have become a part of the propaganda machinery for feeding Jihad to the masses. Mosques and madrassas are in overdrive. The whole valley breathes of lawlessness and terror. People are being sucked into the black hole of Jihad, brainwashed into believing that 'Azadi' is round the corner and those who oppose it will do so at their own peril. Most right-thinking Muslims, euphemistically called moderates, find themselves helpless even as they do not like what is happening, for they foresee how it will engulf and imperil the fabric of Kashmiri society. By remaining quiet they acquiesce to the inevitability of terrorism and the means that are adopted to achieve its ends.

January 1990

In the preceding weeks, it has been impossible to keep up with the pace at which things have developed. We have been witness to endless processions of hysterical masses and their raging anti-India, pro-Azadi, pro-Pakistan slogans that slash the air. People go about with their index and middle fingers raised in a V signifying victory; green flags with crescents breezily wave atop mosques and houses. Everyone seems powerless against the cataclysmic forces of violence.

On the long, dark, wintry night of 19 January, when the whole world was asleep, thousands of loudspeakers hoisted on as many mosques through the length and breadth of the valley suddenly boomed 'Azadi' slogans and war cries, exhorting the masses to come out of their homes and march to Srinagar to capture power in the valley. They were urged to cleanse the land of kafirs, to subdue the Pandit women and drive their men out of Kashmir! This went on until midnight. The Muslims came out on the roads while the Pandits shrank back in terror, watching from behind their drawn blinds, trembling with fear from the shocking slogans that pierced their windows and walls. They were witness to the acme of religious frenzy, a flagrant exhibition of mass hysteria. They saw and heard the threats of genocide coming. The slogans were in question-answer pairs. Two slogans in particular were terrifying:

'What do we want?'

– 'Azadi'

'What do we want?'

– 'Pakistan. Without the Pandit men; with the Pandit women.'

In effect, the Pandits, who had been subject to selective abductions, torture and killing, were finally warned by the whole populace of Kashmir, not just the terrorist groups, to quit and leave their women behind.

Jagmohan, known as a tough administrator, was re-appointed as Governor in place of Krishna Rao the same day. The mass processions marching from different directions were stopped from reaching the historic Lal Chowk. Police were forced to shoot in order to disperse the rampaging hordes. As a result, there were civilian injuries and deaths. Chief Minister Farooq Abdullah, who had lost his grip on the state completely, found an easy excuse to abdicate and resign 'in protest'. He had ordered the release of seventy terrorists from prisons during the previous six months. Governor's rule has been imposed and the State Assembly kept in suspended animation.

The macabre happenings during the night of 19 January have proved to be the turning point in the exodus of Kashmiri Pandits, as it has unleashed terrible forces against them, making it impossible for them to stay back in their homeland.

Poignant scenes have followed, of truckloads and busloads of Pandits in flight, some even barefoot with hardly any belongings—caravans of men, women and children running away from their homes and hearths. We hear frightening stories of escape after that fateful night—how each one of them planned their flight on a short notice as news filtered that there would be mass massacres of the Pandits in the valley.

The attitudes of the Muslim neighbours have transformed overnight into one of suspicion and hostility as if the Pandits manoeuvred the security forces into action against the mass hysteria.

Meanwhile, militants go about in streets and neighbourhoods, brandishing guns and promising 'final victory' against 'Indian occupational forces'. The Muslim masses are awed by their bravado, fearful of their power, hopeful of their success. They compose paeans to their valour and their capacity to deliver! Large processions of militants, with increasing participation from the common people, are the order of the day.

Srinagar rapidly transforms into a veritable cantonment. Military bunkers, fortified with sandbags, are in evidence at important squares and crossings. The long barrels of guns spike menacingly from the small openings in the security pickets. Bridges and public buildings, the special targets of the militants, are heavily guarded. It is a war-like atmosphere. A pall of fear hangs everywhere.

Our predominantly Hindu neighbourhood wears a deserted look except for packs of famished dogs scouring for food in the drains—poor dogs without masters, disowned and hungry! Padlocks stare at you from the closed doors of desolate Pandit houses, some of their signboards tarnished with black paint, the words 'Bagode Pandit', meaning runaway Pandits, painted on their doors.

Islamization of Kashmir, and a switch-over to Pakistani cultural mores, goes on at a rapid pace at several levels. People have been directed to reset the time half an hour behind Indian Standard Time to synchronize with Pakistan time. They must watch only Pakistan TV, listen to the Pakistan radio and resist exposure to the contamination by All India Radio and Doordarshan. The two institutions have been emasculated and ordered to exclude Hindi words from their lexicon, stop allegedly anti-Azadi propaganda and highlight the true meaning and impact of the tehreek The telecast now begins with the traditional Muslim greeting, Aslam-ali-kum, and ends with Khuda hafiz.

Shopkeepers and business establishments have been ordered to observe Fridays as the off days and to work on Sundays; the masses have been reminded of their religious duty to pray five times a day at homes, offices and workplaces. Under an unwritten rule, the State Government employees work only the first half on Fridays, the second half being allowed for prayers, after which hardly anyone returns to work.

There is a great rush for the black veil. Tailors have announced reduced rates for stitching in deference to the writ of the militants.

There is talk of a switch-over to left-hand drive, as in Pakistan. Urdu is encouraged even in homes rather than the mother tongue Kashmiri, believed to help identify with Islam and Pakistan where it is the official language.

I have never before witnessed such congregations for the midday Nimaz inside the hospital premises. Conscious of the overarching reach of vigilantes, every Muslim employee of every denomination, from the most elevated professor to the menial sweeper, rushes out at noontime for the mass prayer, leaving behind unfinished work. In the prevailing Islamic milieu, religious calling has precedence over secular and humanitarian obligations.

February 1990

Our genial Muslim neighbour, with whom we share a common boundary wall, has been keeping a low profile for the last several weeks. The traditional welcome that always greeted us across the fence is missing. A chill seems to have descended, and suspiciousness, even an indefinable alienation. His two kids have acquired a new lexicon, their conversation replete with terrorism-related lingo that betrays wide knowledge and understanding of, and even some fascination for, militancy—expressions and words like tehreek (freedom movement) and jihad (religious crusade), mujahids and ghazis (freedom fighters and martyrs), mukhbirs and soyats (informers and moles), agwa and tafteesh (kidnapping and interrogation), 'action' (the militants' strike) and reaction (the retaliatory police action), Kalashnikovs and grenades, etc.

This morning we found in our letterbox a hand-dropped letter in Urdu addressed to Leela, my wife, that reads: 'It has come to our notice that in spite of our directives to all doctors you have not cut down your consultation fees. We are constrained to remind you that we hate to target any servant of the people in these difficult times.'

So here is an extra-constitutional order, a writ that rules the roost in the present times, that you dare not flout. We hardly see any patients these days except for the neighbours whom we have always seen free. In any case, we have decided not to accept fees from anybody. But the letter leaves us petrified. Is it just a routine warning or a harbinger of worse to come?

A group of medical students came to my chamber and informed me that the staff and students of our medical college were going to join a procession to the office of the United Nations Military Observers Group at Sonwar to submit a memorandum. 'We will appreciate if you join,' said one of them in a tone that sounded like an order.

'Memorandum about what?' I asked.

'Calling for an end to the massive human rights violations by the Indian security forces, and seeking recognition of, and support for, the ongoing freedom movement in Kashmir,' he replied.

'Does it really matter whether I join or not?' I asked.

'It does because you are a senior faculty member. This is a common cause.'

'But this is not my cause. Nor is it my brief to join processions and present memoranda. I am here to mentor you, and to treat patients. And you are here to study medicine, not to indulge in politics and perverse ideologies,' I blurted out, forgetting the gravity of the situation.

The wild expressions on their faces still haunt me.

March 1990

Yet another tragic day in the history of Kashmir! Slogan-shouting crowds clad in white shrouds marched towards the Srinagar office of the United Nations Military Observer's Group at Sonwar to submit a memorandum seeking 'Kashmir's freedom from India'. They blocked the passage of an army convoy, and started heckling and hectoring the soldiers. The hysterical mob soon turned violent and attacked their vehicles including an army school bus carrying their children. In the retaliatory firing 46 civilians have lost their lives. Curfew has been clamped in the whole valley.

I had sensed the ominous tidings when the students approached me last week. I hope and pray that none of them is hurt.

Meanwhile, we wait for more details as we bide our time in the valley.

Curfew is here to stay for quite some time, forcing people to stay indoors for the whole week. We receive news mostly from the valley-based newspapers that have unfortunately turned into instruments of disinformation, weapons of terror, and harbingers of tragedy and death. One shudders with fear and seethes with anger at the inflammatory write-ups. The news is distorted to suit the palate of the local populace and aimed at inciting them to hatred and violence. The security forces are vilified and demonised, painted as wild and hungry beasts that barge into people's homes, snatch food and precious objects, beat people up, and molest women. It is humiliating to go through the blatantly offensive caricaturing of Pandits, and the wild and terrorising proclamations against them. They are portrayed as scheming villains and saboteurs sworn to foil the tehreek. They are blamed for stabbing the Muslims in the back by running away and leaving them to face the army bullets. In fact, the newspapers have become the mouth organs of the terrorists, highlighting their programmes and activities, eulogising their achievements, publishing their directives for the common masses, pouring venom on the 'enemies', and fanning the fires of 'revolution'.

The residual Pandit community lives on the edge as rumours of a backlash against them abound. The desperadoes have already gunned down Pandit Lassa Kaul, Director of Doordarshan, and Pushker Nath Handoo, Assistant Director, J&K State Information Department.

We exist in an ambience of fear as we hear of more killings almost every day. Even the sound of a radio out of tune, of a cistern filling with water, of leaves rustling in the breeze—these everyday sounds—sound menacing at times. The doorbell rings and your heart flutters, a knock on the door and you brace yourself, a telephone ring and you wonder whether it is another unknown caller threatening you to leave or face the consequences. If the call is from an acquaintance, you just whisper or talk in monosyllables or in metaphors lest the phone call gets mixed up with others and your conversation betrays you.

You look into your letterbox and your hands tremble while scanning the mail lest there be another warrant from the terrorists. When you go out, you open the door of your house with trepidation; you furtively look for any pamphlets or letters pasted outside, proclaiming you a mole or an informer, an enemy agent or a blasphemer, a drug peddler or smuggler. You walk the street up to the nearest electric pole or the mosque to watch out lest you figure in the new list of offenders that may have been pasted there during the night.

Meanwhile curfew passes are being handed out to restore essential services that have been totally disrupted. As I drive to the hospital I find the roads almost empty, and driving to work with a curfew pass in my pocket is like a flight through a city turned into a fortress. As I step inside the hospital, the walls of the corridors and the wards look menacing. For there, splashed in bold charcoal graffiti standing out against the white background, are the names of the blacklisted Pandit medical professionals who are under the close surveillance of vigilantes for their suspicious activities. I breathe a sigh of relief; for now, I don't figure in the blacklist!

The atmosphere in the hospital has turned chaotic and scary. All routine has gone haywire. Doctors and others arrive late, leave early, or miss duty altogether. There is no one to ask questions, no accountability whatsoever. The wards are like fish markets; there is no control on mobs that accompany the terrorists wounded in action or civilians caught in crossfire. They barge into the outpatients', wards and operation theatres without any fear or compunction, rough up the menial staff, break hospital machinery, raise slogans of Azadi and threaten the doctors and administrators.

The medical students are missing, except for the residents and postgraduates. I adopt a daily routine of finishing work and returning home, refusing to be drawn into any discussions except the strictly professional. It is gratifying to find some postgraduates still eager to attend teaching rounds and case discussions. Has it dawned upon them that one of these days I will be gone like the other Pandits? I can see that inquiring look in their eyes and it makes me uncomfortable that I might prove them right.

The only contact with our friends and relatives who still brave it in the valley is the phone. They ask your welfare and your plans. They seek your advice even while they might have already made up their mind to run away. You can neither offer advice nor assistance since you yourself are sitting on a huge mound of anxiety, confusion and indecision. How can one maintain equipoise in this miasma of brutality, insanity and death?

I know a number of Muslims who are mortified by the situation but have sealed their lips out of mortal fear. But there are others who avidly support the militants.

This morning a Muslim couple came to see me. The man, a university professor, is a friend. His wife, a bureaucrat, is running a fever. After I examined her, our talk veered to the ongoing mayhem in Kashmir and the stories going around that the militants were lecherous, greedy young men, collecting money and craving virgins.

'They demand money only from the corrupt and dishonest who must spare a percentage of their ill-gotten fortunes for the cause of freedom,' she claimed. As to coveting girls and the alleged rapes, she dismissed the reports as exaggerated even as she justified the actions in fulfilment of the physiological and emotional needs of the young 'warriors' who sacrifice everything, even their lives, for the revolution. 'Most girls feel privileged to offer themselves for a popular, honourable cause—a small return for a much larger sacrifice,' she pontificated. I was stunned.

April 1990

Al Safa, a local Urdu daily, has published a front-page ultimatum issued by Hizb-ul Mujahideen, the dreaded terror group, warning all non-Muslims to leave the valley within 36 hours or face death. The headline reads: 'Leave Kashmir within 36 hours.' It also carries a write-up captioned 'Snake in the grass'—a stinging proclamation of the Kashmiri Muslim perceptions of Bhattas (Pandits). Through a liberal deployment of vituperative rhetoric against Pandits, the writer has likened them to snakes in the grass that have bitten the unwary Muslims at every critical juncture of history.

This is the last straw, the final push to set off the exodus of the residual Pandits. It has sent panic waves all around. Even the Muslims are getting nervous. Sister Dida was jittery on the phone. Her Muslim neighbour had called on her, sounding apologetic but earnest when he said: 'Until now we persuaded you not to migrate. Now, after this ultimatum, none can vouchsafe your security and well-being for we ourselves feel threatened. It is for your own good to leave Kashmir.'

'Brother, we are no longer in a cleft-stick situation, unable to decide; we are hanging from a weak bough that is ready to break any time,' Dida was metaphorical even as she sounded panic-stricken. 'Don't you think we need to take the final call?'

I couldn't agree more. I rushed to her home to discuss it threadbare. We had to choose between the iniquity and fear of staying back and the uncertainty and the travails of exodus.

In the long discussion that ensued, Dida and her spouse argued that we had nothing to lose by quitting our land except the deprivation, the ill will, the hatred and humiliation, the subjugation and terror; that exodus is better than abject surrender to our tormentors; it is the only way left to defend the honour, dignity and chastity of our women, to protect our lives, to preserve our traditions and rituals, and to give a chance to our younger generation to grow up in an atmosphere free from malevolence and fear, free from discrimination and violence.

But the argument fell flat on me like water on a lotus leaf. 'Have we then to bid farewell to all that we cherished through generations—the mountains, springs, rivers and lakes that we worship, the green pastures and golden valleys that nurtured us in their lap since the dawn of history, the sacred pilgrimages that sustained our faith, and all our earthly belongings—our homes and the house deities?' I asked.

'This may be a test of our faith in the Gita that teaches us to shun all attachment, to relinquish craving for material objects, to observe the Karma of action without coveting the fruit of action. Didn't Lord Krishna leave Mathura that had degenerated like Kashmir into greed, hatred, revenge and violence and move to Dwarika to raise a new kingdom on the seashore? Isn't it time to emulate him and move away from a place that has become the bane of our lives, and start life afresh somewhere else?' Dida reasoned.

'But we have no place to go. Let us give ourselves some more time,' I pleaded even as I knew we were on thin ice.

April 1990

Nine Pandits have been killed in the week since the militants' deadline to Pandits to leave Kashmir passed. Everyone is in jitters. Our determination to hold on was already sagging, but now the last straw has broken it. It is the murder this morning of Mr Rajnath, an anaesthesia technician in Lalla Ded Hospital for Women, where Leela works. He was dragged from his home out into the street and shot dead, while his neighbours, to whom he would render free professional services, looked the other way.

Raj Nath was a decent, conscientious, and hardworking young man, friendly with his colleagues, obedient and respectful to the doctors. When the news came, the few Pandits still working in the hospital were stunned.

The Muslim staff—doctors, nurses, technicians, janitors and others—did not even bat an eyelid. Not a whimper, not a word, not a sigh, not a nod from anyone. As if he never existed. It so shocked and angered Leela that she shouted at her colleagues for having done away with even the pretensions to decency. Werc they in such a terrible grip of fear of the militants or had they lost all human values, she fumed. But she only met cold stares from them, even those who claimed to be her buddies! One theatre assistant, however, ventured to open his mouth finally, 'He must have had connections with RAW; we all must know that the mujahids don't kill people without a reason.'

Can you beat that argument? There is a reason for the brutal murder of every Pandit—you are an informer, agent of RAW, blasphemer, political activist, RSS member, or simply just a Bhatta, a Kashmiri Pandit. If you are none of these, then you are the Indian 'dog' that needs to be shot.

Ironically his tragic death has sounded the final bugle; our family and close kin have taken a collective decision to quit the valley as soon as possible. Sister Dida and her husband will start packing the necessary clothes, documents, bank passbooks and other necessities. that can be accommodated in my van, besides our own bare essentials. Leela's mother is already with us since both her sons fled last month after they were threatened that they would be staying at their own risk if they didn't leave.

30 April 1990

I set to working in my lawn soon after breakfast. The gardener has not come for a long time because of the curfews. Tomorrow we are departing. The lawn needs a cleaning, the flowerbeds a de-weeding, and the hedges a trimming. The vines have to be tethered to their supports. The pine saplings have come loose in the soil due to the rains and need firming up. I am quite sentimental about them for I have transplanted them from my customary climbs up the Shankaracharya hill where they grow wild.

Mother Chogtu, my mother-in-law, sunning leisurely on the patio, watches me toiling furiously in the garden like one possessed, now in my second shift after lunch. But I am at peace with myself, with the ambience. I do not for a moment think of anything else besides gardening, certainly nothing about our decision to leave tomorrow. I am only living in the moment. Today is what matters; now is the moment of truth, of eternity. These little eternities that we live hour to hour, that make life what it is.

Leela comes out and joins me. She starts speaking with the tress, touching the flowers, humming a tune, looking for the bird nests, and watching the butterflies.

Does she feel one with me or does she really believe that we will return to Kashmir before the lawn is due for the next mowing? When I suggested last evening that we roll the carpets and store them away, she insisted that there was no need to go through the exercise since we would return in a few weeks, as soon as the situation improves.

Soon, sister Dida and her spouse, Dr Bansi Lal, having done their last-minute packing and loading the van almost to the point of blocking the rear view, also join us, to be followed by Leela's niece, holding cups of steaming tea and snacks for all of us. What a garden party—all of us sunning as we sit on the freshly manicured turf, in silent contemplation for some time, as if in a last farewell!

And then, mother Chogtu, looking amused, half at me and half away, addresses her daughter, a touch of irony in her tone: 'But tell me, are we not leaving tomorrow?'

'Yes we are,' I reply in place of my wife, reassuring her that our plans stand.

'Then why all this toil since morning?' she wonders aloud.

'Just as we can't wait to wash and eat when it is time, this garden too can't wait until we return. What will the plants think of us?'

'The sanctity of this place will be trampled upon no sooner than we are gone. They will come swarming to occupy this place. What use is this labour?'

'At least they will know who we were and what we stood for. That may stop them from desecrating this place.'

It is dusk when I reluctantly put the garden tools away. There is more to do; there always has been every time I have toiled in the garden.

We eat our dinner early and quietly slip into our respective beds. There is no more talk about anything; nothing about tomorrow.

1 May 1990
I had restorative sleep after a long time. There was nothing to lose sleep over; after several weeks of uncertainty, we had taken the final decision. There was no going back; we had taken the long leap into an unknown future.

We woke up before daybreak. The house buzzed with activity as we washed and shaved and dressed and prayed and ate our breakfast and bolted all the windows and doors.

I looked through the window at the Shankaracharya hill, the Siva temple on its crown, and the garden below. I had missed my morning climb up the hill for several days. Will I get to see you again, I asked the Lord.

I picked a small clod of earth from the garden, locked the garage and the main gate as everyone took a seat in the Maruti van. We drove away, looking at our house till it was out of view.

Then there was no looking back, not even looking sideways, as if we were being chased by phantoms. We started our journey while curfew was still in force, and drove steadily on the deserted highway, braving the bumpy road rife with potholes, mounds and rubbish. The fan belt of the van wore out but did not snap even as the radiator started heating up, but we dared not stop anywhere till we reached Qazigund. We had been warned about village folk stoning the vehicles taking the Pandits out of Kashmir. Luckily we found a service shop open. The Sikh mechanic, mindful of our urgency, quickly replaced the fan belt. The Banihal tunnel was close by and we were keen to cross it and be out of the valley.

This rugged mountain range pierced with a 2.5-kilometre-long tunnel has always been the barrier, insulating the Kashmir valley from the rest of the world. In better times I always felt saddened to leave the valley even for a brief holiday, like a child being separated from its mother. How eager that child was to get away from his mother today!

It was light that we saw at the end of the tunnel, literally and metaphorically. Our bodies relaxed, our eyes lit up with relief and we started breathing lightly, freely. The phantoms stopped as we emerged from the tunnel. We were suddenly transported into a different land, a different milieu, out of harm's way. A strange calm descended on us. From here on we stopped at many places, sipping tea, taking in the whole scenery as if we had come on a holiday.

As we descended from the mountains and Jammu neared, it started getting warmer. By the time we arrived, it was evening and blistering hot. It took us quite some time to locate the rented lodgings of Ramji, my brother-in-law, on the Canal Road where we planned to spend the night. We had to stop at many places and ask for directions. On the way we met fellow refugees—yes, we were refugees now, it suddenly dawned on us—some wearing Pherons, fur caps and turbans in this terrible heat, as if they were still in Kashmir, all looking worn out and lost in the busy bazaars, flocking chemist shops, haggling with vegetable vendors or looking for rental places.

Some of them who knew me were happy to see me and pleaded that I stay on in Jammu for they did not know where to go for treatment. There were so many falling ill; so many had succumbed.

We found our destination, a garret Ramji had managed to find after a long search. I parked the van in a side lane a furlong away. As we got out, swarms of mosquitoes rose from the shores of the Canal to welcome us. We walked fast, warding them off, and into a yard and up a steep flight of narrow stairs into a cramped room, twelve-feet-by-twelve, a table fan struggling to whip up the hot air in our direction, its swerving blades striking the protective frame in a jarring cadence. Water was served from bottles chilled in the cold stream of the Canal.

A hearty dinner followed. How Ramji's wife, Pushpa, had managed to cook for all of us in that small kitchen, barely six-feet-by-four-feet, without any running water and no exit for smoke, was a marvel of fortitude and innovation that only our women are capable of. Ramji's landlord offered us his own cooler-fitted room for the night. However, it was not the heat and mosquitoes that kept me awake but the thoughts of what was to come. After all, this was just the beginning, just the first few hours of our arrival from our home in Kashmir!

Leela could not stand the lavatory-cum-bath fashioned out of the small space under the stairs that led to the first floor. There you had to squeeze yourself in or out of the four-by-two-feet door, to bend and twist your body when inside, to position yourself awkwardly when squatting on the toilet seat, to huddle yourself while bathing, to close your nostrils and hold your breath as long as you could to avoid the stench. If you came out from that claustrophobic hot hole without hitting the sloping ceiling that almost came down on you, without getting into a skirmish with the walls or the door, without being asphyxiated, you were lucky.

We drank water sparingly even as we were thirsty, to cut down the need to visit the toilet; we coaxed our bladders to behave and withhold any urge until we were gone next morning. It is a miracle that we managed without having to visit the toilet again. The human body is equipped not only with great reserves but also with amazing mechanisms designed to rapidly acclimatise in adverse situations. We will have to fall back on them from time to time as we traverse the unchartered territories in exile.

4

If we're killed, the gold buried in the earth under that apple tree belongs to you

Ashok Pandit

On a warm summer day in July 1988 Syed Ali Shah Geelani delivered a long lecture to the people assembled in the park near Villgam bus stand in Handwara, Kashmir. I was a young boy then and went to listen to his lecture out of boyish curiosity. In his lecture he directed the Muslims of Kashmir to buy guns instead of television sets to liberate Kashmir. This sounded unusual to me for I heard this kind of thing for the first time in my life. I got a little confused. But fear of a strange sort entered my mind. In spite of this I went on laughing inside. Then he added that he knew that the agents of the government were there. He asked them to report to the intelligence agencies whatever he was saying that time.

I must have been studying in class 9. I was walking on the road. A speeding jeep came and halted in front of the police station. Scores of people had been running after it. I also ran to see what the matter was. A policeman dragged a man out of the jeep, pulled his hair and pushed him into the police station. The onlookers said that he was a bank robber who had looted a bank at Langate and killed the manager of the bank. The people had caught him, beaten him and handed him over to the police. They had been jubilant that time. In no time the people came to know that the man who was pushed into the police station was Maqbool Bhat of the Jammu and Kashmir Liberation Front. Now the same people started cursing those who had caught and beaten him. My consolation was that I had seen Maqbool Bhat who, after many years, was hanged in Tihar jail.

We were used to the hartals observed on the death anniversaries of Maqbool Bhat.

When Zulfikar Ali Bhutto was hanged all the Muslims of Handwara protested and raised slogans against Zia-ul-Haq for a number of days. When Zia-ul-Haq died in an air crash all Muslims went on a pro-Zia demonstration and mourned his death. But an alarming situation took shape. At midday the Muslims pelted stones at the houses of Pandits and even attacked some. I heard that this was the first time such events happened in Handwara since the tribal raid in 1947.

In August 1989 the political climate of Kashmir changed for the worse. Anti-India activities were brewing. Handwara was peaceful because there were no demonstrations, protests and hartals. But I could smell something fishy. I saw the simmering restlessness and that-which-can't-be-explained atmosphere. The mood and attitude of the Muslim community had changed.

I did agricultural studies in Meerut University. A number of Muslims from Handwara were studying there with me. We were best of friends. We used to visit restaurants, watch films, play pranks, talk about the girls, remain standing outside the girls' college, play cricket and other games and eat together. We never thought on communal lines. We were all good although at times we were mischievous. All of us got jobs in the same year and were posted in Handwara, our native place. We used to meet daily, play cricket and then watch films on TV in my home. We formed a unique and interesting group in Handwara. Since my home faced the main road we used to meet in our house, watch matches and films on TV and talk endlessly about everything under the sun. Our relationship was perfect.

September 1989
Handwara, Kashmir

My Muslim friends avoided me. I asked Majid Dar, 'What is the matter? Why are you changed?' He smiled and said, 'Nothing.' Then he left. The peon in my office told me: 'There will be war.' As is the habit with all Kashmiris I urinated near a wall. Two young boys of the neighbourhood came and threatened me. One of them said to me, 'Why did you urinate facing our graveyard?' I kept quiet and then I apologized. I found a menacing look in the eyes of the one named Ghulam. He was known to me. I left crestfallen and insulted.

1990
I saw lakhs of Kashmiri Muslims coming back from Chrar. Women were singing songs in praise of militants called mujahids (freedom fighters). Many persons were serving water and bread to the people on the road. I was stopped and given a bagel. I was driving my scooter. I was to go home. Not a single vehicle was plying on the road from Sopore to Handwara. It was about 9 pm. I was terrified. Darkness added to my fear.

Next day curfew was imposed.

A policeman told me that conditions would worsen. He asked me to remain indoors. My mother and I kept gold ornaments in a lunch box. We buried the lunch box in the earth near an apple tree that stood in our kitchen garden. Then I told a friend: 'If we are killed, the gold buried in the earth under that apple tree belongs to you.'

Frightened Pandit neighbours assembled in our home. We talked and decided to shift Pandit women to the Ganesh temple. We kept some axes and lathis at home, determined to fight if the militants came to kill us. My mother was a very brave woman but I found her tense and dispirited.

From the mosque announcements were made: 'We are free from India. Defy curfew now.' In no time I heard anti-India and pro-Azadi slogans coming from about 10,000 processionists. They assembled in Lal Chowk. I saw one man carrying a gun. An army vehicle came and got stuck because of the crowd. It moved slowly through the crowd. Some people pelted stones at the vehicle. Others broke its panes. Soon they tried to set it on fire. The security personnel got off the vehicle and ran away towards the police station. The people ran after them. Nobody opened the gate of the police station. The security personnel turned back and opened fire on the mob. Later I heard that twenty-one were killed and hundreds injured. I ran towards home. When I entered home I saw the two kids of our family huddled in a corner. Hundreds of people came running towards our home. But they asked for water. They asked us to show them the way towards their village Magam. I did so. They ran away. I saw people carrying dead bodies. The Guest House was set on fire. Flames were rising. The army was everywhere. Crowds of people were running towards Braripora through the paddy fields.

In the evening Muslim neighbours came to our house and asked us to give them shelter for they had heard that the army would kill Muslims.

Next day there was another rumour that some Pandits had fired on the mob. Soon a 'hit list' with the names of seventeen Pandits to be killed was pasted on an electrical pole. This was warning of death. My brother's name figured in the list. He was a medical assistant at the hospital in Handwara. He nursed the wounded persons there. A man who owned an AK47 rifle, used to meet my brother regularly. They knew each other very well. Perhaps out of ignorance my brother was not afraid of him.

On 26 January we saw the Republic Day parade on TV in the house of our neighbour Madan Lal. Around 11 am. two people, known to us and belonging to good families, entered Madan Lal's house and asked us why we had watched the parade. We were speechless. They even warned and threatened our servant from Machil. They told him that he had turned into a pig by eating our food. All were tense and felt terrorized.

On 27 January many Pandits assembled in our house to talk about the fluid situation and chalk out a future plan. Bushan Lal Pandita was also there. He insisted that we leave Handwara till things settled down. He said that he was leaving himself and didn't know what would happen to his orchards and land in his absence. The Deputy Commissioner of Handwara came. He had organised a peace meeting with the prominent Muslims and Pandits in the Town Hall. One Rashid Khan and Ghulam Mohi-ud-Din entered the hall shouting and disrupted the meeting. They loudly asked all present there to leave immediately for 'there is no government and we are ruled by mujahids'. We knew them very well. Everybody was afraid. I ran home in a panic. I did not find my brother there. I left to search for him. I found him walking on the road. He shouted at me to go back home because 'they all say that we Pandits shot at Muslims that day'. He was terrified. Rumours had become a day-to-day affair.

We needed a truck or a bus but Handwara was under curfew. Brother went to Sopore to get any kind of transport and inform my maternal uncle's family that we had made up our mind to leave for Jammu. Brother returned late in the evening and informed us that we were to walk up to Kulangam next morning to catch the bus. We informed our Pandit neighbours about this decision and asked them to come with us. Two Pandit families agreed to send their womenfolk with us. Brother's wife had a one-month-old infant. We asked a Muslim neighbour to carry the mother and child in his tonga up to Kulangam. But he, out of fear, refused. We packed up and carried them in our own load carrier driven by a labourer. It was 4 am. We were experiencing psychological trauma. Fear had conquered us. While passing through a mohalla inhabited by Muslims we kept quiet but the sound of the moving load carrier made us miserable. We thought that we would be killed there and then. When we reached Kulangam, we got down and waited for the bus. It did not come. We stopped a truck which was carrying sacks of coal to Srinagar. The driver was kind enough to come to our help. Two women and the child sat by the driver's seat. The rest sat on the sacks of coal. We got down near the Palladium Cinema Hall and boarded a Jammu-bound bus. There was a bomb blast nearby. We could see the rising smoke. The bus left for Jammu. I don't know what I was thinking so long as I was seated in the bus.

The journey from Lal Chowk up to Jawahar tunnel was agonising. We didn't talk at all. The tunnel was our relief.

We reached Jammu by 9 pm. and went straight to my brother's house in Talab Tilloo. There were already many relatives there. Somehow we managed one night. Next day we took one room on rent. Other relatives came to ours. Fourteen people lived and ate and slept in that room for some days. We met the Divisional Commissioner and asked him to make arrangements for us. We were asked to shift to the Animal Husbandry Department and the adjacent buildings. I paid a visit to Geeta Bhawan to get our family registered as 'migrants' and to get a ration card. I found thousands of Pandits there. There was utter confusion and chaos. I saw old men and women cursing their fate. I saw children who were dumbfounded. I saw parents rebuking their children. I saw Pandits in agony and pain. Some could not recognise one another. The old were shouting for water. I reached my 'new room'. I found mother weeping. She asked us to get the cows and oxen from Handwara, our lost home. This continued for a number of days. Father lost his cool out of frustration and anxiety. Both mother and father talked about the cows, oxen, lands and house endlessly till they got used to the new life. It took them and others, including me, many years to adjust to the climate and the new environment.

In 1991 I got married. The beautiful joint family that we had in Handwara is no more. I now live with my wife in Shalimar Garden in Uttar Pradesh. My son is doing engineering in Pune. But I can't stop my mind from thinking about our village, property, orchards, the medical shop that we owned, cows, oxen, fruit trees and all the other things we had.

5

Ya Allah, they have killed them; pour some water into their mouths

Adarsh Ajit

He was a Deputy Commander of a dangerous militant outfit.

I had no idea of the changing political climate in Kashmir till I was asked to be the polling officer at a polling booth in the 1987 assembly elections. The polling station, in the Shopian district of Kashmir, was a few kilometres away from the place of my posting. A few days earlier, some local groups had issued warnings and pasted posters on the walls and the electric poles asking people to desist from casting their votes. After a few sittings at the election training centres I was given two ballot boxes to be used the next day. I carried them to my relative's house where I was staying as a guest. It was a three-storey building with a balcony facing the road. When the house owner saw me from the balcony carrying the ballot boxes with me he signalled to me to not enter his house with those boxes. I blushed. I hadn't expected this from him. I turned back to go to the bus stand to board a bus and go home, which was about fifteen kilometres away from there. The militants had announced a 'civil curfew' on the day of the election. Hoping that I would be able to arrange a taxi early in the morning I continued to walk towards the bus stand. There I met the presiding officer who was also tense and anxious. He was not able to figure out where to spend the night and how to reach the polling station. We were discussing the matter when Vir Ji, my friend, came and asked me what was going on. I narrated the whole story to him and he invited the presiding officer and me to the house in which he was staying. His house owners did not live there. We were relieved. We spent the night discussing the political situation, playing cards and drinking. In the wee hours, Vir Ji, Mr Mattoo (the presiding officer) and I left for our destination. We set off on foot and reached the polling station. Soon it was polling time. Not a single vote was polled. In the evening the presiding officer gave me the polling duty incentives. I started walking towards the place where I was to spend the night. Mattoo was to hand over the empty but sealed ballot boxes to the concerned authorities.

The results of the elections were declared and, as usual, the government was formed. But the political atmosphere was completely changed. There were signs of turmoil and unrest. A few bomb blasts that took place in the vicinity pointed towards future happenings.

One day I was to board a Srinagar-bound bus at 4 pm. I was late by a few minutes. I heard the sound of a terrible blast. When I reached the bus stand I saw that the bus had been bombed and there were some casualties.

My close friend Kamal was to get married on the fourth of October in 1989. I reached his village on the second of October. The village was a couple of kilometres away from the national highway at Qazigund. I and some other friends were happy to accompany the baraat on 4 October. But that day curfew was imposed. Only five persons were allowed to accompany the baraat and that too on the curfew passes given by the magistrate of the area.

Civil curfews, official curfews, blasts and selective killings became the order of the day.

On 9 October, I was to attend the marriage of a friend Dilip who lived in the same village where I lived. A non-vegetarian feast was to be hosted on 7 October. On 6 October I was asked to go to the butcher's shop and direct him to cut the mutton into different sizes. I reached the butcher's shop by 6 pm and the butcher and his assistants started their work. I and a couple of relatives were shivering from the cold. No one came to see us and offer us tea. But suddenly Mohammad Ashraf came with a samavar in his hand. He was a bearded man and offered nimaaz five times a day. But he used to drink with me whenever we got an opportunity. Dilip's brother-in-law was amazed to see our friendship and that too during those abnormal and disturbing times. He helped us with our work and finally we took the meat and reached Dilip's house. We handed over the meat to the cooks who had managed to come on foot as the bus services had been disrupted. The preparations for the feast were underway. Everybody was expecting four to five hundred guests. But on the day of the feast only thirty to forty guests turned up. They had managed to come on foot with great difficulty. They looked scared and wanted to return to their homes quickly. The separatists had given a call for a hartal. Much of the food that had been prepared was wasted. The food was disposed of in the street where the stray dogs of the village relished it. That was the end of the marriage ceremony.

I was to get married on 26 October 1989. My friend, Muzzaffar, from an adjacent village had arranged a videographer for us. On my father's directions I borrowed fifty mattresses, fifty quilts and fifty pillows from his Muslim friend, a teacher, to be used on the night of 25 October for mehandiraat. Two taxis and a bus were also arranged for the baraatis. Early in the morning of 26 October, the barber, Ahda, came to cut my hair and shave me. I asked him to hurry up. When I was ready, I was asked to board one of the taxis. The two drivers of the two taxis were Muslims from the same village. They fought because each wanted me to take his taxi. Somehow the issue was settled and I boarded one.

When we reached a Muslim-dominated locality of my village, my taxi was stopped by the Muslims. The mother of a Muslim friend brought a huge glass of milk for me. Coins and sweets were showered on me. The Muslim women sang songs usually sung for marriages. I asked them to allow us to proceed because the conditions were not favourable and we would be late as we needed to return in the evening. After an hour's journey we reached the village. When we got down the Muslims received us warmly. It looked as if the bride was their own daughter. Separate dishes had been cooked for the drivers. During the chanting of mantras I felt like defecating. I went out to search for a bathroom but there was none. I found a public latrine but that was very dirty. I went to a Muslim house and asked the members of the family if they had any bathroom. They welcomed me. There were no traces of Hindu-Muslim tension. After relieving myself they offered me lukewarm water to wash my hands with. Such gestures were not unusual at all. At 4 pm the videographer said that he needed to reach his home in Srinagar before sunset. So he urged us to hurry so that he could shoot and capture the parting scene. He said that the valley was going for a complete shutdown for three consecutive days. When I asked him the reason he replied that separatist leader Shabir Shah had been arrested. I did not know how he had come to know all this. I urged my in-laws to hurry so that we would face no problems on our return. But the videographer could not seen anywhere. He had left without telling anyone after shooting the scenes of his choice.

Next day when the valley was under 'civil curfew' two of my Muslim friends and their wives came to see my wife. They handed over gifts to her.

After a week we took the same taxi in which I had gone as a bridegroom and shifted to the outskirts of Srinagar where we took an outhouse on rent. It was a convenient place for all of us ... my father and brothers.

In Srinagar we witnessed bandh after bandh, official curfews, 'civil curfews', for days. Shops opened briefly in the evenings to sell vegetables and other grocery items. Days and weeks passed like this. One day, a neighbour, a retired Army Major, advised me that I should leave Kashmir and find new avenues because there was nothing left in the state of Jammu and Kashmir for the Kashmiri Pandit youth. I did not respond to his advice but felt that he was absolutely right. I was employed in the government sector.

There were selective killings and frequent bomb blasts. The so-called Freedom Movement of Muslims had by now penetrated the whole Muslim population of Kashmir. Processions and anti-India slogans were the order of the day. Time was adjusted in the watches that would then be in tune with the time of Pakistan. The peon of my office asked me what would happen to the Indian currency if Kashmir became a part of Pakistan. Worried, he said to me: 'What will become of my insurance policies?'

National Conference as a political party had lost its relevance. It was nobody's favourite party. Sheikh Abdullah, the tallest leader of the Muslims, who had brought them freedom, was no longer respected. Once the people believed that his name appeared on the leaves of the Chinar trees. I vividly remember the day when the whole population of our village ran towards the neighbouring village to see the crescent and the star that they believed had appeared on a tree. I also went there but did not see anything of the sort.

National Conference activists and even popular leaders were continuously disassociating themselves from the party through paid advertisements. My beloved teacher, who hailed from my native village, had once uttered in front of the wife of Sheikh Mohammad Abdullah that thousands of Kashmiri Muslims were ready to be martyred for her and her son. This teacher too resigned and grew a beard. He assured the masses in the village:

'Insha'Allah we will win our freedom the next Friday'.

There is a particular incident which took place one morning that is etched in my mind. My wife had gone to her sister's residence in the interior of the city. I was sleeping alone in my bedroom. I heard a knocking on the gate of our rented house. I woke up. So did my mother. Both of us went to the gate to see who was knocking. When we opened the door we saw my wife's brother-in-law with a scooter. He was wearing a helmet and seemed to be in a hurry. He had come to drop her off at our place. He said it was not advisable to keep her with them. He told us that the situation was worsening day by day and that most of the Pandits had already left for Jammu. He was nervous and in a panic. He advised us to leave Kashmir as quickly and secretly as possible. He did not enter, restarted his scooter and left. I thought his decision to leave the valley was timely because some days earlier militants had gunned down his cousin. Mother went back into her room where my father was sleeping. I had met and seen my wife after a long time. I wanted to hug her when we heard fierce gun shots. We stood still. Soon after, a Muslim woman shouted: 'Ya Allah, they have killed them.' She went on crying and screaming, 'Pour some water into their mouths.'

We remained standing. We were sure that my wife's brother-in-law must have passed the place from where the gun shots were heard because twenty minutes meant that he would have reached his place. In confusion and mental agony we waited for another fifteen minutes. Then I decided to go out and see what had happened. When I reached the spot, there was no one. There was only blood with some caps and boots nearby. I saw blood-soaked bodies of some men in uniform. Terrorists had killed some officers of the Indian Air Force. Fearing for their lives, no Kashmiri Pandit in the vicinity had dared to offer the dying officers water. Yet a Kashmiri Muslim woman who was passing by had poured water into their mouths.

The result of the killings of those officers was an army crackdown and the imposition of a severe curfew and shoot-on-site order in the entire area. Gradually, Pandit families started to leave the villages. We were not affected by the crackdown. But in our family it was decided that I should take my wife to our village and live there. Father said that the rest of the family would also move to our village later. But before that I had to accompany my wife to her brother's home because one of his wife's relatives had been killed by militants. They spread the rumour that he had been an 'informer' of an Indian intelligence agency.

When we reached our village, I was horrified to see a sea change in the people. Those who knew us very well avoided us and looked at us as if we were strangers. My wife wiped the tilak off her forehead because she wanted to hide her identity from the youths sitting on the banks of a stream. They all knew her. Somehow we reached our home. Father and a few others joined us after a couple of weeks. The atmosphere was charged with anti-India and pro-freedom slogans.

I was baffled at the vacillating nature of the Muslims. They are the people who burnt the houses of Jamat-i-Islami people. They are the people who supported the Congress party. They are the people who welcomed Prime Minister Morarji Desai. They are the people who loved Indira Gandhi. They are the people who stood naked in a park. They are the people who welcomed Indira Gandhi when she was taken around in a procession. They are the people who used to say that Pandits are integral to Kashmiriat. And they are the people who suspected Pandits and wanted them to leave Kashmir.

I joined office after many days. This kind of absence from offices was normal. I came to know that my close friend and colleague, a Kashmiri Pandit, had left the valley without informing anyone. Next morning we received the news that Vir Ji had been killed by the militants in his village. His in-laws lived in our village. We went there to offer our condolences. Not a single Muslim was seen there. Even labourers, milkmen and barbers had been directed not to talk to us Pandits. My maternal uncle who used to play cards with Vir Ji did not come for the funeral. Vir Ji's father-in-law begged me to arrange an army vehicle so that he could salvage some documents from Vir Ji's house. It was the same Vir Ji who had given me refuge during the election duty when my house-owner disowned me. But my parents and my wife did not allow me to go. They feared for my life. They thought the militants would target me. My uncle was worried about my safety. But a well-read Muslim contractor asked me not to worry and act in haste. My parents kept on telling me to leave Kashmir. After some days, my wife and I left Kashmir and went to Jammu.

Years later I came to know that the taxi driver who had taken me in his taxi on my wedding day had gone to Mumbai to become a film actor. He wasn't successful and faced several rejections. After being rejected he had returned to Kashmir and bought a car to earn his living as a taxi driver. Some years ago I heard that he had been killed in an encounter in Kashmir. For many years he had worked as the deputy commander of a dangerous militant outfit.

6

When the time in the clocks was made to go back by half an hour

Bushan Lal Saraf

On March 17 1990, my father, Pandit Saroop Nath, and I boarded a bus at the Reasi bus stop to go to our home in Shopian, Kashmir. Because of the harsh winters in Kashmir, my father would spend the winter months with me in Jammu. I was posted as a Sub-Judge in Reasi near Jammu during those days, and father would stay with me during the winter months every year.

Father had come to stay. He had thought of staying till March and returning to Kashmir at the onset of spring. He travelled alone. After spending some time with me at Reasi my father wanted to return to Kashmir. I accompanied him to Kashmir as the political environment in the Valley had considerably deteriorated. By the time we reached Ramban the drizzle had turned into torrential rain. The National Highway some kilometres ahead of the town was blocked. The road was cleared and, after a couple of hours of halt at Ramban, our journey towards our home resumed. As we were nearing the Valley, we noted a number of ominous signs. We saw many trucks, buses and taxis carrying Kashmiri Pandits out of Kashmir. They were frightened and going to Jammu. Having lived out of the valley for a long time, I hadn't experienced the situation prevailing there. By 7 pm the bus reached Khanabal, Anantnag. A Pandit acquaintance, a resident of Hawal in Pulwama, had boarded the bus at Udhampur. He, too, was on his way to his home. He suggested that we get off the bus at Khanabal and hire a taxi to go to Shopian. We did so and took a taxi to go to Shopian via Bijebehara and Zainapora. We were nervous when the vehicle reached Zainapora, a village inhabited by a large number of Pandits. The taxi driver turned off the cassette player which was playing Hindi film songs and covered it with a black cloth. We saw hordes of young men roaming around the village with guns and weapons. The driver said that while driving the car the lights of the cabin had to be kept switched on. 'What does all this portend?' I wondered.

Finally, around 11 pm we were at the gate of our house. We knocked at the gate and shouted loudly for someone to open it. My brother Virji and sister-in-law heard us, and opened the gate. When we entered the house, we realised that it had been foolish on our part to have shouted loudly. We were told that the area was infested with militants.

I woke up late the next morning. The tiresome journey had exhausted me physically and mentally. The rain did not stop. After the morning tea I set out to have a look at the predominantly Pandit-inhabited locality known as Bata Pora. The sight was extremely depressing. The locality wore a deserted and forlorn look—vacant houses with doors ajar and windows open. Most of the Pandit families had left their houses and the remaining had packed their household belongings and were ready to flee. Incessant rain and the traffic blockage on the National Highway were keeping them from leaving. I met some friends and relatives in the neighbourhood. They were talking in hushed tones. They were a frightened lot. Families were huddled in rooms with doors and windows bolted. The killings of some prominent Pandits in the city had given rise to panic and fear. I returned home in the afternoon in a state of shock. Some Muslims of the town came to see my father. After exchanging pleasantries with us they assured us that there was nothing to fear. Their assurances calmed our nerves momentarily.

I was to collect some papers concerning my service record from a court in Srinagar where I had worked some years back. On March 19 I woke up early to a continual downpour. After having breakfast, I boarded a bus to Srinagar with uncertainty looming large in my heart. The city wore an ominously desolate look. Security barricades were everywhere. The security forces were patrolling the whole city. Frisking of pedestrians on the roads was going on. The situation was very tense. In the court premises, I felt a semblance of normalcy. Fellow lawyers greeted me warmly. I visited the chambers of the Pandit judicial officers who were posted there. They looked unsettled, confused and jittery. They were ready to move out but stood grounded to the place because their jobs demanded it. When I left the court premises with the relevant papers I intended to roam the streets of the city as I used to in the past. But the city looked like a war zone. Frenzy ruled the streets; my confidence was shaken. People waited in long queues outside banks and other financial institutions. I saw some Pandit acquaintances who were withdrawing cash and valuables from the banks. The militants had warned the people of Kashmir to withdraw all their money from other banks and transfer the money and valuables into the lockers of Jammu and Kashmir Bank. The time in all the watches and clocks had been made to go back by half an hour to synchronise with the Pakistan Standard Time. Militants and their supporters beat those who followed the Indian Standard Time. Many Pandits had also changed the time in the watches they wore on their wrists. Some youths who were supporters of the militant outfits were asking the pedestrians to show them their wrist-watches. Those who had not changed the time in their watches to match the Pakistan Standard Time were beaten up. Their watches were smashed to bits.

Before the curfew was imposed I rushed to the Batamalu General Bus Stand to catch a bus for Shopian. The bus was jam-packed. It lumbered slowly and crossed security checkposts at a number of places. Around 4 pm the bus reached Keegam, a village about nine kilometres from Shopian. At Keegam a big contingent of passengers de-boarded and some others boarded the bus. Keegam was the native place of Comrade Abdul Sattar Ranjoor, a veteran communist leader of Kashmir with secular and progressive credentials. He had toiled hard during the rule of the Maharaja and had been incarcerated. My father, a noted political and social activist of the valley, had also played a big part in the freedom movement launched by Sheikh Mohammad Abdullah in the thirties. As such Ranjoor Sahab would often come to our home to see father. In my youth I was a supporter of the Progressive movement too and had come in contact with Comrade Ranjoor. In the past I had visited his house a number of times and I would make it a point to see him while passing through his village. So I got off the bus and reached his home which was on the edge of the road. When I knocked at the gate of his house, someone asked me to show my identity card. I introduced myself and said that I wanted to meet Ranjoor Sahab. My unexpected visit evoked a strange and pleasant feeling among Ranjoor Sahab's family members. Ranjoor Sahab hugged me and then made me sit next to him under a warm blanket. While sipping tea, we talked about the prevailing political situation. Ranjoor Sahab was visibly devastated. The exodus of Pandits had disturbed him greatly. He fumbled for words. After about an hour's stay with him I took my leave to catch a bus home. While bidding goodbye, he uttered something, which, in days to come, proved to be prophetic. He was worried about the safety of my father and other Pandits he knew.

I was home before nightfall. I told father about my meeting with Ranjoor Sahab. He heaved a deep sigh and fell silent. I sensed what was going in his mind. After a long pause, father said: 'Did Abdul Sattar and I toil hard in our lives only to see this terrible day?' The news in the evening shook us. A senior Pandit bureaucrat, AK Raina, had been gunned down in the Food and Supplies Department office at Shaeed Gunj in Srinagar. That time I had been roaming on the streets of the city. We called the children to the room, held them close, turned off the radio, bolted the windows and the doors, drew the curtains and huddled fearfully for a long time.

On the evening of 21 March, my cousin (son of my father's younger brother) came and informed me that his sister's husband wanted to meet me. I went to see him at his house. When I entered their house, I felt that there was something terribly wrong. The house was full of our relatives. The moment was tense and grim. No one was talking. They informed me that they had received a letter from a terrorist organization stating that my brother-in-law, a medical doctor by profession, was part of the anti-freedom movement. In the letter he was warned of dire consequences. Such a letter meant death. Many Pandits who ignored similar threat and warning letters had been abducted and killed earlier. On the previous evening a *Newstrack* team had visited the place and interviewed some residents of the locality. My brother-in-law happened to be one such interviewee. Now the only way out was to arrange a vehicle immediately so that my brother-in-law could leave for a safer place.

The news at 7.30 pm: B K Ganjoo, a Pandit employee of the Telecommunication Department had been shot dead while he was hiding in a drum at his home in Chotta Bazaar, Kanya Kadal, Srinagar. He knew that militants were looking for him. The gunmen had turned his house upside down, found him hiding in a drum containing rice and pumped bullets into his body. The rice had turned red. I returned home but did not divulge what had transpired at my brother-in-law's house lest it should cause panic. In the morning I informed my brother and father and impressed upon them to prepare to leave. They said they would leave in a week's time.

On the morning of 23 March, my brother arranged for a taxi owned by our Muslim neighbour. I boarded the taxi and left for Jammu. The atmosphere was gloomy, heavy and dark. Waving delete goodbye to father and brother I cast a parting look at my ancestral house with a feeling that I was seeing it for the last time. That turned out to be true.

The taxi driver took his friend along with him for company. The scene was quite depressing. Near Kulgam the tension became palpable. People in small groups had gathered on the road. A mob did not allow the traffic to move. We asked the bystanders what was going on. We were informed that the previous night a Kashmiri Pandit police constable had been gunned down in front of District Police Lines, Khanabal, Anantnag. He belonged to Devsar, a locality near Kulgam. We were to pass through that place in order to reach Qazigund. With great difficulty we managed to drive out of the chaos that had unfolded on the road. There was madness all around. For some it was euphoria and for others it was horror. But some signs of sanity could be seen and felt on that strange day. The driver refused to take a bystander who was signalling for a ride. I trusted his judgement. An old man at a distance waved his arms frantically and pleaded with us to stop the car. I reasoned with the driver and requested him to stop the car for him. He was holding the hand of a small girl. We stopped and asked the old man and the girl to hop in. The driver's friend asked the old man the reason for the commotion on the road. He was joyous when the man informed us that some Indian army men were killed during an encounter with the militants. The old man's voice was feeble. But then I heard the him say: 'How much depletion will a sea suffer if a sparrow drinks its water?' The friend of the driver asked the old man to explain. He sighed and said, 'We are the sparrows and India is the ocean. We cannot cause its depletion.' The taxi driver got angry and retorted, 'So what? Our freedom fighters will kill thousands of army men.' The old man sighed and said, 'Yes, but by then the Kashmiris would have been wiped out.'

At around 10 am, we reached Qazigund. After dropping off the old man and his girl there we proceeded towards the Traffic Check Post where we were informed that the highway ahead was blocked for some security reasons. We were asked not to move ahead. But the driver disclosed my identity to the traffic officials who allowed us to proceed. But they warned us that under no circumstance could we proceed beyond Banihal. We went ahead and reached Banihal, a small town on the highway. It wore a completely different look. It was surging with a multitude of Pandits who were on the run to Jammu. The road blockade had forced them to stop there.

We reached Jammu in the evening. Our taxi stopped in front of the Dak Bungalow in Jammu. One of my colleagues, Khalid Nizam, an advocate who practised at the local court, spotted me from a distance and came up. He invited me to his place. But his place was far off and miles away from the town. Then he took me to the branch office of the State Bank of India and offered me food. Mr Nizam was the legal advisor to the bank. The manager, who was from Punjab, was a kind-hearted person. He came to my rescue. He carried my luggage to a room and made me comfortable. His wife greeted me as though I was her elder brother. Khalid left for his home, promising to come see me the next day.

On March 24, I left for Srinagar. Anarchy and mayhem ruled everywhere. I listened to the 7.30 pm news on the radio. It was a bulletin of deaths. A day earlier, Abdul Sattar Ranjoor had been killed by the militants in the same room of his house in which I had met him three days earlier. Then came the news of the kidnapping of the former Member of Legislative Assembly, Mir Mustafa.

On 25 March, I prepared to leave Srinagar. Thousands of people had gathered at the airport to fly out of Kashmir. At noon I managed to get a ticket and, by 1 pm, the plane was airborne. My mind was blank. When I reached Jammu, I regained my senses and felt relieved.

In the evening I took a bus to Reasi.

7

Mata Roop Bhawani will protect us

Susheel Pajnu

At around 10 pm on 14 January 1990, we started calling our relatives and friends on the phone to know what was going on outside our homes in Srinagar. Earlier in the evening, Khankah-i-Sokhta, Safa Kadal, the locality we lived in, had erupted with the clamour of frightening slogans coming from loudspeakers in the neighbourhood. We heard the sound of drums too. People in the neighbourhood were beating drums and shouting slogans. It was the very first time that such an event had taken place. Like other Pandits in the neighbourhood, we were clueless. Everyone said that this was the beginning of something frightening. Things changed overnight. From that day onwards, the entire locality and downtown Srinagar witnessed mass protests and marches against India. Armed militants came from nowhere and prowled the streets. Our locality fell under the command of some area commanders of two militant organisations. We lingered on, despite the fear.

Then, one summer day in June that year, Prithvi Nath Ticku, our neighbour, was shot at by two young boys just a few steps outside his house. The boys had called him out of his house at dawn, and pumped eight bullets into his body. Miraculously, none of his vital organs were damaged. Prithvi Nath had wounds on his arm, shoulder and leg. Two of his neighbours, one Muslim and the other Pandit, took him to the SMHS hospital. The moment they reached the hospital the doctors gesticulated and signalled to each other as if they were communicating in a secret code. The two neighbours who witnessed this sign language didn't understand. They pleaded with the doctors to treat Prithvi Nath immediately. He was bleeding profusely, but was still conscious. One of the doctors prepared an injection and administered it to the patient. He left the ward, assuring the neighbours that the patient would be fine. Thirty minutes later, Prithvi Nath died.

After the shocking death of Prithvi Nath Ticku, the rest of the Pandit families in our locality met the Halqa president of Awami Action Committee, which was headed by Mirwaiz Farooq, one of the prominent leaders of the Muslims. He feigned ignorance about the murder of Prithvi Nath and told them that even he was not aware who was behind these killings. The killers had killed an innocent man just because he was a Pandit. Mirwaiz Farooq advised the Pandits of our locality to shift to a safer place in uptown Srinagar till the situation became normal.

The Pandit families in our locality met in the Ram Mandir in our neighbourhood and discussed the matters concerning their safety in the wake of the threats which had been issued to them by the militants. Even Mirwaiz Farooq had expressed his helplessness. We were left to fend for ourselves.

The next day, Professor Ganjoo, a retired professor, was shot dead outside his house. Soom Nath Sapru, who lived in our neighbourhood, was kidnapped. My father and our neighbours managed to establish contact with some local militants and, with their assistance, got Soom Nath released in two days. The spate of killings and kidnappings of Pandits continued unabated.

From April 1990 onwards, the Pandit families in Khankah-I-Sokhta, Safa Kadal, started shifting to other localities. Some took refuge in Indra Nagar, near the army cantonment in Batwara. Most fled to Jammu. Dr RL Koul was the only Pandit who stayed behind after sending his wife and son to Delhi.

One summer day in June, we packed a few clothes and some utensils and went to Gogji Bagh, and moved into my paternal aunt's house which was vacant. Thereafter, my father and I started visiting our locality to assess the condition there. The situation worsened. Bomb blasts became a routine affair. So did the gun battles between the militants and the security forces. Youngsters defied curfew and came out in the streets to pelt stones at army bunkers.

I went to Delhi with my uncle for my studies and joined a college there, but, during my vacations, I would go to Srinagar on my own. Upon seeing me, my neighbours would hug me and cry.

In July 1992, I visited Kashmir. My parents decided to take the rest of our household belongings out of our house in Khankah-i-Sokhta to my aunt's house in Gogji Bagh. I requested a friend who was a militant commander with Al Jehad, one of the militant organisations active in the valley, to accompany me to my house. We went with a load carrier to my house and started packing the household things. While I was packing, two masked youth barged into my house with guns. Upon seeing my friend, they got excited. One of the youths took off his mask. I recognised him instantly. Much to my surprise he happened to be an acquaintance from the neighbourhood. We used to play cricket in the same team at Eidgah. We hugged each other. Like other militants and locals, he blamed and cursed Jagmohan, the Governor of the state, for the political happenings in Kashmir, and the exodus of the Pandits from our locality. I argued with him, trying to convince them that Jagmohan was not responsible for the bloodshed. He was the Governor, whose responsibility it was to administer the state in the absence of the government. I told them that the targeted killings of the Pandits in our locality had forced the Pandit families to leave.

My friend, the militant, told me that one of his hideouts was just behind my house. The house belonged to one of our Pandit neighbours whose family had left the place. After I packed our household belongings and placed everything in the load carrier, I went to the hideout, and, much to my surprise, I saw many things intact in the house. The cane furniture in the living room, utensils, gas cylinders and other things! I went upstairs to one of the rooms and saw a lot of books on a large bookshelf. I told my friend that I wanted to take all the books with me but felt bad that the load carrier was full. My friend suggested that we come back some other day and salvage the books and other things from the house. I took an old radio set with me. After a week, my militant friend and I returned to the house to take the books. The moment I reached the house and went to the room, I was shocked to see the bookshelf empty. I left the place dejected. My friend, the militant, felt helpless too. After two days, my friend was killed in an encounter with the security forces.

I completed my post-graduation in Pune and started working in a company in Delhi. My father, who was working as an insurance surveyor, was hospitalised in Srinagar around that time. I left my job and went back to Kashmir. I came to know that my father was being investigated for some insurance cases. He knew that the cases were fictitious as they involved some top officials of an insurance company. My father became paralysed. We went to Sona Sahab, a pious saint of Mazhama, to seek his blessings. With his spiritual powers, he cured my father and showered his blessings and grace upon him.

In August 1997, I joined my father in his business. I took charge and helped my father run the business from our office in Srinagar. My work involved dealing with the public and settling insurance claims (mostly related to damage of property). Given the militancy and spate of violence, several buildings and houses were destroyed due to fire, bomb and grenade blasts. Incidents like these were a common affair those days. Several private and government-owned properties used to be targeted, and suffered damage.

For one claim, which was related to the damage of a property at Natipora, the claimant was not ready to sign the consent letter as he thought the insurance amount was less. He started threatening me. One morning, he came to my office with some youth from Abi Guzar and started yelling. 'We will get you killed,' they screamed. I took an iron rod from under my table and bashed the intruders. They got scared and ran away. Some days later, when I was not in office, some militants barged in and stole all the files. When I reached my office, I saw the office boy crying. He, too, had been warned and threatened. The militants had told him that they would kill me. I contacted my friends at Batmaloo who were militant commanders in the area. I called the client to settle the claim the next morning. My friends, the militants, were with me that day. The client came with the same militants who had stolen all the files. They were shocked to see my friends, the militants, who were superior to them in rank and order. My friends talked with the client's friends and soon the matter was resolved, and the files were returned to me.

One September day in 1996, Siddhartha Gigoo, my old neighbour from our locality, came to Kashmir after six years. He had left in 1990. I met him at our place in Gogji Bagh and handed over the antique radio set which I had salvaged from his ancestral house in our locality Khankah-i-Sokhta. The radio set belonged to his grandfather.

In 2000, a decade after moving out of our old house, we shifted back into our old house at Khankah-i-Sokhta. Our Muslim neighbours welcomed us and were happy to see us.

But things had changed. None of our Pandit neighbours and friends were there. Everyone had left. We were the only Pandit family there. I went to Ram Mandir (our temple) where we used to gather in the evenings to play cricket. The temple was in ruins. The idols in the sanctum sanctorum were gone. The walls had been desecrated. It was a very painful sight. The temple had stood there for several decades. Then I went to the Mata Roop Bhawani temple adjacent to our house. This temple, too, was in a dilapidated condition. Everything inside had been looted and vandalised. All the houses belonging to the Pandits were occupied. Some houses were used by the militants as hideouts and others were occupied by the security forces.

I made up my mind to carry out the repair work in Mata Roop Bhawani temple. It took me months to get the temple complex renovated.

I got married in June 2004. My in-laws lived in the quarters at Kashmir University. It was after fourteen years that a Pandit wedding took place in our locality. Our Muslim neighbours came to my wedding and sang and danced. It was a strange experience. We were the only Pandit family living in downtown Safa Kadal in the peak of militancy. And we celebrated my wedding along with the Muslim families.

In 2008, we witnessed hartals for nearly four months. The Muslims protested against the Amarnath Yatra Shrine board. People came out in the streets and pelted stones at the army establishments everywhere in Kashmir. There was violence. Several people got injured in the clashes between the protestors and the security forces. The families in our locality arranged food and other essential items for the needy.

Ghulam Hassan had taken over a small kiryana shop, which till 1990 was owned by Pandit Shambu Nath (known as Shombakak). Shambu Nath had fled the place when the militancy started. None of us knew where he had gone.

My children go to the Kendriya Vidalaya School in Srinagar as none of the schools in the neighbourhood offer Hindi as a subject. The schools offer only Urdu and Kashmiri as compulsory subjects.

The house of Abbas Ansari, one of the leaders of the Hurriyat Conference, is heavily fortified. On many days in the past, I requested his security staff for help. And they always obliged.

In September 2014, a devastating and unprecedented flood ravaged many parts of Kashmir. We lost all telephone and mobile connectivity within and outside the valley. Thousands perished in the flood. Several hundreds became homeless, and sought refuge in temporary shelters. Somehow we survived. Downtown Srinagar remained unaffected by the flood. For weeks, we had nothing to eat. The supplies didn't reach us. We depended on whatever we had hoarded over the last several months to make ends meet. We started community kitchens in downtown Srinagar and fed the homeless. Everybody came together in the crisis. We'd lived through tumultuous times. We'd seen terror. We'd suffered. We knew fear. And during the flood, we stood together and looked after one another. We had learnt how to survive. We prayed for our safety, security and happiness. The waters receded after several weeks.

My father was a member of the Jammu and Kashmir Cricket Association. He owned a cricket club of which I was the captain for more than a decade. Some of the Muslim members of the association wanted to usurp the clubs once owned by the Pandits. They succeeded in taking charge of some of the clubs, and now they were after my father's club. My father was the Joint Secretary of the association from 1972 to 1974 and the General Secretary from 1974 to 1976.

He was also the curator of the two one-day international cricket matches played in Srinagar in 1983 and 1986. The first one was played between India and West Indies and the second one between India and

Australia. Kashmiris will never forget the cricket match played between India and West Indies in 1983. This match became a turning point in the history of Kashmir. Many things came to the fore, such as the political leanings of the Muslims. Their hatred for India became well known. The Muslims supported the West Indian cricket team and erupted with joy every time the West Indians took a wicket or scored a boundary. The Pandits were just mute spectators.

My family continues to live in downtown Srinagar. Ours is the only Pandit family there.

It is very frustrating to not see a single Pandit family around in the locality. I grew up with many of them. We lived in wonderful times. At times when I look at the houses which once belonged to the Pandits I feel miserable. The houses are not the same without their original residents. Each house has a sad tale to narrate. These houses that once belonged to Pandits are now owned by strangers. Without the Pandits, I feel lost in my own homeland, my own neighbourhood, my own ancestral home. No other tragedy can be greater than this.

I'm surrounded by a strange silence. This silence in me has grown.

I wonder if the Pandits will ever return. Probably not! They left more than two decades ago, lost everything, including their home and way of life. However, it feels good to know that many of them have carved a niche of their own and prevailed during the toughest of times in exile.

Whenever I look around, I think very fondly of our old Pandit neighbours, my childhood friends. Many were just like family. I still have ties with some of them who live in Delhi. I miss them a lot and that void can never get filled. This tragedy has left scars in my heart which even time cannot heal.

I have lost a lot. The only satisfaction I have is of living in my ancestral home where I spent most of my childhood. My parents and I derive peace and solace from the presence of the Mata Roop Bhawani temple which is nearby. We're the only devotees in the temple now. We look after the temple as though it is our own temple in our very house. We have full faith in the Goddess. She will continue to protect us, even in the most dangerous of times. Despite the threats that my parents received when militancy was at its peak in the nineties, our decision to stay back in Kashmir and not to ever think of leaving, even though everyone else left, was taken by my father whose love for his homeland overshadowed all fear and insecurity. He did not have any means to support the family for many years during the militancy era. Yet he persevered. 'Mata Roop Bhawani will protect us,' he would say.

Our staying in Kashmir is at a cost. The biggest price I am paying now is that my kids are not getting the right schooling that they would have got elsewhere in India. My kids' education is suffering, due to frequent hartals and the political turmoil which continues in Kashmir. Besides, I don't have any Pandit friends here. Kashmir is incomplete without the Pandits and will always remain so without them.

8

Nights of Terror

Meenakshi Raina

On a cold December night in 1989, a bunch of masked youngsters threw stones at our house in Srinagar. We suspected some of them to be our neighbours. They knew who we were and what we did. They shouted our names and jeered at us. We switched off the lights in the rooms and huddled inside. The din of the stones smashing against the rooftop was so loud that it felt as if it was raining stones from the sky. Most of the window-panes shattered and pieces of glass lay scattered everywhere inside the house. 'Who are these people and why are they throwing stones at our house?' asked my younger sister who was nine years old at that time. Accidentally, she stepped on a piece of glass and hurt her foot. Blood oozed out of the wound and she writhed in pain. She lost track of the question that she had asked. My father was shaken. He didn't understand why someone would do that. That night none of us slept as fear gripped each one of us. Even before this incident, my father had received a threatening letter from a militant organisation, warning him to leave Kashmir.

On the previous day, we'd seen masked men waving guns and shouting anti-Indian slogans in the street. We'd prayed for the situation to be normal. Although we lived in fear, for the first time my father realised that the situation had become life-threatening for us. He decided that my mother, my aunts and all children in the family should leave Kashmir. We had a house in Jammu that was under construction, and only two rooms were liveable. On 3 January 1990, some of my family members and I left for Jammu. We took two suitcases with us and left the rest of our household possessions behind. We couldn't even pack properly. When I was leaving I kept staring at my house; I felt that I was never going to come back.

My father, my uncles and my grandmother stayed back in Kashmir. Throughout the ensuing days and nights they held knives in their hands just in case they had to defend themselves from intruders. They remained confined to one room in the house and became mute spectators, and prayed for the nights to pass without any untoward incident. The anti-Pandit slogans and announcements were loud and frightening.

After some days, my father arranged for a taxi. The neighbours assembled in front of our house. They asked my father if the family was leaving Kashmir. My father replied, 'Mataji chi bemaar, haspatal chi nin.' (My mother is ill and I have to take her to a hospital.) On this pretext, the neighbours allowed them to board the taxi. They carried nothing with them except a small bundle containing some clothes. My father went to his friend's place, which was safer than his own house as he had decided to stay back in Kashmir. The rest of the family fled to Jammu.

When my grandmother arrived in Jammu, the look on her face was horrific. I will never forget that look. I comforted her by telling her that we would be safe now. My father didn't want to leave Kashmir because of his job. He had handed over a satchel containing my mother's gold jewellery to my grandmother. My grandmother held the satchel close to her chest while travelling to Jammu. While handing it over to my mother she mentioned, 'Moklaye Kashmir.' (Kashmir is finished.) She narrated how they had spent the night of 19 January in fear, anxiety and uncertainty. She whispered to us the slogans that were used to harass the Kashmiri Pandits: 'Assi gacchi panunuy Pakistan, Batav rostuy batinen saan.' (We want our Pakistan, without the Pandit men, but with their women.)

The rhythm of our peaceful existence in our homes in Kashmir was broken. A family of fifteen members had to share a two-room tenement. Every day in the neighbourhood I would witness the arrival of trucks full of those who had fled their homes; these were the Pandit families who had managed to escape the terror and taken refuge in Jammu. The number of displaced families continued to multiply and people were rendered homeless. Jammu became a safe haven for the displaced Pandits.

I had noticed the sparks of the separatist movement at my school, when many of my classmates would write on the blackboard 'Happy Independence Day, August 14', which marked the Independence Day of Pakistan. My patriotic instincts would compel me to erase it and that was all I could do. I had always witnessed a different culture in Kashmir; there used to be forced blackouts on 15 August, the Indian Independence Day, and celebrations if the Pakistan cricket team won a match against the Indian team.

My father worked for Doordarshan. After the assassination of Lassa Kaul, Director–Doordarshan, in February 1990, my father shifted to the heavily guarded government accommodation within the Doordarshan complex and worked tirelessly for days. Once when he visited us in Jammu, we didn't want him to go back but he explained that he worked for an essential service and that the show must go on. We were concerned about his safety. He constantly kept on shifting from one room to another at the Doordarshan complex so that nobody knew exactly which room he occupied. He had no option but to continue with what he was doing. During such a crisis, he and his other colleagues who chose to stay within the complex had no access to essential supplies. Many times, they survived on one meal a day and got minimum support from the authorities. My mother would ask my father if he could visit our house and salvage some household items and send them to Jammu. But it was too dangerous for my father to go back to the locality and to our house. He would hardly leave the Doordarshan complex and when he came to visit us, he would not tell us anything.

In Jammu, I would notice my mother climbing the stairs towards the cemented rooftop and crying. One time I followed her, she was sitting quietly on a pile of bricks with tears in her eyes. I asked her the reason for being so disturbed and all she said was that she had worked all her life and saved to build a home in Kashmir and now everything was lost. The news of a break-in in our house in Kashmir had arrived. We got to know that everything was looted. After this incident, a neighbour locked the main door of the house. But it was too late. It was empty. There was nothing left to plunder.

The separatist movement in Kashmir started with anti-India slogans, hoisting of green flags, pro-Pakistani sentiments and exploitation of the youth by the fundamentalist leaders, and support from the radical Muslim population. Mosques meant for religious prayers were used to hide arms and ammunition. There was a well-planned strategy that started with selective killings of prominent Kashmiri Pandits to create fear. The militants killed many Pandits. We lost trust in our neighbours.

The brutality didn't end with killings; the killings of Pandits were celebrated. Those neighbours, who had assured these families that they would protect them, watched them die and did nothing. Many Pandits in our locality were strangulated to death with steel wires. Women were stripped and molested and there was a rise in kidnappings and merciless killings. The bodies of the murdered Pandits bore marks of torture. Threatening letters asking Kashmiri Pandits to leave Kashmir (but leave their womenfolk behind) were pasted on the doors of Pandit houses. Pandits were accused of being the agents of India in Kashmir. Temples were vandalised, destroyed, demolished and set on fire.

The freedom of Kashmir from India became the dream of every Muslim living in Kashmir, and the local masses were absolutely collaborating with the militants by providing them shelter, protection, money and all the help and support they needed.

I was fortunate to have a second home in Jammu, although it was a small house, but it offered shelter and kept us safe. There were many migrant families who had to seek refuge in tents that were erected in vast grounds. The scorching heat was unbearable. With no facilities to fight the intolerable heat, the worst for the camp dwellers came when it rained. Many tents collapsed. The camps had poor sanitation and unhygienic conditions, which created numerous health problems. Due to lack of medical facilities and paucity of medicines, lives were lost prematurely. Unable to withstand the burden of worries and hardships, the displaced Pandits developed heart ailments, diabetes, depression and anxiety. Poverty and lack of educational facilities hit them hard.

Leaving behind their property in Kashmir and deprived of their assets, Kashmiri Pandits became homeless and suffered for no fault of theirs. Throughout the turmoil, the houses of Kashmiri Pandits were set ablaze, vandalised or looted. It caused mental agony and added to their sufferings.

The locals in Kashmir were banned by the militants from buying properties of Kashmiri Hindus as eventually these properties would be grabbed forcibly without any payments. In such prevailing circumstances, our neighbour sent an offer for purchasing our house in Kashmir. The amount offered was not even close to half the estimated value of our house. Yet, my father decided to sell our house in Kashmir because it had already been vandalised twice. Life had become unsafe for my father in his own homeland.

The exodus gave rise to pain, agony and misery. The youth became extremely frustrated; the old were afflicted with depression and trauma due to their suffering and hardships. Abandoned by the political parties and the government, the plight of the displaced Pandit families remained unheard. There was a paucity of employment opportunities in Jammu due to the massive population that had migrated from the Valley. Many families couldn't afford to educate their children.

The state government set up a relief commissioner's office. The migrants who had fled from the Valley were asked to register their names. Once registered, the family was provided with a ration card, identifying them as displaced migrants. On presenting the ration card, government aid was provided to the tent residents and other non-salaried families who had no source of income. The cash relief paid per month was not sufficient to afford the daily commodities.

My parents also registered their names; their black-and-white photograph that was glued to the ration card was stamped and signed by the zonal officer. My mother had worked as a lecturer in Women's College in Srinagar. She was able to collect her salary in Jammu only after presenting the ration card. The ration card became a very important document for every migrant family. Even today I have preserved a copy of the migrant ration card along with my Canadian citizenship. It tells me who I am and where I have come from.

The colleges in Jammu refused to admit the displaced students due to lack of infrastructure. Like other migrant students my future was also at stake. All of us jointly protested and carried out demonstrations at the Divisional Commissioner's office in Jammu. We did so for days. I remember collecting money from the students so that we could arrange banners, posters and placards. It was finally in August 1990 that camp schools and colleges were set up for migrant students to pursue their education.

I failed to understand what led to the situation where life became unsafe for us in our own homeland. How could the intelligence system fail and why was the state government so careless about taking action. Was it intentional? What led to a crisis of such immense magnitude and complexity? How did the intelligence agencies fail to detect the movement of the youth crossing the Indian borders? After getting trained at the training camps in Pakistan, how were the youth able to return with arms and ammunition and execute their plans? When bombs started exploding and bullets were being fired, things became clear, but it was too late to take control of the situation. Militancy had grown over a period of time and stemmed out of the deep-rooted hatred, which the Kashmiri Muslims had harboured against India since 1947. The firing and hurling of grenades on buildings were calculated and persistent. The attackers carefully planned their attack; they fired and then disappeared into the crowd, and finally escaped through the narrow lanes. Fear of law and authority didn't exist; it was evident from the killings in broad daylight. Militants had gained control over the press, the local police, doctors, teachers and lawyers; all of them were at their service. All facilities in the hospitals—from doctors' care to hospital beds—were available for the militants; the hospital administration helped them avoid police interrogation and even to escape from the security forces. Many government employees remained absent from their duties and served in militant organisations, and yet remained on the payrolls of the government and got their salaries. Their absence from duty was never reported by anyone and remained undetected. Many locals became conspirators, informers. Some became informers out of fear and others conspired out of choice and ideology.

What was thought to be a temporary displacement, eventually turned out to be permanent. The properties of Kashmiri Pandits were forcibly encroached on, thus making their return to Kashmir impossible. Weeks turned into months and months turned into years, and we continued living in exile. There was no going back to Kashmir; the government had failed to protect us in our homeland—Kashmir. Most of the population either lived in the camps or rented accommodation, and some sought temporary refuge at their relatives' houses.

One of the deadliest massacres of Kashmiri Pandits happened in 1998 at Wandhama. Unidentified militants murdered 23 innocent Kashmiri Pandits, including women and children. Despite the rise in violence in the Valley, these Pandit families had chosen to stay back. Gunmen had come to their house dressed in army uniform and, after a brief conversation, rounded up all the members of the family and then shot them dead. I was living in a hostel in Mumbai at that time. I made a phone call to my family in Jammu. I felt it like a personal loss and I cried.

In the last twenty-five years, I never went back to Kashmir.

At the time of our exodus, Jammu became the safe haven for Kashmiri Pandits. Over the years, the government has failed to provide justice to around half a million Kashmiri Pandits who were forced to leave their homes in the valley because of persecution by the majority community. Aren't we citizens of India? The government calls us 'displaced migrants'. Those who were born in exile (after 1990) have never known their place of origin.

The middle-aged and senior citizens who left Kashmir during the mass exodus had to face hardship. They were suddenly exposed to a hostile environment. They lived in anger, frustration and with many unanswered questions. However, they consoled themselves with the fact that their future generations would have a better tomorrow. They went through a lot of mental torture and trauma. Despite financial constraints, this segment regrouped and focused their energy and took on the challenge of shaping the future of their younger generation. Some of them managed to secure better education for their children in professional colleges in the state of Maharashtra, with the support of political parties like the Shiv Sena.

The teenagers and youth had to go through trauma at a different level. At that stage of their life, one would expect them to be enjoying life, but they had to struggle along with their parents for space, food, schooling and social stigma. The doors of camp schools and degree colleges were opened in Jammu but the children from migrant families had to attend the camp schools and colleges in the afternoon in scorching heat, with very little infrastructure.

The last decade has seen a new generation of our community lose touch with our own culture, language, tradition and rituals. The new generation, born in multi-cultural cities in India and abroad, find it hard to connect with their roots and moorings, and by the time they grow into adults, they would have no connection with their ancestral places in Kashmir. The revival of the Kashmiri Pandit culture doesn't seem to be happening. One can only relate to a place based on two key cultural aspects: language and rituals. The children born in exile do not relate to Kashmir. They see Kashmir as a tourist place now.

Currently, there are some Kashmiri Pandits who are still living in Kashmir and working for the state government there, but when they retire they might leave. They may prefer to be with their children and grandchildren who are settled outside Kashmir. The migrants, who have settled in Jammu and built houses there, wouldn't like to go back to Kashmir in their old age.

Years from now, we will neither remain Kashmiri nor Pandits. Bereft of the Pandits, Kashmir will become a place with Muslims as the only inhabitants. Everything that stood for the age-old Pandit history, heritage and culture, will stand erased. Deliberate destruction of such places has already taken place. The Kashmir we lived in has changed completely. Over the last several years, the names of many places in Kashmir have been changed. The ancient Shankaracharya temple is now called the

Takht-e-Suleiman. Anantnag is called Islamabad. The young Muslims don't know anything about these places of Pandit heritage. They believe that Hindus never lived in Kashmir.

Kashmiri Pandits have paid an enormous price for their patriotism and the nation still doesn't recognise their pain and suffering; their voices have remained unheard over the past two-and-a-half decades, and they continue to be called 'migrants', a label that was given to them in 1990 when they were forced out of Kashmir.

PART II

SUMMERS OF EXILE

Exilium mors est. (Exile is death.)

– Ovid

Exilium vita est. (Exile is life.)

– Victor Hugo

9

Summers of Exile

Sushant Dhar

The birth and rebirth of my address

	Till 1990
Permanent Address:	Seer Hamdan, Tehsil Mattan, Anantnag, Kashmir
	Summer of 1990
Present Address:	Government School Veranda, Garhi, Udhampur
Permanent Address:	Seer Hamdan, Anantnag, Kashmir
	A year later
Present Address:	Kashmiri Pandit migrant camp, Garhi, Udhampur
Permanent Address:	Seer Hamdan, Anantnag, Kashmir
	Three years later
Present Address:	Kashmiri Pandit migrant camp, Roop Nagar, Jammu
Permanent Address:	Seer Hamdan, Anantnag, Kashmir
	A decade later
Present Address:	Muthi Migrant Camp, Phase 2, E-4, Jammu
Permanent Address:	Kashmir
	Two decades later
Present Address:	Buta Nagar, Migrant Quarters T.R.T H-6, Jammu
Permanent Address:	--

In 2001 I visited my old house in Kashmir, the land of my forefathers. Mother and father took me through narrow lanes, showing me the shops and houses of their old neighbours. I was all stirred up and excited to see my house, the house my mother often boasted about; that it was big and had several rooms, one for everyone; there was a garden too. A brook ran adjacent to our house. We had everything; my mother never stopped talking about our house.

As we went nearer, my father pointed towards our house. 'Look,' he said. We were at a distance; the house was three-storeyed, standing firm and tall, the boundary hedged with firm but old wooden pillars. I looked at the house, and after a few minutes, I was standing at the wooden door of the house, the wood was still intact at the sides and so was the rusted doorknob; the windowpanes were missing though. I saw 'Aum' inscribed on the door and the front wall was visible. Trembling out of excitement, I went inside. The floor was filled with faeces, the wood of the ceiling was coming apart, the stairs to the first floor of the house were missing and a part of the roof was about to cave in. I saw devastation inside. Mother wasn't able to locate her room. The neighbours had converted a part of our house into a toilet, and the other part was used as a shed for their cattle and a garbage-dumping ground. Mother came out quickly, with tears rolling down her cheeks, and then she walked towards the backyard. The garden was a ghastly sight. It was flat and covered with nettles, garbage, filth and cow dung. People from the village came to meet us and hugged us; they started talking to my parents. A few minutes later, father's friend asked us to leave, telling us that it wasn't safe for us to stay longer. We left the place hurriedly.

What wrong had we done? Why were we forced to leave our land? My questions are very simple and for those who inflicted this horror on us (our old neighbours), the answers are as simple as this: 'You were driven out by the government and their conspirators. They are the ones responsible for your eviction. You should have stayed behind.'

'Stayed behind?' I ask. Stayed behind only to get killed?

I was one-and-a-half years old when we were forced to leave Seer Hamdan, our native village in Anantnag in Kashmir. In the beginning, I found it difficult to recollect the torment my parents and relatives went through. My memory takes me back to 1992. I was four years old then.

Some shreds of events and memories are engraved in my mind, the memory of suffering during the early days of exile. After the exodus, my family stayed in Garhi, Udhampur, a small town on the Jammu-Srinagar National Highway. We survived there for three years. We lived there in a shabbily constructed room rented to us by a local resident. For three years we used a makeshift bathroom and a latrine. We lived in fear of the mosquitoes and other deadly insects like scorpions and centipedes. They had invaded the room and the toilet. The summer heat made our skin a pale yellow. My parents shrivelled. The toilet, which was around 200 metres away from the house, was made of sticks, pieces of wood, scrap and tin. The door was made of torn canvas. A dug-out was made to contain the faeces. It all remained there, the faeces, the dirty water and the urine in that little dug out area, faeces over faeces, water over water, all stacked, emanating a foul stench. Two bricks served as footrest; we used to keep our feet firm, steady and balanced on those bricks while relieving ourselves. We feared slipping and falling into the pot full of faeces.

At times, my mother would request the landlady to allow her to use their personal toilet, as she couldn't bear the horrible stench in the makeshift toilet. The landlord's toilet was at some distance from ours. It was terrible; we were bereft of the most basic things of life. Eight of us lived in a small room. A curtain and a sheet were used to create a partition in the room for privacy. It was a room not even fit for cattle. But this is where we lived. We had little choice.

In the mornings and evenings, all of us would carry buckets and small plastic containers to the tube wells to get water. The nearest tube well was half a kilometre away from our hovel. Rainwater was used to wash utensils; fresh water had an unusual earthy colour and odour to it. Rain bought misery and centipedes. Centipedes crawled into our room through the windows, and hid under the bed sheets, below the pillows, in the crevices along the walls. Grandmother called these creatures *sunhari sarap* (colourful snakes). During the monsoon, snakes and scorpions came out of the anthills and other crevices in the ground, and entered our room. The government provided 500 rupees every month as relief. Sahita Samiti, a Kashmiri Pandit organisation, distributed milk, blankets and old clothes. People were reduced to nothing. We lived in extreme deprivation.

I lost my grandfather in the early years of exile. He suffered from depression; his inconsolable longing for his house in his village in Kashmir took a huge toll on his health. His health deteriorated and on the day of Mahashivratri, he left us. My father, the eldest among his brothers, had to bear the responsibility of the entire family.

In 1993, we shifted to Jammu. We sought refuge in the migrant quarters at Muthi. These quarters had domes. There were no windows in the damp and dingy room. Perpetual darkness reigned inside our room. No more than three people could sleep inside. Yet we had to make room for one another. In an adjacent room, a dozen members huddled together. Some people constructed small ventilators in the walls to let the light into the rooms. The ceilings were very low and one could barely stand erect. We had to crawl. We lived for fourteen years in the one-room tenement at the Muthi Migrant Camp. The conditions were inhumane. The dark camp alleys leading to the quarters were frightening. Mornings were gloomy.

Each day was an ordeal; a fight every moment, a fight within. Survival became a struggle; living through the days became a nightmare. The living conditions, the dark locales, pallid days, scorching heat, constricted lanes, mobile water tankers, the din of utensils, long queues for water, verbal spats among the migrants, a tap of water for 200 families. These constituted our dreary days. People scrounged for things as if they had lost their minds. In the camps, the mornings were noisy with people gearing up early in the morning to collect water. Not a single day went by without a fight for water. It was as if everyone had gone mad. The elders looked dreary and burdened, finding their way out of the dark rooms, hoping to escape the appalling conditions in the camp. With each passing day, they grew weak, and pined for shade and cool breeze. They didn't get the comfort they craved, they were anxious, uneasy all the time. They would talk to each other during the day. One could see them on the streets, in the middle of the road, in the shade of a tree, in the community hall, organising meetings, preparing memorandums, thinking of ways to return to Kashmir, hoping for the militancy to end there and normalcy to return.

For years together, my parents woke up early in the morning to line up the buckets and containers for water; the water supply lasted for no more than 15–20 minutes. This extreme mental and physical routine weakened them; they looked as if they were suffering from a long-term illness, and turning into decrepit beings. Sadness engulfed us all.

My parents withered in the endless summers, inadequate spaces and the stifling heat. We slept in snatches during the night. Many of us didn't even have fans or coolers. The nights and the cries of distress were neverending. Our bodies were drenched in sweat all the time. Hiding all day from the blazing sun was a routine game. Finding a corner untouched by the sun on the camp streets was a daily affair for the elders. A raised platform or the shade of a tree became places for the migrants to play cards and gossip. There was nothing else to do. They had nothing to do all day long except discuss the political situation in Kashmir. The elders with ashen faces looked frazzled and wilted as if they were carrying a permanent burden on their shoulders. Elders were often seen loitering in the camp vicinity, expressing their longing through inane soliloquies and monologues.

They were ageing rapidly; many collapsed and died in the streets. The scorching heat was unbearable; many succumbed to sunstrokes and snakebites. Deaths became a daily affair in the camp. The migrants lived through this tumultuous journey, battling desolation, toiling day after day.

The elders were the only connection to my native land. I longed to listen to the stories of the past, to connect to our native land. Their memories were what I depended on. I feared losing them all. I always carry this fleeting fear of losing our language. I fear losing our identity. Kashmir was always a topic of discussion; it never went off our hearts and minds. The elders still carry this undying hope of going back to their motherland.

We waited for the summers to end. Our cramped one-room tenement with the killer dome radiated with heat from the scorching sun. Evenings went by like a flash. Heat was our biggest enemy. The soaring temperatures in Jammu rendered us insane. We had nowhere to go. The rooftops and walls of our room went on baking us throughout the day. Evenings for the camp children, elders, men and women were spent in consoling one another and offering words of comfort. An electric pole stood on the other side of the road where camp people used to sit and discuss the affairs of the community till late evening. The discussions ranged from Kashmir to surviving in Jammu to relief and ration to the apathy of the government.

Everyone ignored us as if we didn't exist. As if we didn't belong to this land and to this country. The authorities didn't care for us as if we were not humans. We became a burden for everyone. Our exodus should have stirred the conscience of the government, both State and Central. But it didn't.

People went on waiting. We grappled with a deep sense of homelessness. They thought that the situation would become normal and that they would return to their homes. Little did they know that even after twenty-five years, their return to the native land would still remain a distant dream.

The children of exile had to bear the brunt of the exodus. Exodus had a major impact on their education. The makeshift room constructed using old bricks, wooden planks and iron sheets was our kitchen, drawing room, study, prayer room and bedroom. The kitchen meant everything to my mother; she had demarcated a part of the room for cooking. The cooking area was lined by a cemented slab, some space created for us to sit, an elevated space used to wash our hands and utensils. Father created a shelf on which he placed pictures and idols of our deities. We prayed.

This cramped little kitchen served us for fourteen years. We shared space with insects, rats and cockroaches. When the lights went off, these little creatures came out of the holes, scrounging for food. Our kitchen served as my study also. I never had the luxury of having my own room; the kitchen was all I had. I created a cave-like corner for myself by placing pillows around myself, and I studied inside this cave. I carved out a little world of mine in these cramped spaces. A friend's father ran a small shop next to his room. The dwelling was blocked from any source of light from the outside.

The toilets reeked and the horrible stench in the latrines made us curse our wretched lives. We were engulfed in a foul smell all the time. There was one latrine for the entire block. In the beginning, these were makeshift latrines, then after years, they were plastered with bricks and cement. One latrine was to be shared by 20 families living in a block. Before relieving ourselves, we used to throw buckets of water inside; the toilet was all stained black, and it was filthy. The toilets blocked every now and then and the municipal vehicles would come once in two months to empty the pit. The pipes of the vehicles leaked at many places, and, at times, the block would be covered with filthy water. For the camp-dwellers, it became difficult to stay indoors all the time; the air reeked of a bad stench all the time. The women folk of the block would clean the area and scrub the surfaces of the block, flushing out the faeces with water. My grandmother once aptly lamented: 'We are in hell, and every day is a struggle—for water, for space, for comfort, for fresh air.'

I did my school homework in our makeshift kitchen; it was so hot in the afternoons that nobody visited us during the day. The roof of our room caved in many times when strong winds blew. Summer storms and lashing rains would destroy our shelters. There were times when we had no roof over our heads. We had to sleep in the narrow alleys in the camp. Powercuts that lasted 12–14 hours a day became a routine affair. In the night, some people slept on the pavements along the roads, on the rooftops of the quarters, and in the narrow alleys between quarters. Our room didn't have a flat roof. The roof was dome-shaped. During the powercuts, children, women and men sat helpless in darkness. They would sit on the roadside and wait for the power supply to be restored.

Herath (Shivratri) brought with it hope and a sense of collective solace. As the most important festival of our community, it kept the camp residents busy for a month. The entire settlement would celebrate in whatever small ways they could. The shops on camp streets were decorated. Cleaning of quarters, washing of the floors of the camp dwellings, and whitewashing of the walls was done a few days before the festival. We always counted the days before Shivratri, waited for the arrival of the auspicious day. The most joyous aspect of Herath for the children was getting pocket money from the elders. The money lasted for quite a few days and we would spend it on our favourite biscuits, chocolates and toffees.

I remember trucks arriving with old clothes and blankets. People would line up to lay their hands on the relief material sent for us by the authorities. The men in the trucks would fling the relief material at us, as if we were beggars. Everyone would get hold of a few things. Some got hold of sweatshirts, old jeans and others pocketed utensils and coarse blankets. Men, women and children ferried something or the other on their backs to their rooms. The Government trucks distributed ration (rice and sugar) only to those who had ration cards. Without the ration cards, nothing was given. Those who didn't possess ration cards depended on others for food and groceries. Leaders from political parties used to visit the camps once a year to assure the displaced of better facilities, better living conditions, better accommodation. Many people believed the leaders and their false assurances.

Once in 1996, it rained for days, and the water from the drains overflowed into our rooms. One morning, we woke up to crowds of people on the roads. As we made our way outside, father was shocked to see our shop at the roadside flooded with filthy water from the overflowing drains. All the things kept inside were soaked in water. Many blocks in the camp were under water. Our household belongings were floating in water, people were crying, many hadn't slept throughout the night, people suffered huge losses.

It was in the summer of 1990 when a politician of the state came to visit the camps, offering promises and all. A month earlier, people had started talking about this visit, as it was normal for them to nurture hope and expect some major announcements about relief and rehabilitation. They were hopeful, ebullient, and preparations were in full swing. Memorandums were drafted meticulously, listing our concerns and demands. The community hall in the camp was decorated with string lights. The camp-dwellers pooled money to make sure the arrangements went as planned, possibly to impress the politician and his delegation. Food, snacks and tea were kept ready on the day of the visit. People were hopeful; they were desperate to hear words of hope from the leader. The day finally arrived, and the politician of the state was scheduled to visit in the morning, but he didn't appear at the stipulated time. People waited all morning, afternoon, and then towards late evening, the politician and his coterie arrived in a fleet of cars. We heard the clamour of vehicles from a distance; people started rushing to the spot of arrival, welcoming the politician, presenting him with garlands. Chaos reigned everywhere. After a few minutes, clouds of dust hovered around and it started drizzling, and people searched for cover in the tent. I made space for myself in the crowd, unaware of the seriousness of this visit. My friends were also keen to listen to the politician. One of the representatives from our camp carried with him a memorandum to be handed over to the politician. The speeches started, and the politician was thanked for showing his concern and agreeing to come over despite his busy schedule. The Camp President talked about the problems we faced, and even quoted a few lines written by an Urdu poet. The politician delivered his speech and there was loud applause; people cheered. I can still recollect his utterances:

'I am here to assure you that before the next rainy season you will be in your new flats. I can feel your pain. Next July, you will be given flats. I assure you.'

People became euphoric, happy and hopeful.

'And yes, take care of your health. You are safe now. We will help you. We will send you everything you need. And we will get the situation in Kashmir to improve so that you may return to your homes.'

The speech ended, and people became happy. Such moments of happiness were rare. During an exile, even a small thing spells hope, every little thing to cling on to means the world. And then began the waiting. The waiting for the promises to be fulfilled!

The years that followed brought mere dejection and anguish among the people. The government provided paltry relief and ration, while assuring us of building better shelters. Little did we realise that these were empty and hollow promises. Our condition was being pitied. We were not even a vote-bank. We were merely a liability for the authorities. We didn't matter. We were as good as the dead.

I became friends with the summer, despite the atrocities it unleashed. I parted ways with the winter; a year-long friendship came to an end. Then came more summers; terrible ones. Summers were devastating, ruthless, showed no mercy. We all looked withered. Years went by and my friendship with the summers strengthened. I faced the torment. I tried to be brave. I waited and waited. Perhaps this was one friendship I never desired, but endured through the difficult years. We became inseparable; we are one now. Though summers showed extreme hostility and tested our mettle in the beginning, we learnt how to grow used to them. Summer days gave me many sleepless nights, all drenched in sweat. My ancestors were the children of winter, of snow, of mountains. I was new to summer. We both were new to each other. The fight in those early years was always one-sided, as I had to wait the whole day to let the fury of my friend pass. A cool breeze would bring respite and scare away my friend.

I cursed the sun, I cursed the heat. I always dreamt of watching the snowfall. I dreamt of snow, of touching it, walking on it. Whenever I heard reports of snowfall in Kashmir, I would dream of leaving my quarters and going back to the distant land, the land of my birth, just to see the snow. I longed for snow. For many years, before sleeping, I imagined myself walking through a land covered entirely with tress and snow, walking through the fields and reaching the top of a mountain; this helped me sleep in the summers.

A Dream of Home

I'm in my native land, my motherland. It has started snowing; I wake up early in the morning. Snow and zephyrs are all around me. I am walking in the snow in my plastic gumboots. I'm one-and-a-half years old and my parents are leaving our house. My mother is carrying me in her arms. It's white all around; this white snow is a sentinel watching over the entire land. I look around at the tall poplars covered with snow, their serrated branches frozen with ice. I'm a boy of ten now. I walk for a while. This silken snow covering the land entices me.

This is a vast land full of trees. I walk through the avenue and reach a garden. My gumboots caress the snow beneath, and I walk slowly. With each step I take, I feel elated. I'm not lost. I recognise everything.

The sight of the snow-clad trees infuses courage in me, and I feel as if they are protecting me. I decide to go on and on. Snow starts falling. I feel happy for the first time in years.

It's all white. I walk a long way, miles and miles. I see pristine beauty around me. The ugliness I'd seen has vanished. I'm enthralled. I'm at peace. I don't want anything else except that this moment should never end.

A House of One's Own

Once some visitors came to meet us in our camp. I discovered they were our neighbours from our village in Kashmir. But why were they visiting us now, for what, after all these years? They brought things for us from Kashmir—walnuts, almonds and other produce from the farms, which once were ours. They talked about old days, when things were normal, when people lived like brothers and sisters. They said that some catastrophe had befallen all of us because of which we got separated. We made room for them in the cramped space. The guests described the condition of our house in Kashmir: 'Your house is broken; it is going to collapse anytime. The people throw all their waste material into the compound of your house. One neighbour has grabbed your land and uses it as a shelter for cattle. The wood inside is rotting. The ceiling has caved in. The rooms are in a dilapidated condition. You must sell the house now. If you don't sell it now, it will crumble soon and fetch you nothing. You must sell it now.'

After they left, our family sat for hours and deliberated on whether to sell the house or wait for some more time. Because the financial condition of my family wasn't good, and father had developed serious health problems, with the entire family depending on a meagre relief amount and some earnings from the shop, the family members agreed to sell the house. With each passing day, the fear of the house falling down grew, a fear that was instilled by the old neighbours. The neighbour visited us again in 2002, as he was desperate to buy our house, owing to the fact that it was big and in good condition compared to other abandoned houses of the Pandits in the village. During this visit, he talked of buying our house and offered my father 3-4 lakh rupees for the house and the plot of land. After getting the consent of our family members, my father sold the house to the neighbour. We didn't know what else to do. We were desperate. But we wondered what would happen if we returned to Kashmir in the future. Where would we go then?

The Elders

I am reminded of an incident which took place during our stay at the migrant quarters in Muthi, Jammu. My great-grandmother first lived in Jhiri, Jammu in the early days of our exile in the 1990s. She lived all alone in a dingy room, which had only three walls; a curtain replaced the missing wall. The place was deserted and full of dilapidated structures, but guarded by policemen. She lived all by herself and never complained. She would often come and visit us in Garhi, Udhampur and stay for a month or two. Her daughter, my grandmother, insisted that she stay with us, but my great granny always refused. She was a lady of profound wisdom. Her son would visit her once or twice a month, giving her money for groceries and other essential things. When we shifted to the Muthi migrant quarters, my father, after deliberations with the officials, got a small quarter allotted to her and she shifted to this new place in our block. But things changed as she started living close by, in her own quarters. At her age, it was difficult to even do the normal daily chores, but the suffering she endured made her tough. She would do all the things on her own, from making food to preparing tea for herself. We would often tell her to avoid doing so much household work, and to eat at our place, but she never agreed. She had a routine of her own, which she followed stringently as she was a very disciplined woman. She always had a coil of thread and a needle in her pocket. In our childhood days, she used to prick the children with a needle, if she found them doing mischievous things. She gave me a five-rupee note every month to buy my favourite biscuit or chocolate. 'Kakni' is what everybody used to call her. Every morning, after visiting the nearest temple, I would get the *chandan tika* (sandalwood paste) for her so that she could apply it on her forehead. In the summers she used to come to our quarters and sit in front of the desert cooler; the horrid heat was unbearable those days. One day, as we were preparing dinner, father came early from the shop. It was 9 pm, and Kakni opened the door and asked father for her bowl of milk. She didn't have her own refrigerator, so she kept the milk in our refrigerator and took it to her room every morning. Kakni whispered and now asked mother to give her the bowl. My mother asked her why she needed milk at that time. Kakni very quickly responded, 'Today I woke up late, and I'm yet to have my bed-tea.' Kakni had fallen asleep for a few hours in the evening, and she had assumed that it was morning as the lights in the quarters were switched on. For Kakni, sleeping at night was impossible; she slept for only one or two hours in the night as the walls in her room radiated heat. She had a table fan. She had developed a habit of taking a nap in the evening and, that day, after waking up in the evening, she felt as if it was morning and she was late for her morning tea.

One sultry morning, as everyone was collecting water from the tap, Kakni came forward holding her small bucket. She was limping in an awkward manner. When the other migrants enquired, she replied, 'Don't worry. This morning, as I opened the door, a snake bit my leg. I caught it in a bag and threw it into the drain. I'll be fine. It was not a venomous snake.'

When my mother heard this, she quickly tied a piece of cloth around Kakni's leg and informed father about the incident. Father took Kakni to a hospital and got her treated. Two years after this incident, Kakni slipped while bathing in the bathroom and couldn't survive the fall. She died that day. The courageous woman is no more with us.

As many migrants often mentioned to me in their conversations, 'Exile did terrible things to us; we became cold in the face of terrible situations'.

For the elders, exile led to misery, anxiety, depression, dementia; our language became an obstacle, we were not able to understand the local language. Once when I was travelling in a bus to some place I saw an elderly woman sitting a few seats away from me. The bus conductor came to collect the fare from the passengers. The elderly woman gave some coins to the conductor. The conductor with a crooked nose seethed with anger and gave the coins back to the old women. The hands of the elderly woman trembled and she couldn't hold the coins in her hands, and the coins fell down. The conductor belched invectives in an alien language; other migrant passengers informed the woman that the fare she had given was one rupee short of the total fare. The elderly woman kept on talking to the conductor in Kashmiri. Bending down, she then picked all the coins off the floor and started murmuring. The expression on her face was grim; she felt helpless.

The Temporary Settlement

The settlement at Jagti, Jammu houses about 4000 Kashmiri Pandit migrants who were made to shift from different camps like Purkhu, Mishriwala, and Bhattalballian. The camp at Mishriwala, where Pandits lived for almost sixteen years facing hazardous pollution and smoke emanating out of the brick plants surrounding the camp, was the filthiest. Many people suffered from asthma and other respiratory ailments during their stay in this camp.

The Central and State governments had promised the Kashmiri Pandit migrants living in camps at Purkhu, Mishriwala and Bhattalballian that the temporary settlement at Jagti would be equipped with all basic facilities like water, schools, electricity, hospitals, and so on. But no such facilities exist. Powercuts are a routine affair. There is no hospital. And the migrants have to store water in buckets, given the acute water shortage. An elderly migrant

I knew would murmur about her old life all the time. 'What a big house I had, the big kitchen garden, all the comforts … the water was sweeter than the water of the Chashm-i-Shahi spring. Now there is no village, no house, no kitchen garden … But it was my home. How many films I used to watch, countless, every film of Raj Kapoor, Madhubala … I have only one wish now, as I know I will die soon. I don't want to go to Nishat and Shalimar gardens, or to Gulmarg, Pahalgam and Tulmul. I wish to go to my village and be in my old house. I wish to roam in those lanes. I wish to breathe that air one last time. I wish to go to my school and bow my head in reverence in front of my classroom. What else I can pray for? I lost everything. I'm a vagrant. Today I have cooked peas and potato for dinner.'

I would listen to him for hours and then mother would call me and I would tell her about the elderly man. He kept telling me about his first house, plunging into grim silence now and then. He repeated the same details with the same love as if he was narrating them for the first time. The torments of exile, the frequent fits of pain and the loss of loved ones had not erased his longing for his old house.

These days I read the teachings of Swami Lakshman Joo, the great scholar and saint of Kashmir. He was a scholar of Shaivism. I watch the video transcripts of the mystic scholar, unfolding ways to attain supra-consciousness. There is much to ponder on.

I stroll around these cramped lanes all covered with wild grasses. One has to find a way to walk through. You gaze around and look up for those fine giant structures; they are all wood, clay and earth. Some have been razed to the ground, some lost hope and came down, others burnt and some converted to urinals and latrines. The Pandit houses are about to cave in. Walls are defaced, doors broken. Idols of worship have been desecrated, temples vandalised.

Dear reader, can you imagine what we went through? The pain of not being in your home, the pain of leaving your home, the pain of parting with your belongings, the pain of that one last glance at your home, the pain of not having a morsel of rice for your children, the pain of sleeping in the veranda of a Government School for years, the pain of living in a tattered tent for years, the fear of losing your life to a snakebite, the fear of dying because of a sunstroke, the pain of living under a killer dome in refugee quarters for sixteen years, the pain of losing your memory, the pain of listening to narratives that create more injustice and more torment in our hearts, the pain of carrying a withered hope for twenty-five years.

I know you can't suffer what I suffered. But can you now try to comprehend the loss? I still wait. There is no justice. It has been twenty-five years. I still don't have an address, a home to call my own.

The Address

For years I carried this uncomfortable feeling of writing my address as Migrant Camp Gole (Round) Quarters, Muthi, Jammu. People would make fun of me, even smirk and mock at me, asking me, 'What is Muthi Camp?' Once a classmate insisted on visiting my place; I took him to a relative's place, pretending that it was where I lived. I was embarrassed to take him to my quarters.

Nothing has changed. Even today, it is the same as well, but the address has changed. Whenever anybody asks me my address, I don't know what to say. I avoid telling people that my parents and I still live in a camp. Even if I build my own house on some plot of land in Jammu or elsewhere, I will still carry a sense of homelessness, of not being connected to my roots. I stand bemused when people ask me, 'Where do you belong? Where do you live?' I tell them I'm originally from Kashmir but our neighbours and yesteryear friends forced us out of our native homes in 1990. Many times when the elders meet at marriages or family get-togethers, they talk about themselves. They say they are doing well in Jammu and that they have their own houses, and that their kids are getting good opportunities. It's only towards the end of the conversations that they say, 'Our hearts don't find solace in Jammu. We don't belong here.' The moment of longing creeps into their hearts and sends ripples of pain, the pain of past memories. They keep on saying that their only home and permanent address is Kashmir. Perhaps it will always be. My grandmother and uncle chant this even now. My grandmother observes that she might not return to her ancestral place, the land of her birth, in her lifetime, so she finds home by recounting memories. Memories, language and our culture are the only strings of hope that keep us alive in an alien destination. We must not let our memories fade away, the memories of home and the memories of intense suffering. We must carry them throughout our lives and nurture the hope of returning to our homes someday. Till then, we must not forget our language and rituals, we must follow them enthusiastically with more vigour, remembering that they are the last connect to our identity. We must endure and at the same time be overly conscious of preserving our memories, culture, and language, that they are the only connects, the only shreds of our remaining identity. We must pass on our stories of sufferings, stories of our parents, of our grandparents; we must make it a point to not let them die with the passage of time, we must all write these stories and pass them onto the generations that follow, generation after generation, these stories must survive and live, our children must carry this longing forward and imbibe this longing, inherit this longing, the longing of going back to our permanent home. Until we return, we have to survive, and with us the memories must survive too—the memories of a lost land, of exile, of the days we lived in tents, of our days in the migrant quarters, of the sufferings we endured, of our lost grandparents, of the ones who were killed in Kashmir, of waking up to news about massacres, of people who lost their lives to snakebites, sunstrokes and other diseases, of my beloved Kakni, of many sleepless nights in camps, of days without water and electricity, of extreme deprivation.

Every morning I read the community bulletin, which is full of obituaries. Here I reproduce a few of them:

> It is with deep grief, we inform the sad and untimely demise of our dear father Prithvi Nath Pandita s/o Manohar Lal Pandita, originally resident of Qazigund, Kashmir, at present living in Muthi Migrant Camp Quarters, Jammu.
>
> It is with profound grief and sorrow, we inform the untimely demise of our mother Dhanvati Dhar w/o Late Sh. Hridhay Nath Dhar, originally resident of Pulwama, Kashmir, at present living in Purkhu Migrant Camp, Jammu.
>
> It is with heavy hearts, we inform the untimely demise of our beloved son Vijay Raina s/o Chuni Lal Raina, original resident of Baramulla, Kashmir, at present living in Mishriwala Migrant Camp, Jammu.

10

My House of Stone

Neeru Kaul

> 'Empires fall. Nations topple. Borders may shift. Old loyalties may dissolve or, without warning, be altered. Home, whether it be structure or familiar ground, is finally the identity that does not fade!'
>
> – Anthony Shadid, *House of Stone*

A friend once said to me: my land is a place where my restive mind seeks new journeys to the world. It was here where it was meant to begin; an exile that would seek to reach its end and trace its origins. Shall I ever know what I am looking for, not expecting to even achieve what I desire? I tried to spoor my origins, thinking I no longer exist. I did seek clues for my quests over the years, in each event leading to that circle, which was or is narrated, and has as many versions to it as the narrators.

Humans have an intrinsic craving to personalise everything that occurs to them. They visit places and leave behind imprints of their presence and embed their identities on everything they come across. And sometimes, in the pursuit of this desire, they create, destroy and re-create recollections. And these embedded thoughts have their impact on collective memory; constructive, destructive or both. But here I wanted to find clues to my own self, not just historical vestiges, or vestiges of times gone by or remnants of memories created or attempting to re-create themselves. Memories are what keep cultures alive and thriving long after we are gone. So, who do I expect to meet from those bygone times? What do they have to tell me? Or do I start afresh?

I greeted a standstill in the arms of the tall clock tower in Lal Chowk, Srinagar. A reprise of the time when I bid adieu to it when I had left what Shadid calls Bayt. Now, I stared at the clock continuously. The woman sitting nearby on a metal bench stared at me as tears streamed from my eyes. I finally arrived at this point in 2012, to my own Bayt, my own hearth, my own Marjayoun to pick up shards of life and my association with this land, which I was forced to leave in 1990. Now, over twenty-three years later, as I set foot in my motherland, the experience left me mesmerised, entranced and spellbound.

I

Civilisations do not last forever but they leave behind their fine imprints, traces and quests for the future to pursue. Which civilisation do I belong to now? Or which civilisation have I drifted from? My eclectic claims to my identity lay scattered in an alien land. A journey in the valley, dotted by remnants of the past, was a pilgrimage for my soul, homage to my parents and their memories, and my own memories.

I ambled through the ruins of the ancient temples at Parihaspura, Fatehgarh, Pattan, Buniar and Martand, where I marvelled at the massiveness of the ancient structures, remnants of Kashmiri architecture. I felt a magnificence standing tall through the ravages of time with remarkable durability, tickling the imagination even in the present time considered much advanced. For me, it was the sense of my glorious history that made me joyful and proud: the sense that the ruins belonged to me and I always belonged here.

As I further travelled through the valley, my gaze fell on the vandalised and desecrated temples and their derelict condition, smudged even more by offensive graffiti inscribed on their walls. Throughout my time in the valley, about a week, a bizarre thought crossed me—my God, almost everywhere, is under lock and key or under guard. My God, is he vulnerable or is it my faith that makes me the other, or the insecurity of the vandal's interpretation of his faith? I wondered. And then at Ganesh Bal, a temple of Lord Ganesh in Srinagar, under the protection of the local police—Lord Ganesh, a deity revered as a protector and guard—I surmised that perhaps God too, is a conspirator.

At Badshah's tomb in Zaina Kadal, both inside and outside, I found Saracenic and pre-Islamic totems merge, a result of failed attempts at iconoclasm. And my mind trailed off to envisage Harsha's and Sikandar's depredations that persecuted my community long before I had come face to face with the sacred pond at Vicharnag—that once was a seat of spiritual learning and discourses, and was also visited by His Holiness Jagat Guru Shankaracharya—dilapidated and in ruins and forsaken by its devotees. I speculated if our faith had anything to do with it or if there was a method to this madness. History of human civilisation is replete with horrible stories where entire clans have been erased, their religious and cultural symbols wiped clean for the sole reason that they belonged to a different ethnic sect, community, faith, nationality, or culture or just over the diversity of being iconic or aniconic—Buddhas of Bamiyan and Sufi shrines. I wondered about the psychological upheavals and erasure of ethos that the survivors are faced with; from Armenia to the Jewish holocaust, to Cambodia, Bosnia, Rwanda, Darfur, many more, scores of surviving stories impelling one to think if it really has to do with just a belief that a belligerent persecutor or a vandal follows to deliberately obliterate the cultural and intellectual roots of a particularity, indulging in *damnatio memoriae* with a view to seek ascendancy. I pondered: what faiths and religious beliefs are meant for humanity to profess?

I couldn't believe that revulsion and instilling fear could be the characteristics and a proponent of a faith—the desire to exist alone and in supremacy. And then I wonder if Camus has the reply when he says, 'The law of this world is nothing but the law of force; its driving force, the will to power.'

My desire to visit the Kali temple took me to the monastery of the evangelist Shah-e-Hamadan. My soul sensed resentment from some unseen spiritual presence which dissipated in a couple of hours, and I felt I was welcomed into the essence of the monastery after I had paid obeisance at the remnants of the Kali temple. And then I reached the ancient Shankaracharya temple. The stoical appearance of the idol filled me with sublimity; something within me felt inebriated and attuned to the mirth of this realisation of unattained but attainable self-awareness. The incipient power of some divine light filled me with joy, which streamed down from my eyes in the form of tears. I felt that the part of my self that had vanished came back and was healed. Even as the environs were pervaded with the fragrance of the marigolds and the leaves of bilva I found a subtle assurance of a resurrection and growth of all; the Pandits, marred with identity crises and a receding sense of belonging and the Muslims, beset with hopelessness and a life bereft of 'freedom'. I felt acknowledged and re-assured and joyous.

Our intertwined histories come into the way of our conflicting memories.

II

Vyeth (Jhelum) meandered through the heart of Srinagar city in silence; the streets crowded now, as then, and claustrophobic but bereft of the people who belonged here. As I sauntered through the old city, my apprehensions blended with the certitude of my belonging, and I returned to echo the poet Milosz:

'... *Says he who after many years, Returned to the city of his youth. There was no one left Of those who once walked these streets. And now they had nothing, except his eyes. Stumbling, he walked and looked, instead of them, On the light they had loved, on the lilacs again in bloom. His legs were, after all, more perfect Than non-existent legs ...*'

Chinkral Mohalla, my old locality in Srinagar, wore a different look. It's deprived of a house for me to enter or claim, the old structure having been erased to construct a new one and later taken over by a neighbour. In the lanes, the memories of my grandparents, the stories of the coming of age of my father and his siblings, his youth, the laughter of my cousins and friends chasing one another resonated, and then exploded into a silence by the sound of a gunshot. And I hear voices and sobbing and the sound of people beating their chests. And somebody whispers into my ears, 'They have killed Taploo.' And I remember that this marked the beginning of what I later realised was forced exile.

Our house in Srinagar, with a *Taaq* type construction, was home to my father and his extended family. It was a four-storeyed building constructed by my ancestors. When my mother came to the house after marriage, my father had specially renovated his room to begin his life with her and to raise their children together. The walls were oil-plastered and ceilings were decorated with ply. Father had a bookcase which he kept locked. It was just below the glass window in the room and stored his exotic collection of books, and I got to lay my hands on some of them only many years later in Jammu, the city which gave refuge to the Kashmiri Hindu exiles. These books were the only possessions he managed to take with him when leaving the place in the dead of one night in early 1990. In Srinagar, I always used to peek into the bookcase thinking it contained some kind of precious treasure. In our house, everyone had a room of their own. Even the birds found their nesting place under the eaves. My favourite was the attic and a small room on the third floor, the *thokur kuth* that was home to the deities. It was separated from the main lobby by a wall made of frames of horizontal wooden shutters. The *shankh naad* always mesmerised me, and here I would often hide to witness the deities appear to take the offerings made by my family, as was narrated to us by the elders. And I would see them appear in the form of crows or sparrows.

Now, the house was defaced and demolished, like a bad dream come true. The coldness of the new occupants greeted me, as did their claims over my house, like stragglers requiring a desperate defence in my solemn assurance that my visit is just a visit and not a claim. I noticed the water tap in the courtyard, a source of water for many in the neighbourhood, including Kaej who used to come over from the other end of Chinkral every morning for ablutions. Her resolve to ignore every other house in the mohalla except mine always mesmerised me. It seemed to me that her ritual had fixed faith coordinates; her morning ablutions were to be performed precisely near our tap. Now, in the new surroundings, only this water source remained as a remnant of the older dwelling.

And I then head out to the highway. Thirty miles north from Srinagar in Palhallan is my *matamal*, where my mother was born and where I spent my early childhood. Palhallan is a place, which carries its own formidable reputation, as a Jamat-e-Islami stronghold.

Scouring the unpaved streets covered with mud, I failed to locate the stone, mud and timber house in which my mother and her siblings were born. And their father and grandfathers and great grandfathers! And then a child on the roadside, noticing my desperation enquired, *'Toh chiv haez Bhattan henz laer tchaandan?'* (Are you looking for Pandit houses?) To my dismay and sorrow, he led me to a ground of unsightly mounds, which I had missed earlier. These were the erstwhile Pandit houses, and now just mounds of rubble. I finally reached a mound of rubble that used to be the residence of Amarchand Razdan, my great-grandfather, whose acts of bravery were part of the folklore of that belt. I remember my grandfather, a teacher, and my grand-uncle, the tough individual who tilled the soil like his ancestors and who in his later years, battling Alzheimer's, remembered absolutely nothing but his hearth and cattle and his land that he cared for all his life. Decades later, he waited for them to appear in his dreams to find out if the cattle had been fed and cows milked and lands ploughed and fields watered. Some years ago, he left us with his last words—*'Gharr chi yirvinaav. Gharr hay gatchav'* (Home is a ruin. Let's go home.)

The villagers converged to greet me. I tried to connect with the women who were my mother's friends and playmates; women who formed the extended neighbourhood that every rural community possesses; women for whom my mother would weep when they lost their children in the conflict.

Scratching at the sketchy memory of my past, my childhood, I conjured up my recollection of how it all appeared in its prime. In the derelict compound, I stood and stared, my gaze reaching far and wide trying to sketch from my memory the erased structures of the familiar landscape. The houses, some for humans, some for livestock, and few for the 'kuj' that was our granary, the small brook, hedged with poplar trees, watering the rice fields ahead, and my grandmother's daffodils and marigolds, a small patch in her vast kitchen garden, that she planted and nourished affectionately to tastefully decorate her gods as if she and her flowers were as immortal as the gods.

The house that Amarchand Razdan had built using *devri* stones, burnt brick, mud and timber had no compound walls. The three pathways—coming from the fields, the small brook, and the neighbourhood—bordered by poplars, walnut trees, chinar trees and flower shrubs, and interspersed by the barn, the kitchen garden and the granary—leading to his abode, all converged at his mighty *devdar* wooden door separating his inner world from the outer that stood witness to the days of yore. Everyone was welcome to his abode with no walls to come in-between. And I could hear the sighs of that glorious and peaceful past of my ancestors from under these melancholic mounds. And I wondered if the people around cared to tell their next generation what these ruinations were and who they belonged to, who these earlier inhabitants were and what their histories were. I knelt down and touched the earth that once was my home and that now was a pile of debris surrounded by filth and wild shrubs. I could visualise that little room on the first floor where my grandmother would vigourously pull the ropes to spin the paddle kept inside an earthen jar to churn butter so devoutly and her vast kitchen from which wafted wonderful aromas from delicious dishes that sated the stomachs and hearts of her family and nourished her soul; and my grandfather's corner where he used to delve into his own world reciting quatrains in Persian and Urdu; my grand-uncle's room where we used to listen to old stories of his and grandfather's childhood, and where he taught me how to count in Urdu; the corners in the compound where my siblings and cousins used to play and giggle chasing calves and ducklings. Everything was buried under these vestiges of irretrievable past—grandeur, honour and repute of the predecessors, their hopes and dreams for posterity, old neighbourhood camaraderie, their stories of evolving together, their beliefs. Nothing remained, except memories.

On my way back I stopped to search for my grandmother's idols near the place where the village temple had stood, but it was now a pile of wreckage. Suddenly realising the transience of it all, I searched for the family well and, as I enquired, only a lone village elder could guide me to the now extinct source of water.

I realised the difference in the rural and urban reactions to my exodus.

On that bleak winter afternoon, as I stood on the mound of rubble, my feelings found an echo in the eloquent evocation of Anthony Shadid's words for his ancestral home, reinforcing my belief in the universality of human feelings: '*I imagined the meals cooked, the dresses sewn, the pillows stitched, the farewells that had taken place here in this house. I thought of the houses empty around me and considered the work, the care of the stonemasons and artisans who left parts of their hopes and beliefs in this place.*'

Nothing from the past remains now—neither my grandparents nor their dwellings in the valley.

And as I remember the conversations I have had with my father, my mother, uncles and aunts over these past twenty-three years, I realise that their memory of home has a greater share of joy unlike that of my generation. My memory now stays preserved only in family photographs and anecdotes. Our lives before the exodus were full of ordinary and fascinating experiences, delightful and humble pleasures and happinesses. Who would have imagined that darkness and gloom would engulf us? We'd failed to see the impending horror.

In the later years, in Jammu, the city that gave us refuge, whenever I used to line up for the assembly prayers in the blazing sun in the afternoon school meant for refugee kids, I always failed to comprehend the meaning of the verse composed by poet Bharat Vyas. What was its import now for me or for all those who, having lost their homes, now led a rootless and hopeless existence?

'Aye maalik tere bande hum, ayese ho humaare karam, nekee par chale, aur badee se tale, taaki haste huye nikale dam' (Oh Lord, we are your followers and pray our deeds be noble and we stride on the path of righteousness and refrain from evil. So smiling we decease!)

Strangely, this verse used to be my favourite as a child when I was growing up in my land, Kashmir.

III

Palhallan was always in turmoil. Twelve boys had died fighting the armed forces that year along with a Panchayat head who had been shot dead by militants. It was in Palhallan where I came across two names, which I had never heard before: Maqbool Ilahi and Ashraf Dar. These two young men from Budgam were, like us, from agricultural backgrounds. They were the first ones to pick up guns after returning from the training camps across the border in Pakistan. They had fought to the end, honest to the ideology they believed in, unlike the publicity-seeking separatists and ideologues who indulge in sloganeering in seminars and on TV shows outside the conflict zone. These two young boys were buried in Eidgah. I—a Kashmiri Pandit—felt compelled to visit the graveyard in Eidgah in Srinagar. Graves! What do these graves mean to me? In that quietness of the graveyard, holding within its bosom little boys and young men, I pondered over what they believed in. At

Shaheed Mazaar, as it's known in Srinagar, I looked for the resting places of these two militants, the forgotten originators of the conflict. When they were alive did they know that their zeal and ideology would one day consume the very people who had lived with them in harmony; people like Sushil Bhat, a young villager from Baramulla who was killed by the militants? Sushil was a school teacher in Gool. His family consisted of his one-and-a-half-month-old daughter, wife and old parents. He was dragged out of a bus and shot dead by militants along with his two colleagues. After this incident, Sushil's mother died of shock, and his father became a recluse. His little daughter now lives with her maternal grandparents in Jammu.

Sitting in the graveyard I thought of the many stories that this war had created within and outside the valley. Does grief have any religion? With shared language, are the wails of bereavement the same? I wonder.

IV

The common story of both the communities, Theirs and Ours, has been one of battles, losses, bereavement and displacement. Life has become what is being fed and offered, and not what it should be.

The place stopped breathing for me, the moment I bid adieu. The houses in the old city and the burnt-out village houses, billeted by soldiers, haunted by the ghosts of the past and turned into mounds of ruin stared awkwardly at me. I remembered an old man I met in Kaavdor, Srinagar near the ruins of houses—destroyed in three days of fighting in 1990 between militants and security personnel—frantically looking for his daughter, abusing militants, security forces and politicians alike. The old man had lost his family including his young daughter, and he now roamed on roads. And this reminded me of another old man who my brother met at a refugee camp in Jammu. Talking about our 'return' proposed by the government, he whispered bewildered, '*Teli kati chi aes? Yi chena kasheer?*' (Where are we now? Isn't this Kashmir?) The state of his mind left me perplexed. I wondered if redemption was a possibility for all such homeless, rootless and innocent people who became victims of vicious political game plans.

One learns from studies conducted by Margoob in 2006[1] that Post Traumatic Stress Disorder (PTSD) is highly prevalent in the general population in Kashmir. And one also finds in the studies conducted by Banal in 2010[2] that psychiatric morbidity, depression and anxiety are more in the migrant population of mixed age, with a major depressive episode being the most common diagnosis followed by depression, post-traumatic stress disorders (PTSD) and generalised anxiety disorders (GAD). Similar results have been found in the Vietnamese, Cambodian and Bosnian refugees. While according to Raina (2008)[3], dementia was rare in the native Kashmiri population in 1986 prior to displacement, later studies revealed dementia in a substantial population of the Kashmiri migrants with prevalence among the elderly Kashmiri Pandit population—6.5% among the Kashmiri Pandit population aged 60 years and above, which is higher than that reported from other parts of India.

In Palhallan, I met a boy whose age was the same as that of turmoil. He was born in 1990 and the only Kashmiri Pandits he had ever seen were my grandparents who had stayed back till 1997 in the hope that their tribe would get a chance to return and till their lands again. The day never came. They too had to migrate in 1997 as old age and violence made it difficult for them to lead their lives there. And then I remember my brothers, having been born in exile, never had the chance to grow and flourish in their own land.

Nietzsche's words reverberate:

'Ah, whither shall I now ascend with my longing! From all mountains do I look out for fatherlands and motherlands. But a home have I found nowhere: unsettled am I in all cities, and decamping at all gates.'

[1] Mushtaq, A., Margoob, M.D., Muhammad M. F., Banal, R., Khan, A. K., Malik, A. K., Ahmad, S. A., Hussain, A., Majid, A., Wani, Z. A., Rather, Y. H., Muzamil, M., Khanday, S. A., Shah, M. S.; (2006); Community prevalence of trauma in south Asia—experience from Kashmir; JK Prac., 13 (supplement) S14–S17.

[2] Banal R, Thappa J, Shah HU, Hussain A, Chowhan A, Kaur H, Bharti M, Thappa S. (2010); Psychiatric morbidity in adult Kashmiri migrants living in a migrant camp at Jammu; Indian J Psychiatry; 52(2): 154-8.

[3] Raina S, Razdan S, Pandita KK, Raina S. (2008); Prevalence of dementia among Kashmiri migrants; An (?)Indian Acad Neurol; 11(2): 106-8.

V

I came across startling notions of the people in the valley. For them, my community through its 'antagonistic actions' and attitudes had effectively erased itself from the society over a period of two centuries and that this extirpation was an inescapable consequence of this self-erasure. A counter argument also exists that a balance could be attained given the religious persecution of my community during the Mughal and Pathan rule. However, this parity fails to justify and answer a pertinent question that nobody either brings up or answers: How can a community's past actions define or judge me, or others like me who had no direct participation in it? My claim on my home and my land is neither notional nor nostalgic. I refuse to be defined by someone else's history.

And then thinkers of all denominations join the fray. Their narcissism nourishes a drive to build up opinionated ideations to sustain competing narratives. All jump on the same bandwagon; rummaging, pilfering and poaching on each other and us. They tell us what or what not to do. They want to make me a stranger to my own history without acknowledging that unlike them I belong to this place and covet its arborescence. I refuse to be a victim. Unfortunately, my own community could never put this forth eloquently. It's only now that the stories are being told. I also refuse to be deprived of my right or be rendered 'irrelevant' on the basis of history and its varying narratives. As an individual of a different social group, my claim springs from my sense of belonging, my ethnicity and my language. The massacres that took place in Gool, Nadimargh and Wandhama to frighten away the minority community reinforces my resolve to not only belong but also to claim.

And then I come across Anthony Shadid, a Maronite Christian, a minority in a predominantly Muslim Lebanon. He was never a part of the deadly civil war which destroyed much of his community's power base in Lebanon, who after three generations in America came back to re-claim his sense of belonging in *Marjayoun*.

VI

Yearning does not end, neither does exile. I walked beside the ruins of my house, realising the profundity of this longing for home. Everything has crumbled down in Palhallan as well as Srinagar. And I try to find solace in the immortal words of Marcel Proust: *"But, when nothing subsists of an old past, after the death of people, after the destruction of things, alone, frailer but more enduring, more immaterial, more persistent, more faithful, smell and taste still remain for a long time, like souls remembering, waiting, hoping, upon the ruins of all the rest, bearing without giving way, on their almost impalpable droplet, the immense edifice of memory."* In my mind, I set off to explore my land, and found myself at peace.

Now I want our next generation to be here so that I can tell them that I too was next to the Chinar tree, and that they should chase calves and ducklings, and feed and milk cows. I want to see their years bloom in their own hearths, not in exile, next to an ancient town where the highway breaks off and leads to a house of mud and stone, which once was ours. I want them to carve their own destinies, and re-claim the land of their ancestors.

In this twilight hour, I'll sing a line from a poem written by the Sufi poet Shamas Faqeer. Singing the verse brings alive the memory of my home:

'Wanyo sir-e-asraar, yino asakh wobale, main vucchh har shayah su yaar, tchano kah zar ti khali.' (I will tell you the secret of secrets. Pay heed to it and don't be inattentive. I have seen my beloved everywhere. Not a single particle exists without him, my friend.)

11

Season of Ashes

Siddhartha Gigoo

The past is never dead. It is not even past.

– William Faulkner, *Requiem for a Nun*

I

On a hot July day in 1994, as I was thinking of leaving Udhampur (in the Jammu province), where I'd been staying with my family since our migration from Kashmir in 1990, I paid a visit to the Camp School where I'd studied and which was located in a vast migrant camp where thousands of Kashmiri Pandit exiles had lived in canvas tents. I'd left the Camp School a couple of years earlier and was about to complete my graduation as a private student. I could not go to the regular college because migrant students were given admission only in the Camp College where the displaced college lecturers taught the displaced students. Unlike the Camp School, which was about a dozen shabby canvas tents erected in the migrant camp, the Camp College was atop a hill overlooking the town. The migrant students attended classes in the afternoon when the regular college closed. The students of the Camp College benefitted from the college library, the playground, the canteen, and most importantly, proper classrooms. Classes in the Camp School were held in tents. There were no benches, but the authorities had supplied blackboards. The migrant students sat on tarpaulin sheets while the teachers delivered the lectures on Physics, Chemistry, Mathematics, History, English and other subjects. During rainy days, most students did not come to school. At lunch break, the students returned to their tents to eat with their families. I was particularly fond of the English teacher and dreaded the Chemistry and Mathematics teachers.

The days were mundane. Whenever deaths occurred in the camp, people assembled for funerals and offered words of comfort to one another. The sight of funeral processions was unsettling. A grim silence would descend upon the families living in the camp. The young and the middle-aged lived in constant fear of losing their elders.

The School Headmaster's office was in a tent with a few chairs, a table and a ramshackle cabinet to store files and documents. The Headmaster had spent several years teaching Mathematics at a senior secondary school in Kashmir. Like other Pandit families in his locality, his family had to flee from Kashmir in February 1990 under the most horrendous circumstances. A militant outfit in his district had warned the Pandit teachers to leave. The militants had threatened one of his colleagues. He spoke fondly of his ancestral house, which he was compelled to desert hardly a year after renovating it. The renovation had cost him a lifetime of savings. He boasted of the intricate and artistic woodwork of the ceilings. His eyes shone when he talked about the cherry and walnut trees in his garden, the magnificent house and the stylish bathrooms. Now he lived with his family in abject conditions in the camp. All they were able to salvage and bring along were the educational certificates, some utensils, clothes and a couple of trunks that contained household belongings.

The Headmaster carried himself with decorum and poise. He wore a suit and his shoes were immaculately polished. He took classes religiously, despite the increasing administrative workload. He was completely possessed of his subject—Mathematics. The blackboard in his class was the most wondrous sight with mathematical problems and solutions, geometrical drawings and equations scribbled all over it. He would solve the problems without referring to any of the textbooks. The look on his face, after solving a problem, was that of a saint's. Nothing gave him more pleasure and satisfaction than teaching and seeing his students solve complex problems. Yet there were a few students who didn't understand anything of Mathematics. He would smile and forgivingly say: 'Mathematics is not everything. There are other subjects too.' After living in the camp for over a year, he took up two rooms, a kitchen and a bathroom on rent nearby. He gave tuitions in the mornings and evenings.

The Camp School was a fifteen-minute walk from our rented two-room house. The camp for migrants had been erected in a derelict stadium where locals used to play football and cricket. A part of it was also used as a garbage-dumping ground. The fence was a shambles. The Jammu-Srinagar National Highway ran close by. Many shops dotted the highway on both sides—repair shops, petrol and diesel stations, cheap tea shops, fruit sellers, and roadside eateries. In the rainy season, thistles grew all over the camp. Anthills erupted in dozens, and buffaloes and cows strayed into the ground to feed on leftovers. The view of the distant hills from the camp was mesmerising, particularly during the evenings. I saw some of the most spectacular sunsets there. During the hot summer days, the camp dwellers stayed inside the tents to keep away from the heat. Going out of the tents meant heatstroke and sunstroke. A wretched barrenness prevailed all over. At night, an eerie silence blanketed the camp only to be broken by the mournful howling of dogs.

I found myself wading indolently through uneventful days and nights. That particular day in July, I stood alone at the entrance to the camp. Overcome with a sense of futility, I'd dragged myself to the camp, hoping for a chance encounter with someone to break the monotony.

The canvas of the tents fluttered vehemently in the wind. The dust storm threw pieces of paper, cloth, leaves and plastic bags in different directions and engulfed the surroundings. Some migrants ran into their tents and fastened the flaps with ropes. Some of the torn tents had plastic sheets stitched on to them.

I stood there aimlessly. Then I sauntered into the camp. The tents of the Camp School were empty that afternoon. At night, some migrants from joint families slept in them. Their own tents were too cramped.

Giant clouds of dust hovered intermittently and eclipsed the sun momentarily, providing succour from the blinding light and scorching heat. Specks of dirt stuck to my face. I wiped the sweat and dust off it. After some time the dust storm abated. Evening fell and the sky turned vermilion. Some migrant men and women emerged to inspect the condition of their tents and attend to them. Fortunately, none of the tents had fallen apart, though some of the bamboo poles holding the fabric had been dislodged, while others leaned precariously.

An old classmate came out of a tent. He was dishevelled. We met after a long time. He greeted me with an unusual expression. His eyes met mine. He lived with his family in that tent. I enquired about the welfare of his family. He looked around desultorily. It was a congested cluster of shanty tents. They looked the same. Each tent had a number. It was difficult for an outsider like me to tell one tent from the other. He had once told me that the most agonising part of his camp life was taking baths in the mornings. Going to the makeshift bathrooms, which were in a pathetic condition, was a messy affair. Every morning, he would walk down to a spring at the bottom of a hill to bathe. On his way back to his place, he would bring along a bucketful of spring water for drinking. I'd also done so many times on weekends. But I had a choice. The boy didn't. For him, it was a torment to see his mother and sister struggle for space and privacy in the scrawny tent.

I'd never been inside any of these tents. During my camp school days, I'd spent evenings loitering and looking for an opportunity to be in a tent, partly out of curiosity and partly out of a sense of purposelessness. What else was there to do after the classes, but roam around in the vicinity and strike conversations with acquaintances!

I stood near one tent. The two canvas flaps were placed on either side of the tent for the light and the breeze to enter. An old man lay prostrate on a bed. He was in his shirt and pajamas. An old woman, his wife, was fanning him with a hand fan. I went closer. The man was in some sort of a delirium. The expression on his face betrayed acute sorrow. He seemed caught in a reverie—a frenzy of sorts. He mumbled some inane words. Nothing made sense. Except the old couple, there was no one else in the tent. The old woman mutely fanned her husband and wiped the drool off his mouth with a towel. Nothing distracted her, not even the presence of a stranger who stood at the entrance. I looked at them for some time until I got bored and left.

Some months later, I left for Delhi. I didn't return to the camp after that, though I travelled past Udhampur twice on my way to Srinagar. Once I had an urge to visit the camp. But it was too late. The entire camp had been demolished a few years ago; the migrants had been relocated to another camp where they were given one-room flats. The 'tent shelters' didn't exist any more. The vast ground had once again returned to its original state—a playground where young boys could play cricket and football.

Sometimes when I look at sunsets in Delhi, I am reminded of the spectacular sunsets at Udhampur. There is only one other image etched in my mind—that of the old man lying on the wobbly bed. And I would wonder what ruminations had seized his mind in that state of borderline dementia. What world must he have been transported to upon losing his sense of reality? A world of fragmented images. Images of his childhood days or a dream-world full of familiar and unfamiliar characters. Different expressions plaited on his wrinkled face.

Twenty-five years have passed. The memory of that scene is still alive.

In the winter of 2011, I wrote a short story titled *Poison, Nectar*. It was about a family of four migrants living in a camp. At the heart of the story was the story of that old man who lingered on that day in the puny tent in the camp. His world was somewhere afar, and he dangled between nostalgia and pain.

In the spring of 2013 I went to Jammu to meet my parents who live there. Their house is next to a camp for Kashmiri Pandit migrants at Muthi. One morning, my father, a friend who is a cinematographer and I went to this camp—an apartment complex consisting of two-room flats. We were greeted by a host of old men sitting on the porches. The president of the camp took us to one flat in which an old couple lived. Their children lived elsewhere. The old man puffed on a cigarette. Wrinkles crisscrossed his sunken cheeks. He smiled a mysterious smile and didn't speak a word. His appearance intrigued me. I tried to get the old man to talk of his house in Kashmir, his childhood and youth, the circumstances leading to his exodus, his early days in the camp and, most importantly, how he felt about the current state of affairs, his life and his wife. He barely spoke a word. Then after finishing his cigarette, he lisped two sentences. 'What else can happen to us? We're ruined.' He turned his gaze elsewhere and puffed on his cigarette. I met another old couple that day. They offered us tea. The old man adjusted his cap and spectacles as soon as he saw my camera. 'Newspaper-wallas and television-wallas used to come during the initial days, take pictures of us, ask us questions and then leave. But there was no mention of us either in the newspapers or the news on the radio. Now no one comes here. What can I do for you?' he said.

The old man reminded me of my grandfather. His karakul cap was exactly like the one my grandfather wore. He sat exactly the way my grandfather sat by the window, holding his favourite transistor in his hand and waiting for a cup of tea. An uncanny resemblance! The cheekbones, the nose, the forehead! My grandfather was bedridden for three-and-a-half years, unable to walk and go even to the bathroom. The trauma of the loss of his home, his clinic, his Kashmir (which meant the world to him) devastated him. The first shock he experienced was when he crossed the Jawahar tunnel, in Banihal. He was in a truck with his family, leaving Kashmir for Jammu in 1991. When the truck exited the three-kilometre long tunnel the entire landscape had changed. Something changed in him that day. And the tunnel became the tunnel of forgetfulness, not just for him, but countless other elders who were leaving Kashmir for an unknown place, possibly for the first time in their lives. Then in 1995, five years after the exodus, he lost his memory. During those five years, he waited for the political situation in Kashmir to be normal so that he could return home and to his clinic (he had a pathology laboratory of his own called The Imperial Clinical Laboratory at Maharaj Ganj in Srinagar). If there was one word he couldn't come to terms with, it was 'migrant'. His condition deteriorated rapidly once dementia set in. We lost all hope when a neurologist diagnosed him with Alzheimer's. 'It is impossible to recover from this degenerative state. It is an abyss. One falls and falls until memory and recognition cease to be,' the doctor said. While studying in Delhi, I read articles about this disease on the internet to understand this state of no-memory, no-recognition. My grandfather mistook my mother for his granddaughter and my sister for his great-grandmother. Once he left the house and didn't return for hours until my father brought him home after searching for him in the whole of Udhampur. He had found him sitting on a footpath by the roadside. But the worst day of our life was when he went to the bathroom one afternoon and came out after an hour smeared with faeces. For him, the meaning of things had altered irrevocably. From that day onwards, my father accompanied him to the bathroom every single time. One day he went to the bathroom a hundred times. He just wouldn't stop. My father was patient. He ensured that nothing went wrong and reassured him that he was around, though he was not sure if grandfather recognised him. My father never left him alone from that day onwards. A few days before my grandfather died, his ear lobe fell off while my father was giving him a sponge bath. His body was full of sores. His skin had become flaky and shrivelled. His fragile skin peeled when we applied an ointment on it. My father cried on some days. So did my mother. My grandmother was a strong woman. She kept on spreading cheer in her own way. She narrated parables to help us stave off depression.

My sister and I were mute spectators to this horror that gripped us, day after day in our lives. As a family we were falling apart. Exile did terrible things to us, as it did to many others who lived and suffered in camps. Love deserted us every morning only to return in snatches, and disappear again. Yet, we waited. We waited for the violence and upheaval in Kashmir to end. We waited for homecoming. Waiting meant hope. Waiting kept us alive.

This hopeless wait for the glorious past festered within our hearts. The present was oppressive. Though the horror of the 'tent life' had ended, the camp-dwellers were not able to get rid of the memory of painful living in tents even when most of them were no longer living in them. When one such camp near my parents' house in Jammu was demolished in 2011, I saw a seventy-something migrant woman sitting on a mound next to heaps of rubble, which till a few days ago were four walls and a roof—a place that the old woman was never able to call her home. It was just a temporary abode where she lived with her husband for almost two decades. The woman held a piece of brick close to her chest and refused to discard it. She had picked it up from the wreckage of the demolished shed. The entire camp was nothing but a huge pile of debris now. Smashed bricks and tiles, blocks of concrete, iron sheets, rusted iron rods, broken frames of doors and windows, decaying wooden pillars, plastic and potsherd covered the plot of land. The migrants had been relocated to another camp. The woman sat there with the brick in her lap. It was the last remnant of the shelter where she had spent one-fourth of her life with her husband. In this place they had grown old together nurturing hopes of a better tomorrow. And yet when it was time to move into a new place that was slightly better, she wasn't able to just leave and forget the old one. The wretchedness had come to grow on her.

After spending some days with my parents in Jammu, my friend and I went to Srinagar, Kashmir. We wanted to shoot some scenes for a short film based on my story. We shot a scene at Ram Mandir in my old locality, Nawa Kadal in Srinagar. The temple is now in a dilapidated condition. I walked through a narrow lane in my locality, a lane where even the rays of the sun didn't enter, a lane sandwiched between clusters of old houses. A Muslim woman came out of a house and saw me taking photographs and looking around my old neighbourhood. She stood in front of me and asked me to try and recognise her. When I wasn't able to place her she slapped me gently out of affection and burst into tears. 'I've carried you in my arms when you were a small boy. You were like my son. Your grandmother was like my mother,' she said and sighed.

During her last years, my grandmother would often say to me, '*Wumber ha gayam zaeth.*' (My life has become long. I want to go now.)

She rediscovered love for her husband, my grandfather, when he was fading away.

II

On the morning of 24 June 2012, my parents and grandmother undertook a trip from Jammu to Srinagar, Kashmir. My grandmother had been to Kashmir four times in the last twenty-three years, each trip lasting five or six days. Twice she had stayed at her brother's place near the army cantonment, a few kilometres from Lal Chowk. On one occasion she had stayed at a hotel in Srinagar; and the fourth time she had accompanied some of her relatives on a pilgrimage there. That time they visited a few temples and a Sufi shrine on the outskirts of Srinagar. During that trip the pilgrims spent some days in quietude found in abundance in temple complexes. The purpose, however, was not to pray or offer obeisance to God and deities but to be in the lap of nature, in a willow grove, by a wistful stream and amid scented gardens. At the end of the sojourn the families returned, not empty-handed, but with presents and mementoes for everyone. Often, these presents and mementoes included packets of assorted dry fruits, condiments like saffron and spices, and decorations made of walnut wood. Upon returning, they talked fondly of their stay in the familiar locales of the land of their birth—their homeland—where once they lived, where their ancestors were cremated, where they dreamt of nurturing their children and grandchildren and where they wished to die in peace. They recounted the days spent there, gossiped about people and then, with a certain degree of certitude, thought of the trip as the last one in their lifetime. Even with the passage of time—in weeks and months—these trips were not forgotten. The memory of these visits became a source of regular conversations during family get-togethers. Nothing about these journeys faded.

Babi, my grandmother, had become old. Yet her smiles were mysteriously radiant. Her eyes shone when we asked her questions about her life and her parents. She came from a vast joint family. She remembered all the details of her brothers, sisters, uncles, aunts and cousins. She could trace the entire genealogy of her family—names of her relatives, their ages, hobbies, tastes, likes and dislikes, the yarns they spun, and the riddles they invented. Every person had more than one name. She knew the intricate details of the relatives of her relatives. Even the distant ones! Her memory was a cage from which nothing escaped. We were baffled by the infallibility of it all. She told me about her father-in-law (my great grandfather, Madhavjoo Gigoo). He was a scholar and traveller. I got to know that he had written a book, *The Serpent in Kashmir*, which was published in Portugal during his travels in Europe. He introduced Arya Samaj to Kashmir. Sadly, his library consisting of rare books was pillaged by intruders in the spring of 1990 soon after my parents shifted from our ancestral house in Khankah-i-Sokhta, Nawa Kadal, Srinagar, Kashmir to Indira Nagar, a cantonment area.

Earlier Babi visited me twice a year. Then, as months went by, it became difficult for her to travel to Delhi, where I live. Travel by train was out of question, given her age and condition. She walked with difficulty and needed support to climb stairs. She became frail. The last time she came to stay with me was a few weeks before the onset of summer in 2012. She had taken a plane from Jammu to Delhi. It was less cumbersome to travel by air. I brought her home from the airport. She spent most of the days in bed, reciting hymns I neither understood nor paid attention to. Upon my insistence she spent an hour or so in the drawing room every evening, particularly after dinner, and looked at the television screen with utter disinterest. We would sit and watch inane programmes on television.

She would sit silently and look for an opportunity to start a conversation about something that had taken place years ago. Sharing anecdotes from her youth fascinated her. When the conversations ended and we got busy attending to the household chores, she lingered on and pretended not to feel bored. Then she would retire to the bedroom.

Over the next few days she didn't come out of the bedroom because of discomfort and fatigue, and complained of indigestion and nausea. She would fish for a sedative in her medicine kit and pop one into her mouth. Even then sleep evaded her. She struggled throughout the nights. I doubt if she ever slept peacefully. Every night, she would get up from her bed an hour before dawn, tiptoe quietly into the kitchen, a few paces from the bedroom, switch on the light, survey the cabinets, take out the saucepan from the tray, turn on the gas stove and make salty tea for herself. The rest of us would be fast asleep. Then she would wash the utensils and sip the tea in the dead of the night, sitting all by herself in desolate silence and stillness and then go to bed, content and at peace. At dawn she would bathe. In the mornings, she would say, 'I made some tea in the night and the stomach ache disappeared.'

During the days, she did nothing. Yet she never complained of boredom. She just waited for the moments to pass. All she owned was a bag full of a few saris, a towel, a small purse containing some money, a coil of thread, a needle, a prayer book, a comb, a bottle of hair oil, a toothbrush and a kit containing medicines. She didn't keep photographs in her purse. Other household things we normally treasure did not lure her. Strangely, she never exhibited signs of attachment to any of her belongings. Talking to people, taking part in conversations and gossip, attending weddings and family functions interested her more than anything else. Even though she narrated the same anecdotes repeatedly, the renditions were different every time. No two sentences were alike. Each narration was a consummate tapestry of enchanting tales about people and strange happenings during her youth. Often I would be charmed by the way she conjured up magical tales of adventure, deftly weaving them partly from strands of memory and partly from her fecund imagination. Often, one wondered if any of those events had taken place. Such events occurred mostly in dreams. In one such story a lion made a grand appearance. She was also particularly fond of introducing a viper in many of her stories. She might have seen a viper during her childhood and it must have remained etched in her imagination forever. The viper was portrayed compassionately in her narratives and she was quite fond of it. Occasionally, she loved to buy gifts for us and slip some money into our hands during festivals.

One night she had an attack. She started trembling; her hands and forehead went cold, her breathing became difficult and her voice turned feeble. Despite the terrifying sight we managed to remain calm and called her nephew, a doctor, who is a neighbour. He came immediately, examined her, talked to her, cracked a few jokes while we watched nervously, and finally reassured her that we were around and wouldn't let anything happen to her. She chuckled and then smiled a tremulous smile, partly out of fear and partly because she was relieved to see all of us around her. I felt a shiver while clinging to her trembling arm. Anything could have happened that time. This wasn't the first time she had suffered an attack at my place. The previous one had taken place sometime a year back because of low blood pressure, cramps, bad digestion, diarrhoea and palpitation. The next evening she called me to the room and handed me a woollen shawl. 'Get this dry-cleaned,' she said. The next morning I took the shawl to the dry-cleaner. After a couple of days, I returned the dry-cleaned shawl to her. I had noticed that the shawl didn't need any dry-cleaning. It was in immaculate condition and reasonably clean. It smelled fresh as well. I made it a point to mention this to her—the fact that the shawl didn't need dry-cleaning. She smiled at my question. 'The shawl is for you to place on me when I am gone,' she said casually. A strange smile played on her lips. 'Who knows, you might need the shawl tomorrow itself!' she added.

She was not prone to anxiety in her life. She was energetic and zestful when it came to visiting her relatives or hosting guests at her place. Her conversations were laced with wit and humour. Her laugh was hearty. The anecdotes she recounted were fabulous and racy and held us spellbound. Many of our relatives visited her only to listen to her charming accounts. We marvelled at her uncanny ability to cast a spell during her storytelling sessions.

In 2010 when I'd gone to Kashmir, I hadn't told my grandmother about the trip, thinking she might get worried. But when my father told her that I was in Kashmir, she insisted on speaking to me on the phone. She called me and said, 'You didn't tell me that you were going "home".' I was struck by what she said. She referred to Kashmir as her home. Twenty years in exile, yet Kashmir was home.

As she grew older, her memory became stronger, her renditions more burnished. She always talked to my wife in Kashmiri at home and even on the phone from Jammu. The result was that my wife and my daughter learnt many Kashmiri words. She had been very beautiful in her youth. Her only son used to call her Zeenat Aman. One day, at the wedding of her relative, she wore a new blue saree and looked like a bride. She survived both attacks miraculously.

She even survived the third one at her place in Jammu, when my father was away. She was hospitalised and administered medicines intravenously for a night. But family and friends had come and helped. A couple had even stayed at her place for the night.

When it was time to return to Jammu, her home, she was both excited and morose. Excited because she would get to be in her room there, and sad, thinking that she might not live long to see me again. She held me in a warm embrace for a long time and left for Jammu. At her house in Jammu she seldom came out of her room. Sometimes I spoke to her on the telephone. She would say a few words and then hang up. I grew worried on account of her deteriorating health. She kept on complaining of indigestion and headaches. Her personal physician had prescribed one tablet in the morning and one before each meal.

When I got to know that my parents were taking her to Srinagar to spend a few days in solace, I didn't even for a moment dissuade them. I was delighted at the prospect of their journey. My sister's family took everybody in their car. They were to stop briefly at Srinagar and then proceed on a pilgrimage to the Holy Cave of Amaranth. I made a few calls to them while they were on their way to Srinagar. They talked excitedly about how fragrant the air had turned the moment they crossed the Jawahar tunnel at Banihal.

They had arranged for a couple of rooms in a developing residential locality in Srinagar. A visit to our old ancestral house was on the itinerary. It had been twenty-three years. Ever since the exodus in 1990, my grandmother had not visited her old house. Despite having visited

Srinagar four times previously, she had not been able to visit the house in downtown Srinagar. The place was the hub of militancy, and it wasn't safe for the Pandits to go there. I always wanted Babi to visit the house. This time I was hopeful that the visit would materialise. I was more excited than she was and wanted to be with her that time, particularly the moment she would look at her house (which belongs to someone else now) from a distance for the first time in twenty-three years. I was not sure if she would be able to enter the house though.

That evening, when they reached Srinagar, I telephoned my father to inquire about my grandmother's health. She was fine throughout the journey. She had braved the ordeal. At her age, being on a drive through a meandering mountainous road for hours together was not easy. A grand plan awaited them the next day—a drive through the roads in the city and the visit to the old locality and then her 'home'. A visit to other places too.

Earlier that morning, a 200-year-old Sufi shrine of Sheikh Syed Abdul Qadir Jeelani—locally called Dastgeer Sahib—had been set ablaze in downtown Srinagar. That afternoon, a violent clash between the people and the police forces had broken out and snowballed into a city-wide protest. Curfew had been imposed in some parts of town. Hundreds of policemen patrolled the streets. The residents remained indoors as unrest gripped the city.

I kept telephoning my father every hour to find out how grandma was doing. In the night my father called me and said, 'While taking rest in the room, Babi experienced pain in her stomach. The pain didn't ebb for a while and she vomited. When the discomfort didn't abate for two hours, we took her to a private hospital nearby. The doctor examined her, administered dextrose intravenously and said there was nothing to worry.'

I spoke to my mother. She was worried that Babi had fallen ill in Kashmir and that they had to take her to a hospital where they didn't know anyone. But mother was relieved when she saw my father's Muslim friends. They had come to the hospital and insisted on staying there. Mother said, 'Two Muslim nurses attended to Babi. One of them was kind and compassionate. When her shift ended, the other one took over. For some reason, this nurse hesitated in staying close to Babi. She feigned ignorance when it came to changing the drip. But later she changed her attitude and attended to her with utmost care.'

At night my father telephoned me. 'We've taken her to the government hospital in the city. There were a few complications,' he said.

'Which hospital? How is she doing? What do the doctors say? Shall I take the next flight to Srinagar?' I asked.

'SMHS Hospital! Don't worry. I will keep you posted.'

I looked at my watch. It was half past one. I gave the phone to my wife. She talked. I couldn't sleep and kept thinking about the situation.

An hour later, the phone rang again.

'The doctors say she needs surgery immediately. But the chances of survival are slim. Her intestines are a mess. If she survives the surgery, she won't live for more than a few days. We've to decide fast.'

'What do we do?' I asked.

'What do you suggest?'

I was clueless and didn't know what to say. I remained silent.

'We should opt for surgery. It is the best thing to do. We should take a chance. Miracles happen,' my father said.

I concurred and prayed. Within a few minutes the phone rang again. Father said that Babi was not doing well. She had gone into a semi-conscious state. 'Let us not go for surgery,' my father said. A nursing orderly in the ward had walked up to him and said, 'Why take the risk of surgery when she might not survive? Keep your mother with you. Serve her well in this difficult time. Let her live a few more days. Let her be with you.'

The man spoke wisdom. It was the wisdom of an illiterate man who saw life from close quarters every day and lived through tumultuous circumstances every moment. Our life is superficial. The man saved us from ruin and lifelong regret and guilt with his wisdom.

'Let us bring her home tomorrow. To Jammu,' I said. 'But in case she is in no condition to travel, either by air or by road, then we stay at the hospital there. For as many days as it takes.'

At half past two in the night, I booked a flight to Srinagar for the next morning.

I couldn't sleep that night. In the morning I got dressed, packed many clothes and set off for the airport. The flight was on time. It reached Srinagar at 1:30 in the afternoon. It was a strange journey. I didn't know what awaited me. At the airport taxi stand in Srinagar, I asked for a taxi to the hospital. To my dismay, things started falling apart. The taxi drivers and the taxi booth operator said that no taxi would go to the hospital because the area was under curfew due to the violence the previous day. The taxi drivers refused to take the risk of taking any passenger to the city. I made frantic inquiries and pleaded with the taxi drivers who were taking tourists to other places in the Kashmir Valley. After moments of desperation, one kind-hearted middle-aged taxi driver relented. 'I'll take you to the hospital. Hop in.'

The roads wore a deserted look. Fortunately, the policemen who kept vigil in the armoured vehicles parked on the roads didn't stop us. The taxi driver talked to me and, sensing my anguish, tried to comfort me. 'God will be kind to us,' he said. 'Humans are powerless, but we must be fearless in times like these.'

When the taxi reached Lal Chowk, I spoke to my father's uncle on my mobile phone. He asked me to rush to the hospital. I got worried and, helplessly, fixed my gaze outside the window and waited for the destination to arrive. My mind went blank. I reached the hospital in forty minutes. I paid the taxi driver and ran to the ward. My father's uncle was waiting at the gate. He had bled from his nose earlier in the day. It took me another five minutes to reach the general ward on the second floor. I entered the ward, which was a vast hall with beds on both sides. Some injured persons with bandages and casts on their bodies were being wheeled into it. We walked twenty or thirty steps and reached the end of the ward. A matron came out of an adjacent hall on the left. My father's uncle greeted her and pointed towards me. 'This is her grandson,' he said.

The matron looked at me with compassion and said, 'She just died a few minutes ago.' Her eyes were watery.

I entered the hall and neared the bed on which my grandmother lay. My mother sat next to her and wiped a tear from her eye. She lifted the white cloth from my grandmother's face and asked me to pour a spoonful of water into her mouth. I struggled to keep my hand steady while pouring water into my grandmother's mouth. Her lips were grey and her tongue was curled. It was a moment of uneasiness. There were strangers around the bed, looking at my grandmother's body.

I called my wife and asked her to take a flight to Jammu.

I went to search for my father downstairs. He was standing outside the hospital gate, talking to some people and making arrangements.

Upon seeing me, he broke down. We consoled each other and got busy with the preparations for taking my grandmother out of the hospital. The matron and her staff wrapped my grandmother carefully and meticulously in white cloth.

A thought crossed our minds … that of cremating her in Srinagar, the place of her birth, her homeland, where she was born, got married, gave birth to her only child (my father), reared her grandchildren and lived for years there. The crematorium was not far from the hospital. It was the same crematorium where her parents and grandparents had been cremated. But the area was under curfew. Then we thought that Jammu was our home now.

The ward staff saw us off at the hospital gate. They hugged us. Some cried. 'She died in her home,' a woman said.

We couldn't get hold of a hearse or an ambulance that afternoon. Ambulances didn't go out of the Kashmir province. A private Chevrolet SUV was available for hire. We laid down my grandmother in the middle seat. At about half past four, my father, mother and I set off for Jammu. On the way, we stopped briefly at the house my parents and sister's family had rented to pick up some of my grandmother's belongings. A bag and her sandals.

We made calls to friends, neighbours and relatives in Jammu. Some of them started preparing for our arrival. It was the strangest journey I have ever undertaken in my life. Bringing my grandmother home! A day earlier she had plans of visiting her 'home' in Srinagar. But it was not destined to be so. She had survived three attacks previously. Why couldn't she survive this one? Or live just one more day to be able to see her old house one last time and spend some time talking to her neighbours, some of whom would certainly have recognised her. But then she had survived the three previous attacks only to have lived till that day. She didn't die anywhere else but in the land of her birth, her homeland. These thoughts crisscrossed my mind. I drifted into a maze of bizarre thoughts, thinking of my grandmother, regretting that I couldn't make it on time and was not able to see her or talk to her during the last moments and kiss her one last time. A kiss in return for those thousands of kisses she had gifted me since my birth. A familiar scent wafted in the air. I could smell the hands of my grandmother. Her hands were always fragrant.

En route home, we spoke briefly about my grandmother's last day at the hospital. I wanted to know what her last words were. I wanted to know if she had asked for me. My father mentioned that she wanted to be in her room. That morning at the hospital, she had vacillated between bouts of wakefulness and stupor and experienced flashes of momentary consciousness. My father had told her that she was in a hospital at Srinagar and that the doctors were treating her. When she was conscious she had been able to see the people around her, the hospital staff, the nursing orderlies, the matron, the team of doctors, attendants of other patients and strangers. She was very happy to see her younger brother and his wife. She knew the persons in the hospital were Muslims. Everyone around in the ward knew that she was the only Pandit patient and exile the hospital had ever had. In response to one of the remarks, she had said, 'Muslims are responsible for our plight.' Everyone had laughed and understood the deep humanity hidden in her caustic expression. They called her 'Mother'.

Dusk fell as we left the city behind. We drove through Pampore, famous for its saffron. During her youth, my grandmother used to visit this town every summer and stay for days with her relatives. She must have passed through this road a thousand times and always been certain of returning to the town. Now, perhaps, she was looking at the town from a different realm. Now she was reunited with her husband who had left us many years earlier.

My father fell asleep soon after we had tea at a highway tea shop. He had not slept for 63 hours. My mother's tired eyes refused to steal a nap. She didn't eat or have water. I clasped my palm around my grandmother's feet which were tied together firmly with a string.

The vehicle sped past through the countryside amidst a sudden hailstorm, leaving behind the Valley and everything else that was precious only a day before. We reached home at half past one in the night.

Family friends waited outside our house in Jammu. I spent the night next to my grandmother in her room. Tired and drowsy, I fell asleep.

My wife and daughter reached Jammu the next morning.

After the last bath, my grandmother was draped in a shroud and a shawl, and decorated with flowers. We took her away for cremation amid the chanting of Vedic hymns and prayers. While touching her bare body, I grew numb. I knew that this was the last time I was touching her, caressing her, showing my unbounded affection for her, not just as a grandson, but as a person who knew her as one of the greatest storytellers. Despite her failing health during the last few months, she never betrayed signs of ageing. She grew old, but slowly. Her hair never turned completely white. It was grey in patches and some strands were the colour of henna. She was a great cook, a raconteur, obstinate at times and full of practical wisdom. She would crack jokes about her death. During the last few months, she would always say, 'Why am I not dying? I have lived enough. This life is long.' She must have told my father hundreds of times: 'I have only two wishes. I shouldn't fall ill for a long time. You should be by me at the time of my death. I want you to carry me to the crematorium and light the pyre.' My father used to tell her in his own characteristic manner: 'I will burn you with my own hands.' And she used to laugh and bless him.

The shawl she had asked me to get dry-cleaned months earlier adorned her cold body. At the crematorium, I pretended to be brave. The burning pyres at the crematoriums have always fascinated me. The smell of burning flesh and bones, the crackle in the flames, the cinders and the ashes that remain in the end! The deep loneliness of the pyres when the mourners leave. The flames take some time to consume the bodies. And at night, the embers, the last traces and the remnants—pieces of bones—remain intact. These remnants crave a human touch. The bones crumble in our hands when we pick them up and put them into earthen pots. The warm ash settles down in a small heap. It grows less warm as the night progresses. Nothing else exists. Yet a strange scent wafts through the air. A scent quite distinguishable from any other scent one has known. It is the scent of neither life nor death, neither being nor non-being. At the crematorium, people become spiritual and philosophical. It is as though wisdom and enlightenment dawn upon them, not by chance or accident, but by means of some divine intervention. This feeling is transitory and vanishes the moment people step out of the crematorium. For a moment, I found myself caught in this magical spell of transient wisdom and knowledge. Of all things material and spiritual the unsettling knowledge is that everything perishes in the end and that life is not to be lived worrying. If only we could spend some time every day in the crematorium, many beautiful secrets of life would be revealed to us. Revelations that would lead us to a more fulfilling and purposeful existence! One would become detached and, therefore, experience joy and bliss. Death perhaps turns us into beautiful beings.

After two days, just after dawn, we went to collect my grandmother's ashes at the crematorium. A small Vedic ritual was performed. The ashes were still warm. We poured water on the ashes. One more family was performing a ritual. A young woman cried inconsolably. She still referred to the mound of ash as her loved one. Nothing could console her. Soon she gathered courage and became quiet before commencing the ritual.

We collected my grandmother's ashes in two earthen pots, decorated them with marigolds and set off for Akhnoor, a village not very far from Jammu. River Chenab runs through this village. Mango trees dotted the road. Alongside, a canal, in which children were swimming, ran serenely. We crossed a steel bridge and reached the ghat of the river Chenab. During the monsoons, the transporters who work for timber merchants throw hundreds of logs of timber into the river and the waters ferry these logs from one place to another. Some youngsters dive into the river, even when it is in fury, to gather driftwood.

The water of the Chenab was cold. It was greenish grey in colour and a lot cleaner than what we find in most other rivers. I held the ashes in my hands one last time before placing them back in the pots. Soon, we immersed the ashes in the water and saw them float instantly. The water changed its colour for a moment. The flowers floated in a zigzag movement and slowly moved away from the riverbank. I watched the flowers for some time till they were visible no more.

Where does this river go? I asked myself. I remembered that the river flows into Pakistan. For many of us who saw their elders pine endlessly for one last homecoming, it was Pakistan we always cursed for creating a mess in Kashmir—our homeland—and for making us leave and spend the rest of our lives in waiting and exile. For many of us, it would take years or even decades to fathom the impact of the loss of a generation, which traced its ancestry to a unique people who originated from the land of *rishis* (sages) more than 5000 years ago. And now the descendants of these people struggle to keep alive the consciousness of this fabulous ancestry. The people of my grandmother's generation are fast fading away into oblivion and nothingness. My memory of that generation is eroding. For me the death of my grandmother made me realise how little I knew of her life which spanned more than eight decades. And I was overcome by a tearing urge to preserve what was on the brink of extinction. Like many of her contemporaries, my grandmother had lived an eventful life full of vicissitudes.

In the context of the lives of an exiled family, I came across an unsettling ambivalence. Three generations looked at their ethos, condition and aspirations in three completely different perspectives. The old nursed a yearning to return to their homeland; the middle-aged and the young vacillated between a strange past (which once was beautiful, then changed for the worse) and an uncertain present; the children born in exile grappled to assimilate into the new and carve a new identity, yet grew up amid a shared and fragmented memory, that of their parents and grandparents.

In a cameo titled *36 Hours*, my father, Arvind Gigoo, summed up the story of Kashmiri Pandits in two sentences: 'He gave me freedom for thirty-six hours; I gave him freedom for ever.' (In 1990 a militant organisation, through the columns of an Urdu daily, issued an ultimatum to Kashmiri Pandits to leave the valley in thirty-six hours.)

The river took my grandmother far away beyond the imagined borders of hope and despair, of pain and longing. Yet there existed some more places where she would have desired to go. For her, there always was one more place to set foot on and explore, even when, for many of us, there was nowhere else to go.

Some days later, my cousin wrote me a line to comfort me. It read: 'She never planned her journeys and always landed somewhere else.'

A day after my grandmother's death, my father wrote an obituary for her. It read:

Uma Shori Gigoo passed away in Srinagar, Kashmir. She was cremated in Jammu and the ashes were immersed in Chenab at Akhnoor. The next day, a havan was performed at home. That was the last day of mourning. Rice and water are not offered to the deceased. Neither a lamp is lit in the evenings. Other rituals will not be held at all. The dead don't eat anything; they don't drink water, and they don't need a lamp when the evening sets in. They don't hear the melodramatic, horrible, fearful and weird wail. This family tradition should and will continue.

12

From Home to Camp

Santosh Kumar Sani

My uncle Mool Chand Sani was working as a Sub-inspector in the J&K Police Department and was posted at Tangmarg in Kashmir in 1990. One wintry day a young Sikh girl, Neelam Kour told us that my uncle's life was in danger and that some people had told her this. When we asked her to tell us whatever she knew about it she said that some unidentified young men had come to our village Biyawa in Pattan and met and talked to her and made enquiries about the whereabouts of my uncle. The group of five militants had left the place after asking the girl not to tell anyone in the village about that meeting and conversation. But the girl showed courage and great presence of mind. She came to our home and narrated the story of the unidentified persons to my mother. Obviously they were militants who wanted to kill my uncle.

After half an hour, at about 7:30 pm, my father Jagar Nath Sani returned home after the day's routine work and was informed about the conversation that the militants had with that Sikh girl. We were all struck with fear and panic. That evening nobody in our family could eat dinner. Uncle, the target of the terrorists, was with us that night while his family had already left for Jammu. Another Sikh family, who were our neighbours, too, told us about the terrorists' plan to kill our uncle. This further terrified us all. We sat terror-stricken and confused, not knowing what to do. My father hurriedly went to a Sikh boy, who owned a car, and asked him to take uncle to a safe place. At about ten in the night the boy came to my uncle, managed to take him to a place in another village, and the following day took him to Jammu.

At about 1:30 am, we heard the sound of footsteps in and around our house. Some people started knocking at the main gate of our house. They shouted 'Darwaza kholo' (Open the door) a number of times. We sat silent and paralysed in the balcony of our house. The terrorists went on shouting, 'Darwaza khol do varna marey javogay' (Open the door otherwise you will be killed.) My father and I came down and as soon as we opened the door, they pointed their guns towards us. They asked us threateningly, 'Where is Mool Chand?' My father told them that he had been with us only up to 9:30 in the night. These words did not satisfy them. They said, 'We will search each and every room of your home.' They searched the house but did not find my uncle there. They left telling us that they were after the blood of my uncle, who, they believed, was an informer of the government and of the intelligence agencies. They threatened the rest of our family members and warned us not to leave the village for they were seeking 'revenge only against the informer'. It was a ghastly scene. I shiver when I recall it. I will never forget that night. Sister, brother and I were petrified. Father trembled out of fright.

The militants issued threats to the Pandit community and asked all of us to vacate the valley in 36 hours. Posters were circulated throughout the valley and announcements were made: *'Kashmir Mein Agar Rehna Hai, Allah-ho-Akbar Kehna Hoga / Azadi Ka Matlab Kya? La Illa Hi Illa La.'* (If you want to live in Kashmir, Allah O' Akbar should be chanted / What is the meaning of Azadi? La Illa Illa La.)

The brutal killings of several Pandits in our village shocked and frightened us. Father and three neighbours managed to hire a truck. Four families including ours left our village without carrying any belongings. My mother, brother and sister were silent throughout the journey. This was the effect of terror on them. It was March of 1990. I was studying in class 12. We took a room on rent and lived a very miserable life in that room. It was simply horrible. Then we shifted to Purkhoo camp. We lived there for many years. These days we are living in the camp at Jagti. We have been living on relief and the mercy of God all these years.

I studied in the camp school and then the camp college. I went to university and got an MA in Economics. After that I completed my PhD.

For some time I taught Economics at the Government Degree College for Women, Gandhi Nagar, Jammu. Then I taught at the Government College at Badarwah in the Jammu province. I learnt much by interacting with the students, teachers, professors and other people from Jammu. Like all other families we also faced extremely bad and pitiable conditions. But I am happy that I was able to achieve in migration something which I would not have achieved had our family been in Kashmir. I get complete satisfaction in the classroom where I deliver lectures to my students about what they want to know.

The thought of our family's life in the camp at Purkhoo shatters me. It calls up a nightmarish picture of degradation, humiliation and decline. I have been an unhappy spectator of the miseries of other displaced Pandits who were forced to run away from Kashmir for no fault of theirs. A peace-loving community suddenly found itself on the road. It lost its moorings and everything. I will describe the details below so that the reader gets an idea of what life in a camp means.

Initially the Pandit migrants were put in makeshift camps, schools and temples. Later they were shifted into tents at various places where they had to face tremendous hardships like extreme heat and torrential rains. The camps were bereft of proper sanitation and other necessary facilities like bathrooms and toilets. In one camp in Udhampur, one makeshift toilet block was to be used by a dozen families. In the initial years hundreds of Kashmiri migrants perished due to inhospitable weather conditions and lack of proper facilities at the camps. The government built one-room tenements for those Kashmiri Pandit migrants who could not afford rented accommodations. These tenements were built at a number of places in Jammu city and Udhampur. Life in the newly constructed camps was not free from sufferings and difficulties for the camp dwellers. The structures built were not hygienic. Nor were they suitable for the hot climate. There were acute problems of sanitation, water shortage, latrines, and so on.

However, the migrants who were housed in the camps at Purkhoo, Mishriwala, Muthi and Nagrota bore their sufferings with an exemplary patience and forbearance until the government built a huge and the biggest camp for them at Jagti. The camp at Jagti became operational in 2011 when all migrant families living in other camps were shifted there.

Jagti Mini Township is a government-run camp for displaced Kashmiri Pandits at Jagti, a place about fifteen kilometres from Jammu city. The camp comprises 178 blocks. Four thousand and two hundred families of Kashmiri migrants have been living there since 2011. Kashmiri Khatris, Sikhs, Rajputs and a few Muslim families also live in the camp. The total number of people is between twenty and twenty-two thousand. Besides, a hundred shops have also been constructed by the government and handed over to some inmates of the camp. The allotment of these shops was made on the basis of a lottery system against a security of Rupees 15,000. An agreement demanded the person, to whom the shop was allotted, to pay a monthly rent of Rupees 600. In the second phase of construction, which is underway, one hundred more shops are being constructed.

There are no adequate medical facilities available for the camp dwellers. A small dispensary under the charge of one doctor can in no way cater to the health problems of twenty or twenty-two thousand people. Most of the residents in the camp are poor who cannot afford medicines for treatment. The government dispensary is always short of even the most ordinary and cheap medicines. Tap water is supplied to the residents only twice a week. The quality of water has been found to be inferior and even hazardous to health. In view of the short supply of water, residents have been forced to set up their own hand pumps built at their own cost. Electricity and its supply is a big and painful problem for the residents. The camp dwellers have to spend days and nights in darkness without fans and coolers in the scorching heat of Jammu. Road connectivity to Jagti is far from satisfactory. The condition of the road from Nagrota to Jagti is extremely bad. The residents have to face immense difficulties of transport particularly in the rainy season.

The homeless Kashmiris living in the Jagti camp face innumerable economic difficulties. Most of the residents come from a rural background. They are unused to urban living. Bereft of their agricultural holdings in their places of origin they find it difficult to live a life of dignity. The relief provided to them by the government is a pittance in these days of inflation. No NGO has ever bothered to remove or lessen the miseries of the unfortunate community. The majority of the residents cannot afford to provide quality education to their children. Although the government has set up a higher secondary school at the camp, nothing has been done to ensure higher education for the meritorious students. Only 5 to 10 percent of young boys and girls living in the camp have managed to get higher and professional education in or outside the state through their own efforts. Most of the youths at the camps are frustrated. There are no means of employment. They are idle. Some of them have fallen prey to gambling and drinking. This has given rise to some kind of moral laxity among the youths. Residents of the camp are victims of uncertainty and social tension. Most of the people suffer from stress-related diseases like high blood pressure, heart ailments, diabetes and the rest.

Twenty five years of life in exile have brought many behavioral changes in the members of the displaced community. These changes have been mostly negative and have in no way improved the quality of their life. The youths have adopted new customs and ways of living which have in no way benefitted them. They are rootless and bereft of their traditions. The displacement has also affected the religious and spiritual life of the young camp dwellers. Their faith has become more phony and unreal. They suffer from inner emptiness, mental agony and confusion.

Lack of adequate living space is also a grave problem for the migrants of Jagti camp. In the one-room-one-lobby-kitchen-and-bathroom setting, there is very little space to spare. It becomes very hot and claustrophobic for the residents during summers and on the humid monsoon days. The material used for the construction of the buildings is quite inferior. In some of the apartments walls have cracked.

The camp is cut off from the life that one finds in a city. There is no interaction with the people belonging to the other sections of society. The camp dwellers live in a closed system. They are not exposed to other aspects of life. Their life is boring. The elderly and the old live in their memories. Some of them spend time in gossip. A handful of them play at cards. Most of them were landowners in Kashmir. They lived their beautiful, contended and simple lives in Kashmir but are devastated because of migration.

In spite of these drawbacks we feel that Kashmiri Pandit culture is safe in the camp. We follow rituals religiously, participate in all the festivals, pray in the temples in unison, distribute walnuts and sweets among the neighbours and relatives and attend marriages and other functions. Being co-operative we help one another. It is a small world where the old, the young and the middle-aged live in harmony. In the tents and one-room tenements there were conflicts because of frustration and unhappiness but slowly all those things disappeared. Our youths are very hardworking and ambitious. We are sure that in spite of the change in our lifestyles, they will ultimately do well in life and remember the difficulties and the tortures faced by us in the camps.

13

Camp Schools and Colleges for the Displaced Students

BL Zutshi

The tragic and sudden migration of about four hundred thousand Pandits from Kashmir to Jammu in 1990 put thousands of school and college students in a cesspool of hopelessness and despair. Like all other government employees the teachers, lecturers and professors found themselves in a slough of meaninglessness and insecurity. There were no schools and colleges where education could be imparted to the displaced Pandit students. The students of the medical college, engineering college, BEd colleges and university found themselves at cross-purposes. Initially everybody thought that the displacement of Pandits would last for a few months and that all would go back to Kashmir once the political climate changed for the better. But that did not happen. The future seemed bleak and dark for all. It became a painful human problem which demanded immediate attention. The government issued orders about the salaries to be given to the displaced government employees. The announcement to this effect was made by Vijay Bakaya to an agitating crowd of employees. The case of the 17000 unadjusted government employees was very grave. They went to the court of law to seek justice. Monthly relief was sanctioned in favour of those who were in the private sector or were running their own businesses in Kashmir.

HL Chatta and ML Malla were with me when we discussed our problems with the then Divisional Commissioner of Jammu division,

Vijay Bakaya, who in turn discussed the issue with the governor of Jammu and Kashmir state. In March 1990 the displaced college teachers made me the president of the migrant teachers' association. My job was to put the issues and problems of the college teachers and students before the government. The veterans like Prof BL Fotedar, Prof HL Misri, Prof MK Kak, Dr (Prof) RL Kaul, Prof Ashok Munshi, Prof PN Handoo, Prof Indu Kilam and others did their best to solve the problems faced by about 3000 displaced Pandit students. It was decided to open two camp colleges for the displaced students in Jammu and one camp college in Udhampur. We discussed the importance of these colleges with Prof JN Bhan and Prof MR Puri (former vice-chancellors of the University of Jammu), and Balraj Puri, an eminent journalist of Jammu. They agreed that the establishment of these colleges for the displaced migrant students would solve the problems connected with their education. Prof GS Dassi, Prof AN Bhan and Prof Pooran Kachroo were extremely helpful at every step. Vijay Kashkari, MK Tickoo, MK Jinsi, Sanjay Saraf and others of the Displaced Employees Association played constructive roles throughout and came forward with advice, suggestions and help. They worked very hard for migrant Pandit students.

Mr Vijay Bakaya arranged a meeting of the college teachers association with the then chief secretary, Mr RK Takkar who readily agreed to the proposal of the establishment of camp colleges and camp schools and sought approval from the governor of the state. In July 1990 camp colleges, camp schools, a camp university, a camp regional engineering college and camp B Ed colleges (Gandhi Memorial College of Education and Vishwabharti College of Education) were established. In spite of the lack of infrastructure the school teachers, lecturers and professors managed to give the best possible education to the students. All teachers and students tolerated the inhospitable climatic conditions with patience and perseverance, faced acute financial difficulties with strength and heroically rose to the occasion. There were innumerable problems all around but the spirit of the sufferers did not fail them. They proved that their nerves were made of steel. They had their dreams to guide them.

All the undergraduate and other educational institutions were affiliated to the University of Kashmir and the schools were affiliated to the J&K board of school education (Kashmir division). Because of the political upheaval, social unrest, turmoil and militancy in Kashmir it took the students five years to complete the three-year degree course. The examinations were not held in time. We took the matter to the National Human Rights Commission where our tales of woe and pathos were heard with sympathy and understanding. I presented the grim story of the migrant student community before all at the Abhinav Theatre in Jammu. The event was attended by students, teachers, the civil society and members of the bar association. The chairman of the National Human Rights Commission, Justice Venkatchalia, who had come from New Delhi to listen to us, assured the students that their problems would be put before the government of India. In this connection we took up the case with IK Gujral. In 1999 the examination schedule of the migrant students was delinked from that of the Kashmir division. Zafar Saif was made officer-in-charge of the migrant cell at Jammu. His help at every step proved exemplary. Thereafter the annual university examinations were held on time and even the results were declared in a timely manner.

The camp schools, camp colleges, the engineering college and the BEd colleges produced brilliant students who are working not only in India but in various countries of the world. Most of them are doing very well in the fields of fine arts, journalism and electronic media. These educational institutions became centres of cultural and literary activities. Writers of repute like Dr RL Shant, Prof Hari Krishen Kaul, Dr BL Kaul, Prof CL Saproo, Dr Amar Malmohi, Dr Tej Raina, Dr Soom Nath Kaul, Dr GS Dassi, Prof Arvind Gigoo and others were on the staff of these camp colleges. Many school teachers and lecturers were established poets, essayists and short story writers. Makhan Lal Saraf (of GGM Science College), the distinguished playwright and stage and TV actor, directed plays. Kailash Mehra Sadhu sang Kashmiri and Hindi songs in and outside the country. Prof Usha Baghati organised musical concerts. The contribution of these litterateurs and artistes to art, culture and literature has been immense. Among the migrant Pandit students who carved niches for themselves in various fields we can proudly name Raj Koul, Deepali Watal (singing), Sunita Raina Pandit (poetry), Meenakshi Raina (writing), Smriti Kak (journalism), Sidharth Zarabi (electronic media), Reshmi Kher (social activist and political analyst), Rahul Pandita (writing and journalism), Varad Sharma (writing), Siddhartha Gigoo (writing and filmmaking), Kalhan Mattoo (architecture and design), Sushant Dhar (writing), Raj Nehru (social activism), Anil Bhat (journalism), Parakshit Koul (social activism), Sanjay Ganjoo (social activism), Sanjay Kachroo (political activism) and others.

In 2002 the state government converted the camp colleges into evening colleges where other students too were given admission because by that time the number of Pandit students had dwindled. And that was the end of the camp colleges which transformed the lives of thousands of Pandit students.

The mass migration of the Pandit community from Kashmir in 1990 saw families facing tremendous financial problems. It became impossible for people to pay income tax. We went to New Delhi and met, Chandra Shekhar the prime minister of India at the time. We discussed the income tax issue and other things with the leaders of the Congress party, BJP, CPI, CPM and others. We talked to Kedar Nath Sawhney, Vasant Sathe, Saif-ud-Din Chowdhary, DP Ray, LK Advani, JP Mathur, Sushma Swaraj, Ramesh Chenithala, Yashwant Sinha, Somnath Chatterjee, Atal Behari Vajpayee and many others about our fate. All of them showed sensitivity towards our miserable plight and promised help. In December 1990 Vasant Sathe spoke in the Lok Sabha about us and told the finance minister: 'They (Pandits from Kashmir) have become refugees in their own country.' Chandra Shekhar was very warm towards us. He received us with affection and respect. He told his secretaries (in chaste Hindi): 'How can they pay income tax under such circumstances?' He asked us to meet the finance minister who heard us patiently. We conveyed the exact words of the prime minister to him. Kedar Nath Sawhney asked us to create awareness in the people of the whole country about our plight. He suggested that we create a lobby of political-minded persons and project our agony and tragedy of such a big magnitude before the nation and the world. His suggestion and advice proved very beneficial in the long run.

On the 8th of February the government of India issued 'the income tax deferment letter' for the year 1990-91. We met PV Narasimha Rao and the chairman of the Central Board of Direct Taxes. We talked to Dr Manmohan Singh, who was the finance minister. He welcomed the fifteen-member delegation warmly and listened to us with patience. We said to him: 'Three generations are living in one room. If the deferment order is removed we will be forced to withdraw our children from the educational institutions.' He was kind enough to say that the concession would continue. Besides, Maqbool Dar, the state home minister at the Centre, was extremely helpful. We can't forget the help and guidance that RN Kaw rendered to us. A handful of cynics tried to create hurdles in our way but the sufferers won. This concession and kind gesture lasted till 2008.

Other problems of great magnitude have been those faced by the 437 teachers who had worked in the government-aided private educational institutions in Kashmir. Those teachers, mostly women, lost their jobs and means of livelihood. The government refused to listen to our point of view. It was a legal battle (Usha Manwati versus the State of Jammu and Kashmir) which ended with a meagre amount paid to these teachers. Then everything was stopped. These teachers are still dreaming of their salaries and fighting for a just cause. Most of them are in the late sixties and even seventies now. They are victims of injustice and callousness of the state government.

We arranged educational tours for the young Pandit students who had not visited Kashmir. The non-governmental organization SABZAR distributed books, computers, sports material and other stationery among the students studying in camp schools. The students projected their sad condition through art and theatre. They participated in plays, painting competitions and other activities enthusiastically. The ex-President of India, Dr APJ Abdul Kalam was the chief guest at a function in India Habitat Centre in New Delhi. The camp schools still exist and produce good students. Their role in the education of young minds cannot be undermined. It is because of them that Pandit technocrats and engineers are working in multinational companies.

Only a handful of Pandit college teachers are left now. They teach at a couple of the government degree colleges in Jammu. Most Pandit professors have retired. They are scattered throughout the country. Some are living with their children. Others spend time in their own way. Some visit their children who are settled in other countries. The younger generations among Pandits don't go for teaching jobs. Besides, they have come out of the 'government job syndrome'. Pandits were very able teachers in Kashmir. They had dominated the education sector there.

Twenty-five years is a long period in the life of a minuscule community living far away from their own land. The young students faced tremendous hardships and untold miseries. They saw the conditions that their grandparents, parents and other members of their families lived in. In spite of the miseries of the life of a migrant they devoted time to studies in tents, one-room tenements and the rented accommodations. They did not let the mud of life dampen their spirits. They digested the shocks but kept their honour and dignity intact.

The Pandit youths are the hope and future of our community. Future generations will be proud of their achievements. They have a rich and honourable tradition behind them. They will contribute to culture and show to India and the world that a displaced and uprooted community is capable of doing meaningful work and herculean tasks even under conditions that are adverse, crude, hard and inimical.

14

Life in the Camp

Sushant Dhar

(I listened to the experiences narrated by a seventy-year-old Kashmiri Pandit woman, Pyari Dhar; one young boy, Sagar Pandita; and one young girl, Vishali Dhar, living in the migrant camp for Kashmiri Pandits at Muthi, Jammu. This is what they told me.)

Pyari Dhar

My house was in Seer, a small village near Martand Tirath in the Anantnag district of Kashmir. Many decades ago, the village was called Seer Kanligund. Then its name was changed to Seer Hamdan. In 1989, when militancy started, the political climate in Anantnag changed. Letters were dropped in the houses of Pandits threatening them to leave Kashmir. Announcements were made through the loudspeakers of the Jamia Masjid. Muslims came out in the streets and shouted slogans against India and us. My husband owned a shop near our house. Normally he used to close it around 9 pm but when the law and order situation became bad he began shutting the shop at 5 pm every evening. On some days, he didn't open it. The situation in our village was very bad, especially for our community. Many Pandit shop owners were fearful of the militants.

Every evening, we would switch off the lights in the rooms of our house and stay in the dark. None of us would go out in the evenings. One day my husband went to the toilet located in the courtyard of our house. He was hit by a stone thrown at him by someone in the street. That night we heard strange voices in the neighbourhood. Bayaji and his wife and kids tiptoed from the ground floor of the house to the first floor. Bayaji told us that some people were knocking at the door. They stayed in our room till morning. Nobody talked. We heard some people shouting outside our house. My husband thought they might come with guns and terrorise us. Fear ruled everywhere. In the days to come, militants tortured many Kashmiri Pandit youths from our village. The Pandit boys would come home with torture marks on their bodies. Every day we woke up to the news of killings of Kashmiri Pandits in the villages nearby. Then one day our neighbours came to our house and told us to leave the village to save our lives. 'We can't assure your safety. Even we don't feel safe here,' they said to us. We started packing our things. After a few days my husband arranged a truck so that we could leave with our household belongings. As we were about to leave, one of our relatives died. We performed the last rites hurriedly and left our house and the village. I had never imagined that this would happen to us.

The truck took four families including ours to Garhi, a small town in Udhampur where one of our relatives, who had left Kashmir earlier, was waiting for us. Many Kashmiri Pandits who had left Kashmir before us were already living in a government school in Garhi. The school had been converted into a camp for us. There was nowhere else to go. We occupied a small corner in an overcrowded room in the school. We struggled for space. Many families had to share a single room. These rooms were classrooms. Each room housed two to three families. We set up small kitchens in the corners. The school building was old. There were no toilets or bathrooms in the compound of the school. We used to go to an open field nearby to relieve ourselves. It was not safe to go to the field. The field was full of stray animals and insects. During the night we felt miserable. There was little choice. Sometimes local people would watch us when we were in the field nearby. At times hoodlums and drunkards loitered in the field. We didn't have access to clean drinking water in the school. So we depended on a mobile water tank. This continued for a few months.

Then one day, the school authorities asked us to vacate the classrooms as the school had to be reopened. We were told that alternative arrangements were being made for us. After a few days, canvas tents were erected in the school playground and many of us were made to shift into tents. We lived in a tent for a month before finding a room near Narayan Mandir in Garhi, Udhampur. We stayed there for four years before moving to Jammu where we were allotted a room in the Gole Quarters for Kashmiri Pandit migrants at Muthi. It was difficult for all of us to stay in one room. We constructed a kitchen adjacent to the room and also took another room on rent.

In the camp, we faced water scarcity. There weren't too many water taps, and for years together we used to collect water from a water tank nearby. People scrounged for water all the time. In the rainy season, we would store rain water in large utensils and buckets. Many families had to share one bathroom. We had to clean the toilets ourselves. The toilet was nothing but a shed without any water supply. There was no drainage system in the camp. There was a horrible stench all the time, though my family worked hard to always keep our quarters neat and clean. I would sweep the room many times in a day. It was a small room and all of us had to be patient with one another. I decorated my kitchen. Initially, we prayed for the situation in Kashmir to become normal so that we could return to our house in the village. But year after year nothing happened. Then we lost hope.

My family lived in the Gole Quarters at Migrant Camp Muthi for sixteen years and suffered a lot. The happiest day of my life was when we were allotted a two-room flat in a newly constructed migrant camp. We shifted into our flat a few years ago. The one-room tenements in the Gole Quarters were demolished. It is not an open field. But you can still see some walls of the rooms which are intact. The rubble is still lying there.

For the first time in twenty-five years, we have two rooms, a kitchen, a bathroom and a balcony. We have water and electricity. We saw comfort after twenty-five years. The government should have done something for us earlier. Wonder what took the government so long.

Now we just live quiet lives. We talk, socialise and think of our children's future. They will not go back to Kashmir. They have moved on. But we still have ties with our motherland. I went to Kashmir three times in the last few years. But I went as a pilgrim. At the end of every visit, I came back to Jammu.

Sagar Pandita

I was born in a one-room tenement called the Gole Quarters at Muthi Camp in Jammu. I lived there with my parents for sixteen years. My parents tell me that they lived in Kupwara district of Kashmir and were forced to migrate to Jammu in 1990 when terrorists attacked some people in our village.

I spent my childhood in our one-room camp at Muthi. We did everything in that single room. We survived in Gole Quarters. We can now survive even in the worst of places. A few years ago we were allotted a two-room flat in the camp for Kashmiri Pandit migrants at Muthi. I have a room of my own now where I study. This flat is government property. We can't say it's our own home. The government shifted us from one camp to another in the past twenty-five years. They can shift us from here as well.

My parents took me to Kashmir some years ago. It's scenic there. I love the beautiful landscape, but beauty is not the only thing in our lives. The people there abuse our country. I saw anti-India slogans written on the walls of many buildings. It's not safe for us there. The temples at our old village have been desecrated. Why have they done this? I respect every religion and they must do the same. It's so simple.

What's there for us to go back? My parents' house in Kupwara was burnt. They sold it some years ago. They told me that ours was a big house surrounded by apple trees. My parents owned an orchard too.

They went through tough times in the last twenty-five years. We still live on relief provided by the government.

The government does everything for Kashmir but nothing for us. Now I see Kashmir only on television. It is on the news all the time. If I do anything, I will do it for Jammu. Jammu gave us refuge when there was nowhere else to go. The government only supports Kashmir. Jammu and Ladakh have been totally ignored.

I will never go to Kashmir. What will I do there? Kashmir can never be stable. The young kids throw stones at army men. Life is dangerous in Kashmir. I don't trust the government there. They have never done anything for us. Every day I wake up to the news of bomb blasts and killings of the security forces. Even the local population is not safe.

I want some support from the government.

I'm a Kashmiri Pandit but my generation does not identify itself with Kashmir. It's not important to go back to Kashmir to preserve my identity. I can preserve it here as well. I follow all our rituals. I will not forget what happened with my elders when they were in Kashmir.

I have no love for Kashmir. My parents have memories of what happened to them. We don't talk about it too often. I'm studying in Jammu and planning to go to Pune for higher studies. I will settle somewhere in India. India is my home now.

Vishali Dhar

Many years ago when we were sleeping in our one-room camp at Muthi, dirty water from the canal outside came into our room. It was raining heavily. That night I thought that we would drown. I was ten years old at the time. My parents took me to my grandmother's quarters nearby. Our room was close to the canal running across the camp. The next morning I came back to our room and saw our household things floating in filthy water. The water from the drains had overflowed into the canal and then entered the rooms. Some of our neighbours in the camp were crying on the road. Water had flooded their rooms too. Our bedding, utensils and clothes were floating in dirty water. My school books were damaged. I started crying. My parents comforted me. But they were sad. I can never forget the look on my mother's face when she saw our clothes, bedding and utensils floating in water. The rain didn't stop for days.

When it stopped raining, it took my parents a week to remove the water, dry our clothes and bedding, and set things up again in our room. The stench of filthy water from the drains remained for a month. It was not possible to get rid of the stench. It was tough living in a single room.

Everything about the camp was bad. I used to see the local children play in the courtyard of their houses in the neighbouring locality. But I had no place to play. I used to spend my evenings with other children living in the camp. But we didn't play. We used to talk about school. On hot summer days, some people in our camp used to sleep on the pavements next to us. Insects and mosquitoes were all around us. The door of our room was made of rusted tin. The roof had holes. My father would get the walls repaired. Inside the room, there wasn't much space. I had a small corner to myself in which I kept my books and clothes. Our kitchen was in another corner. My mother had arranged a gas stove and some utensils in that corner. It wasn't a proper kitchen. It was just a corner.

Every day I lived in fear. I feared that the roof might cave in. I feared that deadly insects might enter the room and bite me. Luckily, I survived the tough times.

I want to complete my studies and pursue my dreams. I would like to go to Kashmir some day just for an excursion.

PART III

DAYS OF PARTING

'Farewell, my great one, my own, farewell, my pride, farewell, my swift, deep, dear river, how I loved your daylong splashing, how I loved to plunge into your cold waves.'

– Boris Pasternak, *Doctor Zhivago*

15

Days of Parting

Arvind Gigoo

A day in 1989
Residency Road, Srinagar
In the India Coffee House 'intellectuals' discuss everything. Here a political happening is 'invented' and debated upon endlessly. There was a bomb blast in the bathroom of the coffee house. Discussions are going on about this blast. 'This is the work of Pakistan.' 'This is the doing of Indian intelligence agencies.' 'CIA is active in Kashmir.' 'KGB is doing all this.' 'India is a strong country.' 'Pakistan is no less.' 'What is the Indian occupational force doing here?' Highly imaginative theories are propounded. India, Pakistan, US, USSR, etc. are discussed. Pandits say that the 'Indian army is here to protect us (Pandits) and Kashmir'. Others laugh at this bomb blast of 'no significance'. I am among the laughers.

Another day in 1989
The words on the signboards are written in green paint. Some years ago it was the three colours of the Indian national flag. Cinema halls have been closed down. The shops which lend or sell film cassettes are closed. People have been asked not to play cards. I know a Pandit child who said crying to his parents: 'Will they take away my pack of cards?'

Another day in 1989
In the evening my wife, who teaches in a private school, tells me: 'A few students of class 9 and 10 have not been coming to school for many days.

Today I asked my students where they were. One student said that he had "crossed". I didn't understand anything. Outside the classroom he told me that he had crossed the border. I understood nothing.'

I tell her: 'Your students are naughty.' And I laugh.

Wife tells me: 'A lovely child studying in Kindergarten said to me: "We make crackers in our home. Abba has told me not to tell anyone."' I give a hearty laugh.

Another day in 1989

Wife tells me: 'Today some students fainted in the classrooms. They were admitted to SMHS Hospital for treatment. When some of the women teachers went there to enquire after them we were asked not to enter the ward. But we entered the ward and saw our students. I don't know what the matter is. The police came to school and inspected the classrooms. Someone said he smelled gunpowder. School has been closed for one week. The school management is worried.'

This sets me thinking for the first time. What is all this?

Eid Gah, Safa Kadal, Srinagar, Kashmir

I am in Eid Gah, a ten-minute walk from my house. So many Muslims are here. A man from Spain tells me: 'I am a convert to Islam. It is the best religion in the world. Why don't you embrace Islam?'

What is going on here? I find Muslims from other countries here. Muslims from other states of India are also here. What do these people want? I understand nothing.

And I don't care.

Eid celebration in Eid Gah, Srinagar

I go there with my daughter Henna. Suddenly there is panic. People start running. There is total confusion. I lift my daughter, sit her on my shoulder and run like the others. They say even the Chief Minister left quickly. I am panting and reach home breathless. What was the matter? I can't even guess. Nobody knows.

A day in the 1970s
Hotel Ahdoo's, Srinagar
Today I am having tea with my friends. They are well read and well informed. They are talking about the politics of Kashmir. One person, who is an engineer, says: 'Kashmir is the best place for guerilla warfare. We have to fight for freedom from India.' Basheer says: 'Kashmir neither to bloody India nor to bloody Pakistan. Kashmir is only ours … I mean of Kashmiris.'

A day in the 1980s
I watch Moustapha Akkad's *Lion of the Desert*. It is about Omar Mukhtar, the Libyan tribal leader who fought the Italian army. People are distributing posters and leaflets asking everyone to watch this movie. Suddenly hundreds and thousands throng to the Regal cinema hall. People say: 'We watch this movie because Omar Mukhtar of the movie resembles Sheikh Mohammad Abdullah. Both had been teachers. One laid down his life for his country; the other betrayed his people.'

One day in November 1989
I am walking through Hari Singh High Street. I hear the sound of a gunshot. People run away. I see a dead body on the road. Somebody has been killed. I walk up to the bus stand and board a bus that takes me home.

Next day I get to know that the person killed in Hari Singh Street was Neel Kanth Ganjoo, a retired judge.

20 January 1990
I am in Delhi. The newspaper is very disturbing. I read and reread the news.

30 January 1990
Wife, son, daughter and I leave Delhi for Jammu. We reach Jammu on 31 January in the morning. On the Residency Road, Tej Krishen tells me: 'Call your parents to this place. Don't go there with your children.' I ask him: 'What happened?' He replies: 'Nothing happened. But I can't describe the night between 19 January and 20 January. It was simply horror.' Moti Lal also says the same thing.

What?

31 January 1990
We are on our way to Srinagar. Pandits in taxis and trucks are going to Jammu. There is one young Pandit lady in the bus. We reach the Tourist Reception Centre in Srinagar by 7 pm. A policeman doesn't let anyone leave the premises. A State Road Transport Corporation bus comes and everyone boards it. There is one policeman with a rifle in it. Security! He asks the passengers the names of the localities they are to go to. We reach Safa Kadal in downtown Srinagar.

10 pm, 31 January 1990
When Babi (mother) sees us she says: 'Why did you come to this place?' We have dinner and then talk. Father is calm. He doesn't say anything. A few persons shout from the mosque through the microphone and ask the people to enter the mosque. It continues till late in the night.

The atmosphere is very bad. Muslim neighbours—men and women —ask my wife where she was, why she has come back, etc. 'You know that I go to Delhi every winter.' 'Yes. But why did you return early this time?'

Interrogation on the road! The same person asks the same questions to wife, daughter, son and me separately and weighs the answers.

A day in February 1990

Shaha, the old Muslim woman in our neighbourhood, tells me on the road: 'What nonsense is this! We are fed up.' A Muslim gentleman joins us. Shaha shouts: 'We are prepared to die one by one for independence.'

Searches and searches. Deaths. Killings. It is horrible. A Muslim neighbour tells me in confidence: 'I am afraid of my own son. Strangers are his friends. I have never seen them.'

Pandits whisper to one another: 'There will be an army crackdown. Run away.'

A Pandit organisation, through the columns of an Urdu daily, asks JKLF: 'What are we supposed to do in these conditions? Please tell us in ten days.'

There is no reply. One Pandit is killed near Habba Kadal. Pandits think that this is the reply.

Everybody says: 'We must leave by the 5th of March.'

'When are you leaving?' This is the refrain of Pandit conversation. There is terror in the minds of all Kashmiri Pandits who are called Bhattas.

Every morning mother says: 'That family has left for Jammu. Their house is locked. When do we go?'

She knows nothing about Jammu. Father has heard that there is a place called Jammu.

Another day in February 1990

In the evening the newsreader of Radio Kashmir says that Lassa Kaul, Director of Doordarshan Kendra, Srinagar, has been killed outside his home in Bemina. He is a friend.

I reach his place in Bemina in the morning. Many people, mostly Muslims, are there. His young brown-haired daughter is hysterical. I accompany the funeral procession from his place up to the crematorium in Karan Nagar. Hundreds of Muslims are carrying placards which read:

'*Lassa Kaul ka qatil koun? Jagmohan.*' (Who is the killer of Lassa Kaul? Jagmohan.) The central minister for information and broadcasting comes surrounded by security personnel. One man is carrying a wreath. The people shout: 'Nobody should go near him.' The minister places the wreath on the pyre, joins his palms and leaves. He senses the atmosphere in one second.

I had known Lassa Kaul, a real Kashmiri, for many years. One day while walking on the Bund he talked to me about his officers in Delhi, Jagmohan, the threats that he got and how 'I am thinking of leaving this place now'.

Second week of March in 1990

Shiban Dhar, a neighbour and friend, is terrified and wants to go to Jammu with his wife and son. He has arranged a horse-drawn cart. We board the cart by 5 in the morning. The CRPF jawans see us seated in the cart. They laugh and tell us: 'Pandits, leaving for Jammu?' We say nothing. The driver asks us: 'Pandit sahib, why are Pandits going to Jammu?'

I am horrified at the scene unfolding in the Tourist Reception Centre. I see thousands of Pandits board the buses there. There is a long queue at the ticket-booking counter. I go near the small opening and see an old classmate inside. I shout my name. He directs the peon of the office to open the door for me. I enter the room. There are three persons there. One man accepts the money, another person hands over the ticket to the Pandit standing in the queue and the third person writes the amount in a register. All three persons are nervous. They are shaking, trembling. My old classmate, a Muslim, asks me frightfully: 'Are you also going to Jammu? What do you know? Please tell me. Will we be killed when all of you leave this place?'

'I am not going anywhere. My neighbour-and-friend is going. I want tickets for the family.' The ticket is handed over to me. I see terror and death in the six eyes. The other two persons don't talk.

I watch the horrible scenes. What is all this? I had never imagined this. Where are these Pandits going? I am very angry. I see coolies setting the luggage on the roofs of the buses. I leave the place with a broken heart. I walk the distance from the Tourist Reception Centre up to my residence. I am quiet at home.

A day in April 1990

Nazir Gash (a well-read shopkeeper and a friend) comes to my place with a copy of an Urdu daily and reads: 'Pandits are directed to leave the valley in 36 hours.' Another clipping from an Urdu daily: 'The Kashmiri Pandit is a poisonous snake.' I accompany Nazir to his shop at Safa Kadal. One young man shouts: 'Some men haven't come to their senses yet.' Nazir Gash enters his home and I turn back.

A night in April 1990

Wife and I hear some sound. We peep through a chink. A family is dumping arms in the earth. We don't sleep. Wife says: 'What now?' I say: 'Silence.'

Daytime

I am walking in the lane adjacent to my house. A young boy is coming from the opposite direction. He has a beautiful black and red pistol in his hand. I turn my head and ignore him.

Night

'Who is walking in the lane?' Wife and I look. Two young men are standing near the gate of our house. They share one cigarette. They walk a few steps and then come back. The two young men walk to and fro. One hour has passed. At last they go.

Morning

I am standing near the gate of our house. I see three young men walking fast. I hear one man saying to the other two: 'This is the professor.' Their shoes tell me that they are militants. Ratni, our next-door neighbour, has also heard these words. She comes to our place and reports to my mother and my wife. I tell her: 'Don't worry.'

May 1990
The bus I am seated in is on way to the Government Degree College for Boys, Anantnag. At Bijabehara an old student, a Muslim, sees me, greets me nicely and says to me: 'Aadaab araz, mahara.' I remember this man. He was a very nice student who respected me during college days. All the passengers seated in the bus turn towards me with looks of all-Pandits-have-gone-and-you-are-still-here. I feel uncomfortable but I am not scared. I enter college. I see students loitering. Others are sitting on the turf. Nobody talks to me.

Muslims die at the hands of the security personnel. Pandits die at the hands of militants. When a Pandit is killed a rumour is spread: 'He was an informant.' When militants kill a Muslim the same rumour is spread: 'He was an informant. An identity card was found in his pocket.' Every evening we hear that someone or so many have been killed.

One evening Fazi, our neighbour, says in a very low voice: 'Uma Shori, Uma Shori, don't drink water. Poison has been mixed with it.' There is gloom in the family. Some persons continue to shout from the mosque during the night.

There is firing from many guns in the lane adjacent to our house. We sit in the corridor. Henna rests her hand on my father's head.

I am in a minibus that is going to Safa Kadal. In Karan Nagar there is a dead body on the road. Nobody says anything. When we reach Kak Sarai the conductor of the vehicle gets down and shouts loudly: 'Hum kya chahtay?' (What do we want?) People shout back: 'Azadi.' (Freedom.) Aslam, a neighbour, looks at me, smiles, shakes his head and moves his lips. I also move my lips.

The news reaches that a security person has killed the son of Takai, a neighbour. There is terror when the dead body is brought and kept in the compound of our next-door Muslim neighbour. One woman shouts: 'May the seeds of Pandits perish!' I dare not move out of my house. When Maulana Farooq is killed the same woman shouts: 'May the seeds of Pandits perish!'

Hassan, a good friend, comes to my home. We are having tea in the living room. He picks up a biscuit and tells me: 'I swear by this … tell me … if you have any sort of connection with the CBI … I will save you.'

I am silent but unafraid.

Ghulam Nabi, a dear friend, tells me: 'Some persons were asking me about you. They have seen you walking near Safa Kadal and having tea at a tea shop.'

I am silent but unafraid.

I find an empty bottle of whisky near the gate of our house. I know who has done this. He is a highly sophisticated man. I can be in trouble. I go to his place and tell him all this. He smiles and apologises.

Mohammad Amin, a businessman, came from Sharjah to visit his family. A security person killed him because he did not stop his car. I liked him. Kak's head was hanging from the branch of a tree. Radha Krishen Handoo, an old man, was killed near a butcher's. The two cycle mechanics, 'bachelor philosophers', have been killed. Every morning we hear that two or three Pandits were killed yesterday.

My father is running the Imperial Clinical Laboratory in Maharaj Gunj. He is a highly respected man in that locality. Today he is home with the microscope in his hand. He is perspiring and nervous. He drinks water and then says: 'All the women asked me to go home and not to come in the future.' I have never seen him so tense and terror-stricken.

KHANKAH-I-SOKHTA, NAWA KADAL/SAFA KADAL, SRINAGAR, KASHMIR

I live at Khankah-i-Sokhta in Nawa Kadal/Safa Kadal, Srinagar, Kashmir. Pandits have an ideal relationship with all the Muslims living in the locality. We help and trust one another. Pandits celebrate marriages in the houses of those Muslims who have big houses. Carpets and furnishings are lent to the Pandits for use on all the days. Very wealthy and poor families live side by side. Sunnis, Shias and Pandits live in perfect harmony. One Sikh lives in a room adjacent to the Ram temple. He looks after the temple. The street urchins pelt stones at the houses of Pandits when a cricket or hockey match played between India and Pakistan is over. Nobody takes such things seriously. Many Muslim families have leanings towards Pakistan. There are families which are supporters of Sheikh Mohammad Abdullah and the National Conference. Others, especially the Shias, support the Congress party. Many families support Maulana Farooq. There are no conflicts among them. 'Lions' (supporters of Sheikh Mohammad Abdullah) and 'goats' (supporters of Maulana Farooq) don't quarrel. Pandits living in the new colonies wonder how we Pandits live in the downtown. Life here is beautiful and interesting. I have never seen any kind of division on communal lines between Muslims and Pandits. There was no such trouble even when a very decent, gentle and intelligent Pandit girl married a Muslim neighbour. Elderly Pandit men had tried to dissuade her from doing so but her love for her Muslim lover proved stronger.

One finds all kinds of people here. Educated persons and illiterates rub shoulders together. All steal electricity. On the two Eids most of the Pandits go to the Eid Gah and 'participate' in the festival. My friends Amin, Rashid, Ajaz and Manzoor come to my place on every Shivratri and have lunch with me. Hamid also comes whenever he feels like it. Pandit women, girls and children are safe here. But young Pandit boys and girls are not seen on the roads after 5 pm anymore. The idle spend some time talking near the shops. Political discussions are held on the roads and in the shops. There are no ugly scenes. Goodness, humour and love rule the hearts of all. Some young Pandits and Muslims steal hens and cocks belonging to a few Muslim families, kill them, cook them and then eat them. The owners of the hens shout curses on the 'cock thieves' and the onlookers enjoy these curses and instigate them to curse more. There are scores of Pandits and Muslims who spin yarns. They think that the listeners believe in their fabricated stories of adventures. Pandit and Muslim youths play cricket in the Eid Gah. Others fly kites there. In the evenings some Pandits smoke charas in the Janam Bhumi or the compound of the Ram Mandir. A handful of Pandits gamble in the Ram Mandir.

The old name of this locality is Didda Mar. A khankah (mausoleum) was erected here in the past. It caught fire and perished. Then the mohalla was called Khankah-i-Sokhta (the burnt mausoleum). Madhav Dhar and his daughter Roopa Bhawani, the Bakshis (Bakshi Ghulam Mohammad), Rai Bahadur Shyam Sunder Lal Dhar, Maulvi Iftikar Ansari, Maulvi Abbas, Aghas (grandparents of Dr Agha Ashraf Ali) and Akbar Haidri were born here. Madhu Ram Gigoo, a Sanskrit scholar and one of the founders of Arya Samaj in Kashmir, lived and died here. He opened the first laboratory in Maharaj Gunj and named it Imperial Clinical Laboratory. Nand Lal Gigoo was the first RMP in this locality who opened the first medical shop near Fateh Kadal. Radha Krishen Dhar, one of the first dental technicians in Kashmir, lived and practised dentistry in his house here. Dwarka Nath Gigoo Rajkamal was a Hindi poet and painter. His contribution to Hindi literature in the late 1940s, 50s and 60s was commendable. Prof. S L Dhar, Prof. Badri Raina and Prof. Sadaf Munshi were born here. Siddhartha Gigoo, a novelist and short story writer in English, was born here and lived here up to 1990. Henna Gigoo was born here and lived here till 1990. She joined People for Animals and was very close to Maneka Gandhi. She wrote poems in Hindi and short stories in English. Badri Nath Mattoo, a very good Urdu writer and journalist, was the editor of *Martand*. Sri Kanth Kaul was another Urdu writer on the staff of *Martand*. Krishan Joo Dhar was the director of Food and Supplies Department. He translated the *Gita* into Kashmiri. He collected money and rice to be distributed among the Muslims during the strike launched when the holy relic was stolen.

From the third storey of my house I have seen Habib Painter sing qawalis in the compound of the house of Bakshi Abdul Rashid, who lived there for many years when Bakshi Ghulam Mohammad left. I have seen Sata Lal (lovingly called Sata sitarist) dance and play upon the sitar to entertain Bakshi Ghulam Mohammad. Ram Chand Tickoo, the founder of cricket in Kashmir and the first Ranji player, was born and lived here. He formed the Kashmir Cricket Club (KCC) and played with most of the noted Indian players and film actors. The other Ranji players were Girdhari Lal Tickoo, Rattan Raina, Prithvi Nath Tickoo, Girdhari Lal Raina, Omkar Nath Pajnoo, Autar Krishen Dhar, Badri Raina and Autar Raina. Rattan Raina, nicknamed 'Ajit Wadekar of Kashmir' was a remarkable batsman. Omkar Nath Pajnoo, apart from being a good athlete, was the curator (in charge of the pitch) when the cricket match between India and West Indies was played in Srinagar in 1987. Soom Nath Saproo was the ablest swimmer. Niranjan Nath Raina opened the Merchantile Press in the Residency Road in front of Ahdoo's Hotel and Restaurant. Books in Kashmiri, Urdu, Hindi and English were printed there. Niranjan Nath Raina was a good painter and designer himself who, in his youth, had gone to Bombay to become a film actor. In the fifties Prithviraj Kapoor asked Girdhari Lal Pajnoo to join Prithvi Theatres which he declined. We have many teachers, some doctors and a few engineers. In the past most of the Pandit parents did not keep a watch on their sons. Nor did they care about their education. The result was that some Pandits remained semi-literate while others became good and selfless vagabonds who always helped all—Muslims and Pandits.

The shopkeeper Shamboo Nath (known as Shombakak) is the soul of the mohalla. He is the confidant of all Muslims and Pandits. Some married Muslim women come to him for advice on matters of sex. He enjoys the conversation with them because he is a bachelor. Pandit women keep the keys of their houses with him when they lock their houses. On Sundays young and middle-aged Pandits assemble on the road in front of Shombakak's shop and gossip.

Many persons gossip in the medical shop owned by Radha Krishen who is lovingly called 'Ashok Kumar' because he resembles the noted film actor. He is romantic with beautiful black curly hair. There are some hoodlums here and there. They don't disturb anybody. The quarrel of boatwomen lasts for days together. For the onlookers it is entertainment of the highest type. A few Pandits and Muslims drink in stealth. They pose no problems to anybody. There are many budding romances in our locality—boys and girls, Muslims and Pandits. In the summer evenings, young girls of the boatmen swim in the Jhelum. They laugh when they see young men watching them.

Every evening Rahman chacha sits in the shop of the Pandit baker Niranjan Nath (called Nerakak and Nera Kandur), has his one quarter of whisky, urinates into the drain for a long time, goes home, has his dinner and sleeps. He works as a 'driver' for the J&K Road Transport Corporation but doesn't know driving. He has a tremendous sense of humour. He can fart anytime. When the children ask him to produce the lovely sound he lifts his right leg in the air and farts to the merriment of all. He did so for the Prime Minister of J&K State Bakshi Ghulam Mohammad on the road in the late fifties. Even Bakshi laughed, called him 'Rehmaana' and gave him a five-rupee note. This event happened in my presence when I was in school. Bakshi had got him appointed as driver in the JKRTC. The whole mohalla—Sunnis, Shias and Pandits—sank in grief when he died. Rahman chacha, a Shia, was a good man. He used to say: 'Worry is an insect which eats one up. Therefore, live a carefree life.'

The lanes, kochas and roads in our locality are filthy and covered with garbage. Faeces flows in the dirty drains. The latrines in the compounds of all the houses have a foul smell. Only three families own cars. The people are not ostentatious. Very wealthy Muslims also believe in simple living. Only one Pandit is conceited. Everybody avoids him, and he doesn't care.

Many years ago three Muslim families owned many donkeys. Rehman Gur's family is large. They have many cows and sell milk and curds. Who doesn't know them? One day in the 1950s Bakshi Ghulam Mohammad shouted outside the house: 'O Rehmana, where are you?' Rehman Gur emerged with a glass of milk and offered it to the prime minister of the state. He drank the whole thing in one draught.

Almost all the Shia families make papier mache things in their homes. Here are many carders, excellent carpenters and masons, makers of designed wooden ceilings (khutumbund), bench saw machines, sellers of logs of wood, master craftsmen who make various things of wicker and carpet weavers. The brick house of Rai Bahadur Sham Sunder Lal Dhar was the biggest house in Khankah-i-Sokhta. Many years ago it was dismantled by the person who bought it.

I have seen Pandits selling their houses and buying plots of land in the new colonies and constructing modern houses. Well-educated youths left the locality in search of jobs. Extremely poor Muslims and Pandits live here. There are some illiterates even among Pandits. Some Pandits, idlers, have done nothing in their lives. Some married men and women are carrying on with affairs. Some Pandit girls and boys have affairs with those living in other localities. Decency, carefulness and respect for elders are practised.

Jagan Nath Saqi, the well-known radio artiste and film actor, shifted to this mohalla and died in the house of his sister (the mother of Omkar Nath Pajnoo). He used to sit in the shop of Shamboo Nath (Shombakak) and talk about his past. One day he told me: 'Raj Kapoor and Balraj Sahni wanted me to come to Bombay and act in films.' I said: 'Why didn't you go?' He replied: 'I would have been asked to leave after having acted small roles in one or two films.' I saw Pushkar Bhan and Soom Nath Sadhu weeping the day he passed away. The whole locality felt very sad that day. He was loved by all.

The barbers' shops here are the most interesting places for idle gossip, humour and politics. The posters of film actors, actresses and cricketers 'decorate' the walls. People love Imran Khan. The drivers and conductors of the trucks are very careful about their hairstyle. They are keen about their sideburns. Those who drive the buses and trucks to Ladakh look down upon the drivers who drive short-distance buses. Marriages, family problems, businesses, future plans and even divorces are settled here.

A unique feature of this locality is the high musical sound/whistle which a Pandit or a Muslim makes by forcing his breath out with his lips closed when he has to call someone who is sitting somewhere in his house or walking on the road or playing in the field. The listener can make out the maker of the sound in no time. I do it even these days in Jammu when I have to call an old neighbour walking on the road at a distance. My children and wife respond to my whistle in a second.

17 May 1990

Soom Nath Saproo, a neighbour, has been kidnapped. Neighbours—Shias and Sunnis—leave their homes to talk to the various organisations about him. Mohammad Shafi tells me: 'I am going to get our brother Soom Nath back.' There is no news of him on 17 and 18 May. He is home on 19 May in the morning. Muslims and Pandits go to his place. I find Soom Nath dazed. He doesn't speak. He is sitting like a statue.

Hafiz, who some days ago, had confided in Soom Nath about the possibility of his kidnapping, is kidnapped. He is freed in the evening. I visit Hafiz. While turning the pages of *India Today* Hafiz tells me: 'In the future I will not tell anybody anything.' I ask him: 'What do you suggest to me and my family?' He replies: 'I don't know.' Silence of tension and mistrust!

20 June 1990
About 8.00 pm
Chand Saproo's little son played with my little daughter in my home. I hold the left hand of the little boy for I have to hand over the boy to Chand Saproo. We walk through the lane and reach the road. More than twenty Muslim neighbours are sitting on the road. When we step on the road they abruptly keep quiet. All of them know me, and love me. But this time they look at me in silence. I experience terror for the first time in my life. When I recall that minute I shiver.

21 June 1990
Morning
People are running in the lane. I am standing near the gate of my house. I ask a running neighbour: 'What is the matter?' He replies: 'Pritha Tiku has been killed.' I tell my mother, father and wife that Prithvi Nath Tiku has been killed. They are terrified. Nobody allows me to go to Tiku's place. When my mother and wife come home they raise a hue and cry. There is total rebellion now. They want that we, too, should leave. Wife tells me: 'Why don't you understand? We have two children. Babu ji is old.'

'Give me a minute to think,' I tell them.

In that one minute I decide to leave.

We pack our things. Father is weeping.

22 June 1990
11 am
I ask Hafiz to arrange a truck for us. He says: 'Go home. A minibus will come to you in twenty minutes but don't talk to me on the road henceforth.'

A minibus driver comes with a young boy. We stuff the vehicle with the beds, bedding, utensils, etc. The minibus reaches Indira Nagar, Srinagar, where my cousin, who is in Delhi, has his house. I find hundreds of Pandits in Indira Nagar. I go back home to shift the remaining luggage. When wife sees me she is very tense and says that in my absence a young man had been asking for me. She says that she has never seen the young man before. We put other things in the minibus very quickly. One almirah full of old books belonging to my grandfather remains untouched. I will come some day and carry them. These are rare books which my grandfather had bought in Italy, Turkey and other countries. The other books are mine.

Through the window the daughter-in-law of Mohi-ud-Din tells me: 'Forgive us. Go wherever you want to go. May God protect you!' She is weeping.

I see hundreds of Pandits in Indira Nagar. Some families are living in a temple. All are relieved. Father is a shattered man. Pandits talk freely about everything. My friends Amin and Ajaz come to see me and my family. I join Amar Singh College and even take some classes. I don't go there now. Son is in Delhi. Mohammad Abdullah Challoo, a close friend, came one day and took me with him to the boulevard on his scooter. Near Nehru Park, CRPF personnel stop us and ask us to show our identity cards to them. When one of them sees my identity card he gives me an intrigued look. He doesn't seem to understand our relationship. There are no bathing boats in the Dal Lake. There is only one small boat with a naked young boy in it.

I want to go to my abandoned house and salvage grandfather's and my remaining books, my collection of stones, the latticed windows (that I had purchased), the portrait of my great-grandfather painted by SN Dhar, the books and other things of my son Siddhartha. Nobody allows me to go there. One Pandit, Bansi Lal Bazaz, left Indira Nagar on his bicycle. When he reached Habba Kadal he was shot.

My friend and neighbour Neel Kanth Raina has been killed.

Quereshi tells me: 'Azadi would have been the best thing. Pandit is a venomous snake.'

I tell him: 'We are leaving this place tomorrow.'

The goods looted from the houses of Pandits are for sale by the road in Khanayar. Some people have collected manuscripts in Sanskrit, Persian, Sharda and even Arabic. Some others have collected original artifacts. Pandits had hidden them in boxes and in the small puja rooms in their houses. Some people have collected original paintings and portraits. Where is the portrait of my great-grandfather painted by SN Dhar, who was a portrait artist in those days? He was paid five rupees for it. I remember the eyes, white beard, white turban, long-sleeved pheran of my ancestor, the holy book on a low desk in front of him, brown curtain and landscape through the open window.

And then one day in the summer of 1995

'A black dog bit Sanju one day? He has concealed this thing from all of us,' father says to me one evening.

'Babuji, what are you saying? You are mistaken.'

'I want the seeds, the white cloak, the cigar and the watch.'

I don't wait. I take father to a doctor who says: "This is mental degeneration. It could be Alzheimer's.'

Medicines and medicines which father always hated.

'Who taught you to fly airships? What did you find on the moon? The sun shrank, became a dot and entered into me. I have to talk to Saadam. Kakaji stole my clothes. This small girl is my wife. Where did the doctor get that cigar from? Kuwait! Did it hurt the little girl? Saadam, Saadam, where are you? Get me Salama, the tongawallah. Get me Ghulam

Ahmad. Where are they? I owe Sofi five rupees. Who will pay him? These prostitutes have a mission.'

I listen to all this for nights and days. My mother, wife and daughter are spectators. I manage patiently.

One day he forgets his way home. I search for him in the town. By 2:30 pm. I find him sitting on a pavement. He doesn't recognise me. He is violent when we reach home. Injections and sleep.

It is 2:10 am. Father enters my room naked. Wife watches the scene in silence. He tells me: 'Come on.' I say: 'It is night.' He doesn't agree. I engage him in conversation till it is morning. Then I clothe him. Things get worse.

Father is confined to bed now. Bed sores. One day I try to straighten his earlobe. The earlobe falls into my hand. Tubes and tubes. Injections and medicines. And then death. The whole thing lasted for three years and nine months.

Father is no more. Death was deliverance for him. I inform his Muslim friends in Maharaj Gunj. They feel very sad.

Father was a very simple man without any possessions and money. He loved cleanliness and order and his transistor set. He was addicted to the evening news. Muslims were his best friends. He was comfortable with them.

My dear Kashmiri Muslims,

Right from 1947 your leaders and politicians lied to you, confused you and exploited you. The crafty politicians used you for their selfish ends and the Indian leadership took you for granted. Pakistan played upon your religious sentiments. Then some other countries started playing their own games with you. When George Bush condemned Muslim terrorism you became sad. When Barack Obama praised Muslims you became happy. When Pakistan mentions Kashmir you feel elated.

You are a gullible lot. You believe in false promises. Nobody trusts you. Your tragedy is the result of the politicking of your leaders and of those you consider your well-wishers.

Kashmir is an issue of betrayal, blunder, falsehood and mistrust. It is a confusing admixture of plebiscite, Pakistan, India, independence and ambiguous ideas and theories. Once it was jana gana mana; then it was nizam-e-mustafa. You turned so naive that you thought Azadi was a question of some days. Now things have degenerated into a miasma of stone-pelting, drugs and things you have no control over.

In the last twenty years you lost hundreds of thousands of people—young boys, men, women and children. You lost your humanism and your cultural ethos. You lost Pandits. You are living in lies. You are a victim of depression, repentance, sorrow and defeat.

Pakistanis have a very poor opinion of you. Indians don't trust you at all. Your leaders don't care for you.

Militants, double agents, suspects, informants, spies, looters, freebooters and con men thrive in Kashmir. Nobody knows who is doing what. You suffer from political and societal schizophrenia and civilisational dementia.

You have lost your freedom of speech. The cunning among you talk one thing in private and change their stance in public. Some have chosen silence, and silence, during a period of political unrest, is dangerous. Political blackmailers, extortionists, security forces and greedy opportunists have devastated you. Now you are insensitive to your own suffering and to the suffering of your own people. Rumours and farcical slogans have placed you in a quagmire of directionless aspiration, purposelessness and psychological trauma. You have yet to fix your goal.

Your educated youth have intellect, vision and dreams. But unemployment, uncertainty and lack of opportunity have frustrated them. How long will they and you go on waiting for the outcome of 'meaningful and composite dialogue'?

Answer your own questions. Question your leaders, politicians and think tank. Everything is in your hands. Shifting loyalties and short-term plans will lead you nowhere. For sixty-three years your leaders did nothing for you. Pursue only one goal. Politics of doubletalk is bound to fail. Kashmir is not safe in the hands of its clever rulers.

Letter to Pandits 100 Years Hence
(Read it on 19 January 2090)

My dear Descendants,

You are rootless. You belong to no place. The base of your life is a vacuum. The language you speak is not your own. Your festivals are borrowed. You live by proxy. You are half machine. Machines and robots wait upon your parents. You are unaware of your children. You visit other planets. There is a place called Kashmir on this planet. Fly to that place and find your scattered selves there. What is your religion? You don't know. You are lost in this world peopled with cold and callous half-humans. You have no love and compassion. You don't celebrate memory because you have none. Your life is some digits and speed. What do you want? You will never know. You are unpersons.

Thousands of Kashmiri Muslims and security forces, hundreds of Pandits, Sikhs, Hindus and others have been killed. Several thousand Muslims have disappeared. Nothing is known about them. What has been the gain? NOTHING. The political turmoil in Kashmir caused a catastrophe of unimaginable magnitude. A Muslim lady told me on the phone: 'This is God's curse on us.' Saints and mystics were watching Kashmir and Kashmiris. Or they collided with one another. Thousands of Pandits died in exile. I see old Pandits living alone in their houses and the camps in Jammu. Their children are working either in other Indian cities or are abroad. I see many Pandits living in old-age homes there. The condition of these Pandits is pathetic. They are a lonely lot.

I don't know whether Pandits shall prevail or perish.

16

Gul Gulshan Gulfam

Pran Kishore

On November 29 1989, Ved Rahi and I, along with Sunil Mehta and Prem Krishen, who were the producers of Cinevista Ads, Bombay were waiting for the camera crew at Hotel Asia Brown, Srinagar. Ved and I had been commissioned to direct the serial Gul Gulshan Gulfam, which was based on my then unpublished Kashmiri novel bearing the same title. We were identifying the locations around the Dal Lake to shoot the serial. We had already received permission from the state government for shooting. As required under the rules, we had submitted the complete script to the government, and were waiting for a written approval from them.

Keeping the beauty of the locale and the soft light of autumn in mind, we had decided to shoot the serial on Eastman Colour film. Steven Fernandez, one of the finest cinematographers of the film industry during those days, was the Director of Photography for the project. With the cast led by Parikshat Sahni and Radha Seth supported by Pankaj Berry, Reshma Singh, Ravi Kemmu, Vishal Singh, Upender Khashu, Bashir Dada, Tariq Sheikh, Hriday Nath Gurtoo, Jyoti Fotedar, Bharti Zaroo and Anjana Sood, we were all geared up and excited to commence the shooting. But before that the first alarm for caution was sounded, when one of the owners of the three houseboats that had been booked for the shooting came to me and called me aside. On enquiring, he told me that two men wanted to talk to me, and that they were waiting for me in the lobby of the hotel. I went with him to meet the strangers, thinking that they were officials of the Tourism Department.

When I approached the two men, they stood up and greeted me with rather undue respect, and said that they were from the Tehreek (the resistance movement). I knew what that meant. I asked them to come inside where the producers were sitting.

One of them addressed me directly, and said, 'Pran Ji, they are strangers. We have come to talk to you, and not to them, as you are one of us.'

I said, 'Then let us talk. What has brought you here?'

'We have come to know that you are going to shoot a serial about the boatmen of Kashmir.' I nodded. Without mincing words, they said that they wanted a copy of the script. 'We've already sent it to the state government and they are fine with it. In fact, we are waiting for the written approval which may reach us soon.'

'We are not concerned with that. We want a copy, and without our approval, you won't be allowed to shoot.' Their tone was aggressive. So I thought there was no point in beating around the bush in this matter.

I cut the matter short and said, 'OK. As soon as we get the script back, we shall send it to you.'

'That is all right. But don't start shooting before we provide you our approval.'

'Don't you trust me?' I said with a forced smile.

'We do. That is why we have come to you.' After saying this, they instructed Ghulam Qadir, the houseboat owner, who had brought them there, to see to it that the script reached them. Shortly afterwards, the men left.

I did not want to create any unnecessary panic among the members of the crew as the situation was almost normal in Kashmir that time, and my old friend AM Watali, the Deputy Inspector General of Police in Kashmir, had assured us of protection and security cover. But still I discussed the matter with Sunil Mehta and Prem Krishen, the producers. After due consideration, we decided that there was no harm in giving the script to the men from the Tehreek. The next day, after consulting Watali, we handed the script to them.

After a few days, two other young men from the Tehreek came to the houseboats, where we were about to start the shooting and where we had arranged for the stay of the artistes from Bombay. They brought the copy of the script back and said, 'We have been directed by our leaders to inform you that you can carry on with your shooting. But it must strictly be in accordance with the script that our leaders have gone through. There should be no deviations.' We assured them that there would be no deviation. The two youngsters seemed to be very curious as they kept on peeping into the houseboat, probably to look at the actors from Bombay. One of the boys turned to me and said, 'Now as everything is settled, can we come to see the shooting?' We could not reject their request and said that they were welcome. And thus, after this first encounter with the grim ground reality, we began the shooting, first in the backwaters of the lake, and then in the marshes full of lotuses. These two young men accompanied the unit wherever it went. We sensed that they had been directed to keep a watch on us. But they gradually became a part of the unit, and even helped the spot boys in shifting the equipment from one location to another. Being young, they were enjoying the shoot, and even throwing hints that they too were keen to act. But after a few days they vanished, and after that nobody came to disturb us. So we relaxed and put all our energies into our work, trying to complete the shoot well in time and in accordance with the schedule.

As the shooting progressed, I came to know through a shikarawala (boatman) that one of the most respected houseboat owners, a former president of the Houseboat Owners' Association, a member of the Citizen's Council and an honorary Wildlife Warden, Haji Abdul Samad Kotroo had fallen ill. Haji Sahab was a very dear friend of mine. The character of the protagonist of Gul Gulshan Gulfam, Malla Khaliq, was based on Haji Sahab's persona. Many of his houseboats were near Nehru Park and the three houseboats in which we were shooting were parked near the backwaters of the Dal Lake. Hearing about Kotroo Sahab's illness, I asked the shikarawala to take me to his house, which was situated on a small island in the Dal Lake. I found him resting in his room. He was very weak, but on seeing me, he insisted on sitting up. He enquired how our shooting was going and kept on thanking me for writing about his neglected clan.

He pressed my hand tight, bent a little closer and asked me, 'Pran Ji, is it ever possible that you will come with a gun and then kill me?' I was stunned. I looked into his eyes. They were moist. He repeated the question.

'What sort of question is this? How on earth can you ever imagine that such a situation will arise?' I said.

He sighed and wailed, 'These misled brats! How can one make them understand that Kashmir is the abode of rishis and saints?' He looked away and said, 'I see dark clouds hovering over us. I pray to Allah to give these people some sense.' I comforted him, saying that he was unnecessarily being pessimistic. Kashmir had always come out unscathed in the worst of turmoils. Though I was consoling him, in my heart of hearts, I was shaken. I knew the political and social situation wasn't stable. The unrest was very much visible. Fear lurked all around. I held Haji Sahab's hand, kissed it and, after having a cup of tea, took leave of him.

While returning, I tactfully asked the shikarawala to give me some news of what was happening in those parts. He confided that an armed uprising was slowly brewing up in secrecy. The youth were getting trained in arms and ammunition. There was uncertainty all around. The boatman was worried that the tourist season would be spoiled and they would lose business. To add to his miseries, winter was just a month away. His assessment of the situation added to my apprehensions and anxiety. But in spite of all this, I put up a brave face, and our shooting went on according to the schedule.

During that very time, the well-known film director Muzzafar Ali was shooting his film *Zooni* there. It was based on the life of Habba Khatoon, the great poetess of Kashmir. Dimple Kapadia and Vinod Khanna were the lead actors. Prem Krishen would drop in at our houseboat in the evenings to have a chat. One evening when he came, he looked disturbed. He told us that he had received a letter from the Tehreek, ordering him to stop the shooting of the movie and leave Kashmir. He wanted to know about our schedule and progress. We told him that we should continue and not be intimidated. He said he was confused, and that the artistes, too, were reluctant to continue. That had made his situation more complicated. After saying this, he left. The next day we came to know that the entire unit had left for Bombay without finishing the shoot. It was alarming. The owners of the three houseboats in which we were shooting came with one of the two persons who had asked for the script. They assured us that nobody would disturb us or create any hurdles during our shooting. Once we got this assurance, we relaxed and continued with the shooting. But after some deliberation we decided to complete the work quickly in and around Dal Lake because the situation was changing rapidly.

By this time, protests, agitations and demonstrations had started to gain momentum in Srinagar. Curfew was imposed in the city. This started affecting the pace of our work. But we persisted. Luckily, we had already shot the wedding sequence, which needed big barges and motorboats. But the Mehndiraat scene was yet to be shot. For this sequence we had decorated the banquet hall of the Asia Brown hotel. That day the Tehreek had announced a hartal in the evening. We panicked, as we had choreographed the sequence with the help of Haseena Akhtar, the most popular folk dancer of those days. She had to be brought from Ganderbal, fifteen kilometers from Srinagar. Our gritty music director Krishen Langoo travelled in a wagon to her village and brought her safely to Hotel Asia Brown. It was a great relief and we started shooting, keen to wrap up before sundown. During the shoot, the receptionist of the hotel came to me and said there was a telephone call for me. I went to receive the call. A gruff voice spoke to me. The tone was harsh. 'Didn't you people know that there was a hartal today?' I lied and said that we were not aware of it and offered my apologies. 'It is all right,' he said. 'You must finish the shooting quickly. There is a hartal on the 14th. Don't commit the mistake of shooting on that day. Otherwise you and your crew will be in big trouble. Do you understand?' I assured him that such a mistake would not be committed again. I informed Prem Krishen about the telephone call and the diktat. And we did not shoot on the 14th.

After a couple of days, one of the houseboat owners came with a letter written in Urdu. It was amateurishly written and contained a threat. He had been ordered to drive us away. Though the other houseboat owners tried to convince him that the letter was not from the Tehreek but was the mischief of one of the neighbouring houseboat owners, who was jealous of him for earning a living, even in a 'failed' tourist season. But reading the content of the letter shocked us. Even the artistes from Bombay were scared and keen to leave Srinagar. Two more horrifying incidents added to the scare.

The next day, when our production team members were returning after dropping the local women artistes to their homes in the city, a big stone hit their wagon, and they had to rush back, nervous and worried.

Another terrifying thing happened a couple of days later on the Boulevard, just a little distance away from where our generator van was parked. A tourist bus that had arrived from outside and was parked some distance away from our generator van was blasted by a grenade. Luckily, there was nobody in the bus at that time. Though we felt that our generator was not the target, yet it was an ominous sign, a warning, meant for us to pack up and leave.

The entire unit was happy as soon as the schedule wrap was announced. Early next morning, the luggage and equipment were loaded and the caravan was ready to leave. I can never forget the scene when the three houseboat owners and their families bade the members of our unit farewell. Tears flowed from their eyes when they hugged us. They continued waving their hands, bidding us farewell, till the bus and the cars went out of sight.

As it was decided that I would join the unit later on in Bombay, I picked up my car from the parking lot of Hotel Asia Brown and drove to 'Pragash', my ancestral house in Raj Bagh in Srinagar. My wife, Shanta, a broadcaster, poet and writer, was anxiously waiting for me, as the news of another bomb blast in the city flowed in through the radio. I had recently retired from the Radio Station but she was still in service. Her annual leave had been sanctioned and she was geared up to go to Delhi and Pune to spend some time with our children there. I was planning to return to Bombay where my projects were in the pipeline.

Our air tickets were booked. My wife and I spent the next few days packing our things and praying for peace as the law and order situation was deteriorating by the day. One day when we finished our breakfast and were basking in the sun on the second floor of our house I saw a car pull up near our gate. The driver opened the car door, and helped an old man wrapped in a blanket get out of the car. I was shocked to see my ailing friend, Haji Samad Kotroo. I rushed down to receive him and brought him to the second floor. Haji Sahab gestured to me, asking me not to speak. Shanta was surprised to see him and offered him a kangri to keep warm. When I told him that I was planning to visit him to seek his permission to leave, he smiled and said, 'Is it ever possible that I would not come to meet Shanta and you? She has always given me the love of a younger sister. I can never forget the interview about the Hangul and its habitat she recorded in Dachigam for the Children's Programme of Radio Kashmir.' After saying this, he took out a bag from under his pheran and handed it to her. 'What is this Haji Sahab?'

He pulled out two wild ducks and said, 'Since you won't be here on Shivratri, I thought of getting these ducks for you so that you remember us on that auspicious day.'

'But we are just two of us here. Even my brother and his family are not here. Who will eat them?' Shanta said.

Haji Sahab smiled and said, 'You know that I gave up hunting ducks several years ago. My grandson accompanied an American tourist who was keen on trying his luck as a duck hunter in the wetland of Hokarsar. This is his share. I am old now, otherwise I would have roasted them myself. Take them to Bombay for your children.'

While sipping tea, he expressed his anguish over what was happening. 'Doctor Naseer says that I have no ailment. My main problem is stress and tension. I wasn't sure if I could meet you again, keeping my failing health in view. That is why I came to see you one last time.'

While listening to him, a strange fear lurked in my mind. Wouldn't I be able to return and meet my friends again? After Haji Sahab left, I told Shanta that I wasn't sure of meeting him again in the future.

On the day of our departure, there was no hartal and no curfew. We left Kashmir without any hassles. After spending some days with my daughter in Delhi, I travelled to Bombay to join the unit. The unit had decided to complete the indoor shoot after building a set of three houseboats in the lake in Film City in the suburbs of Bombay. Our art director, TK Desai, was a wizard. He got the set built to the exact specifications of the originals in Kashmir. Thereafter, Kashmiri artistes were called from Srinagar, and the shooting resumed. But the news from Kashmir was very disturbing. Militants had taken over most parts of Kashmir. Reports of violence and clashes reached us through newspapers every day.

As the shooting progressed in the studio of Film City, Sunil Mehta and I started editing the portions that had been shot in Kashmir. To our utter disappointment, we found that the director had not shot the opening scenes written in the script. The opening scenes were set in the houseboats. Without these, we couldn't establish the ambience of the houseboats. So I decided go to Kashmir and shoot the missing portions. I needed some persons from the unit to complete this task. But nobody from Bombay was willing to accompany me because of the situation in Srinagar. I telephoned Lassa Kaul, who was the Director of Doordarshan, Srinagar. He assured me of all his help as the serial was for a Doordarshan-sponsored programme. So I embarked on this mission. My brother, Manohar Kaul had returned home along with his wife after spending some time in Delhi. I had a place to stay in Srinagar.

After landing in Srinagar, I went to meet Lassa Kaul in his office. He was not worried as much about the militancy as he was for his ailing father. His father was bedridden at his newly constructed house in Bemina, Srinagar. He had undergone an operation of the fractured femur bone. Lassa Kaul told me that the militants had ordered him to stop relaying film programmes from Delhi. After being threatened several times by the militants, he had talked to the Director General, who had advised him to take his own decision. 'Nobody wants to take the responsibility. I am at a loss. I don't know what to do,' Lassa had said to the Director General. The Director General had advised him to think of his staff's security and stop relaying film-based programmes. I gave Lassa an official letter requesting for technical assistance and camera equipment for the shooting. He sanctioned everything immediately. I had already contacted Wani, the best cameraman from Doordarshan Srinagar, and Shabbir with whom I had already worked. I decided to start canning immediately from the next day itself.

The next day, I reached the houseboats earlier than the camera crew. Ghulam Qadir, the houseboat owner, who even in the days of our shooting spent hours fishing, was already there with his line cast. Without getting up, he greeted me and said, 'Pran ji, you must eat the fish I have cooked today.'

'What is the special occasion?' I asked him. He got up and said, 'These vagabonds, who call themselves freedom whisky fighters, raided all the houseboats yesterday and poured all the whisky we had kept for the foreign tourists into the lake. The fish must have absorbed all the alcohol. That is why you must taste the fish today.' His jocular mood disappeared and he started cursing everybody—the militants, the leaders of the militant outfits and his own fate. I tried to console him by saying that the anarchy wouldn't last long. He threw the fishing rod away and said, 'Forget it. You'll get late. Let us bring down the signboards of our boats and replace them with yours. Luckily, they are still here where you had left them.' He called others for help and the boards were fixed in no time. Ghulam Qadir cast a glance at them and exclaimed loudly, 'Look! GUL GULSHAN GULFAM.' Everybody there laughed except me. I was worried because the camera crew was missing. Many hours passed and there was no trace of the camera team. Meanwhile a few shikaras passed by hurriedly and the boatmen informed us of a gun battle between the militants and the military near Dalgate. Upon hearing this, I gave up all hope of resuming the shoot. The houseboat owners too got worried and advised me to leave before something untoward happened. I called a shikarawala and asked him to take me across the lake, where my car was parked.

As I reached the embankment, I saw Shabbir, Wani and the camera assistant speeding up in a jeep towards the ghat. They were in a state of shock and told me that violence had erupted in the city and that they had somehow managed to reach the film set. We rushed and rowed back to the houseboats. Luckily, the signboards had not been brought down. With Wani Sahab's help we finished the entire shoot before nightfall. The gun battle had ended, and we reached our homes safely.

Next day, I went to thank Lassa Kaul at about noon. He was terribly upset. He said to me, 'I am caught in a whirlpool. This morning a group of burqa-clad women came to meet me. They told me to stop relaying the programmes from Delhi, particularly the programmes in Hindi. I tried to explain my position to them and told them that I would have to discuss the matter with the Doordarshan headquarters in New Delhi.'

Lassa Kaul told me that the women had given him a warning. 'While leaving, one of the women told me to obey the order otherwise I should be prepared for a bullet,' he said frightened out of his mind. I asked him what he would do to tackle the situation. He said that he had informed the Director General but his reply was the same. 'Tackle the situation as you deem fit.'

Lassa continued, 'I rang up Governor Jagmohan. His reply was that the safety of Doordarshan and the Radio crew was the responsibility of the Central government.' I advised Lassa to do what Bashir Butt, my friend who was the director of Doordarshan Jallander, had done during the militancy in Punjab. After Ramesh Chander, the editor and proprietor of the popular daily, *Hind Samachar*, was killed, Bashir Butt had received a letter from Bindranwale warning him that after Ramesh it was his turn. Bashir Butt had packed his bags and fled to Jammu. After reaching Jammu, he had spoken to the Secretary of Information and Broadcasting, Government of India and told him about what had happened. He had told him that he was proceeding on leave and going to Kashmir with a request to make an arrangement to run the show from there.

Lassa Kaul told me that he was thinking of going to Delhi to seek a transfer. But he could not leave his ailing father behind. We talked about the situation for some time. Before leaving I asked Lassa Kaul to be careful. We hugged and parted.

That very night Lassa Kaul was killed by militants near his house. He was going to visit his ailing father. It was the greatest shock of my life. The next day I left for Bombay with the cans of the exposed stock. Reaching the airport was an extremely risky thing with a civil war kind of situation in the city. The sight at the airport was horrific. Thousands of crying and wailing men, women and children, old and young, with dishevelled hair and crumpled clothes were begging for tickets. When the plane took off, I felt a lump in my throat. I wanted to cry. I did not even have the courage to look down at the valley below which at that time I felt I had lost forever.

By the end of June, Gul Gulshan Gulfam was ready. But there was uncertainty about its telecast, as the militants did not allow Doordarshan Kashmir to function normally. Even the News unit had shifted to Delhi. We held a couple of meetings with the Secretary, Information and Broadcasting. Finally it was decided to telecast the serial. From the very first day of its telecast, the serial was received well in every household in India. It was out of that fateful 1990 that G3, as the serial came to be called in the industry, bloomed and became a landmark in the history of Indian television. The most important achievement was that it brought the viewers back to Doordarshan and helped in evoking nostalgia of the glorious old days of Kashmir that helped foster the desire and longing for peace.

Twenty-five years have passed. I see hope, but the wounds inflicted by two and a half decades of violence are still raw. I haven't been 'home' ever since.

17

Dear brother, our part in this story is over

Tej N Dhar

When I was pushed into leaving my home in Srinagar in 1990, I could not get over what I went through in the early months of that terrible year. It sat so heavy on me that I had a compelling urge to write about it, to take it out of my system, as it were. I tried to do that several times, but with no success. Every new attempt died at paragraph one, and the shape of the paragraph too changed every time. It took me several years to get over the agitation that the effort caused within me and to write about what I experienced then. And when that happened, the act took on a creative hue. The result was a narrative mix of memories of people and happenings, of the present and the past. It resulted in a book that appeared in 2002.

When I go down memory lane, once again, to write about what I experienced and felt during that time, I find that some happenings, places, and faces have acquired faded edges, but some are acutely imprinted on my soul.

In the welter of images that crowd my mind, I see my friend Lassa Kaul, the then Director of Doordarshan, Srinagar, in his office, in the last week of December 1989. I had gone to see him and to ask him if it was safe to let my wife and children be on their own, because I had to go to Hyderabad to work on a research project. I believed that as a respected media person and one who had close links with the high-ups of the city, he was the best person to advise me on this.

I needed his advice because 1989 was marked by a steady decline in governance and a large scale disruption in the life of ordinary citizens. Militants made steady inroads into public space by ordering people what to do and what not to do. They ordered the closure of cinema halls, video stores, liquor vends, and beauty parlours. Schools, colleges, and even offices too remained closed for days. They also killed some known and respectable Pandits, in broad daylight, and there was neither any public outcry nor any action from the government. This was enough to spread panic waves among the community. When the government released five top militant leaders in exchange for Rubaiya Sayeed, the daughter of the Home Minister of India, who had been kidnapped by a militant group, the militant movement acquired a new respectability in the popular imagination.

Kaul knew it all, and conceded that conditions in the Valley had deteriorated during the past several months, but he seemed quite sure that they would take a turn for the better. I remember his parting words: 'Go, and be at ease. Things will improve soon.'

So I left for Hyderabad to work in the American Studies Research Centre. While I was there, I had no contact with my family because I had no phone connection at home. After four weeks, I went from there to Chandigarh to attend the marriage of my cousin. There I met some of my relatives, who had come from Srinagar and Jammu. They snubbed me for being stupidly careless and told me to rush back to Srinagar immediately, for conditions there were too bad. So I took a flight from Delhi to Srinagar. On reaching Srinagar, an old friend gave me a lift in his car. From where he dropped me on the way, I took an auto-rickshaw to my home. When I asked the driver why all the shops were closed, he said it was because some militant had been martyred.

The moment I put my foot inside my home, my wife and children clung to me in one tight embrace and wept loudly. Then they told me how they had had been living with threats and rumours, and how right in the middle of the night of 19 January, the whole of Kashmir Valley had erupted into a loud booming of pro-freedom slogans relayed from mosques. The incident was so traumatising that more than half of the Pandit families of the mohalla had left in the early hours of the morning. My wife had watched our Pandit neighbours leave the city, till she was the only one left behind.

Courtesy: Kashmiri Pandit Sangharsh Samiti

Ruins of Shri Bahkateshwar Bhairav Temple, Chattabal, Srinagar. This temple was destroyed in the 1990s.

Photograph by Muhabit ul Haq, 2013

An abandoned house of a Kashmiri Pandit family, Village Haal, Pulwama

Courtesy: Kashmiri Pandit Sangharsh Samiti

Remnants of Vichar Nag Temple, Soura, Srinagar

Photograph by Muhabit ul Haq, 2013

Abandoned and dilapidated houses of Kashmiri Pandits, Village Haal, Pulwama

Courtesy: Kashmiri Pandit Sangharsh Samiti

A destroyed idol in Shri Vaital Bhairav Temple, Motiyar, Rainawari, Srinagar

Photograph By Siddhartha Gigoo

House of Madhu Ram Gigoo, who introduced Arya Samaj in Kashmir, and his son Omkar Nath Gigoo, in Khankah-i-Sokhta, Nawa Kadal, Srinagar

Photograph by Siddhartha Gigoo, 2012

Abandoned Ram Temple, Safa Kadal, Srinagar. This temple was looted and desecrated in the 1990s.

Courtesy: Kashmiri Pandit Sangharsh Samiti

The derelict Shiv Temple, Kakpora, Pulwama

Photograph by Seema Bhat

Ruins of an abandoned house of a Kashmiri Pandit family, Village Haal, Pulwama

Courtesy: Kashmiri Pandit Sangharsh Samiti

Wreckage of Shivlingam in the ruins of Shiv Temple, Naidyar, Rainawari, Srinagar

Photograph By Muhabit ul Haq, 2013

The crumbling façade of a deserted house of a Kashmiri Pandit family, Village Haal, Pulwama

Courtesy: Kashmiri Pandit Sangharsh Samiti

A destroyed idol in the ruins of Shiv Temple, Bijebahara, Anantnag

Photograph By Muhabit ul Haq, 2013

Remnants of an abandoned house of a Kashmiri Pandit family, Village Haal, Pulwama

Wreckage of Raghu Nath Temple, Fateh Kadal, Srinagar

Remnants of the interiors of an abandoned house of a Kashmiri Pandit family, Village Haal, Pulwama

Remnants of an idol in Shiv Temple, Kulgam

Courtesy: Kashmiri Pandit Sangharsh Samiti

Remains of the desecrated idols inside the ruins of Kameshwar Temple, Karfali Mohalla, Habba Kadal, Srinagar

Photograph By Muhabit ul Haq, 2013

Dilapidated house of a Kashmiri Pandit family, Village Haal, Pulwama

Photograph By Muhabit ul Haq, 2013

Abandoned houses of Kashmiri Pandits, Village Haal, Pulwama

Courtesy: Kashmiri Pandit Sangharsh Samiti

Abandoned Shri Pingla Devi Temple, Pinglen, Pulwama

Photograph By Seema Bhat

The crumbling façade of an abandoned house of a Kashmiri Pandit family,
Village Haal, Pulwama

Courtesy: Kashmiri Pandit Sangharsh Samiti

The dilapidated Shiv Temple, Chinkral Mohalla, Habba Kadal, Srinagar

Courtesy: Kashmiri Pandit Sangharsh Samiti

The desecrated Shivlingam in the ruins of Shiv Temple, Kupwara

Photograph By Muhabit ul Haq

Remnants of an earthen oven inside the kitchen of a deserted house of a Kashmiri Pandit family, Village Haal, Pulwama

Photograph By Vijay Dhar, 1994

A group of displaced Kashmiri Pandits in front of canvas tents in Garhi, Jammu Province where they lived from 1990 to 1997

Photograph By Vijay Dhar, 1994

A Kashmiri Pandit family in front of a canvas tent in Garhi, Jammu Province where they lived from 1990 to 1997

Photograph by Sushant Dhar, 2015

Gole Quarters, Migrant Camp for Kashmiri Pandits, Muthi, Jammu Province. Hundreds of Kashmiri Pandit families lived in such camps from 1993 to 2011. Many of the structures in this camp were demolished in 2011.

Photograph By Arvind Gigoo, 2013

A one-room tenement in the Migrant Camp for Kashmiri Pandits, Muthi, Jammu Province

Photograph By Arvind Gigoo, 2013

One-room tenements in the Migrant Camp for Kashmiri Pandits, Muthi, Jammu Province

Photograph By Vijay Koul, June 1991

A Kashmiri Pandit woman living in a canvas tent in the Migrant Camp for Kashmiri Pandits, Muthi, Jammu Province

Photograph by Arvind Gigoo, 2013

A one-room tenement in the Migrant Camp for Kashmiri Pandits, Muthi, Jammu Province

Photograph By Sushant Dhar, 2015

Gole Quarters, Migrant Camp for Kashmiri Pandits, Muthi, Jammu Province

Photograph By Sushant Dhar, 2015

A toilet block for Kashmiri Pandits living in the Migrant Camp for Kashmiri Pandits, Muthi, Jammu Province

Photograph by Vijay Koul, 1991

Kashmiri Pandit men sitting outside the one-room tenements in the Migrant Camp for Kashmiri Pandits, Muthi, Jammu Province

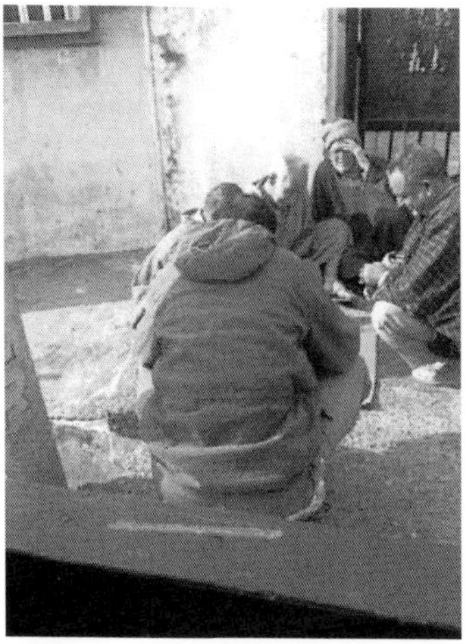

Photograph by Arvind Gigoo, 2013

Kashmiri Pandit men sitting outside the one-room tenements in the Migrant Camp for Kashmiri Pandits, Muthi, Jammu Province

Photograph By Vijay Koul, 1991

A Kashmiri Pandit girl outside a canvas tent in the Migrant Camp for Kashmiri Pandits, Muthi, Jammu Province. Hundreds of Kashmiri Pandit families lived in canvas tents in this camp from 1990 to 1993. In 1993, the tents were replaced by one-room tenements, where the families lived till 2011.

A Kashmiri Pandit woman in her one-room tenement in the Migrant Camp for Kashmiri Pandits, Muthi, Jammu Province

Photograph By Arvind Gigoo, 2015

A Kashmiri Pandit girl filling water from a canal outside a one-room tenement in the Migrant Camp for Kashmiri Pandits, Muthi, Jammu Province

Photograph By Vijay Koul, 1991

A Kashmiri Pandit girl storing water outside a canvas tent in the Migrant Camp for Kashmiri Pandits, Muthi, Jammu Province. Hundreds of Kashmiri Pandit families lived in canvas tents in this camp from 1990 to 1993. In 1993, the tents were replaced by one-room tenements, where the families lived till 2011.

Photograph By Sushant Dhar, 2015

Temporary settlement for Kashmiri Pandit exiles at Jagti, Nagrota, Jammu Province. About 4000 Kashmiri Pandit families were relocated here from different camps in Jammu in 2011.

The incident had also led to a spurt in militant presence among the public, which had its impact on ordinary folks as well. After fighting the police and security forces during the day, some of them would look for good food and some relaxation, too. Soon after darkness set in, they would seek shelter in any home, order the inmates to cook food for them, and some would seek pleasure with the female folk. My wife told me how she had been advised by one of our friends to let the militants in, if they knocked at the door. These young men lived and worked under constant threat to their lives, so they deserved some moments of leisure and pleasure! She told me that several families had put up with these visitations quietly, but some had left their homes the very next morning.

When I switched on the TV to listen to the evening news bulletin, the lead story was about Lassa Kaul's shocking death. He had gone to see his aged parents from his office. The moment he touched the handle of the main gate of the house, bullets were pumped into him and he had fallen dead.

I had left the city after hearing Kaul's reassuring words and I was back in the city to see him die a gruesome death! A worthy son of the soil had to pay with his life only because he occupied a high central government office.

Next morning, I went to see my parents and other close relatives. My parents and my brothers were all packed to leave. My brother-in-law was also ready and he wanted that we all should go with him. I told him that I had to stay back, because I had to attend to my job and the obligations it entailed.

I remember some bits of my visit to my department in the University on the day of its reopening after the winter vacation. While walking towards the main building of the Arts block, I saw an elderly Muslim colleague from another department talking to a small group of Muslim teachers in loud and angry tones, saying that many teachers from my community had left the city, causing problems in their departments. When I told him that I had come primarily to do my duty, his tone mellowed and he stopped complaining.

Some hours later the Vice Chancellor called a meeting of the department heads. While it was going on, one of his assistants walked in to whisper something in his ear, and he called off the meeting. We learnt outside that heavy firing had been reported from some area of the city and transport services had been disrupted.

I rushed to the bus station, and got into the only available bus that was there. I had barely been inside for some minutes, when the bus slowed down and came to a grinding halt. There was a long line of stranded vehicles ahead of it. The driver got down to see what had happened. Within seconds he rushed back to tell us that a large procession was heading towards Lal Chowk, and he could not say for certain when the traffic would resume. So all the passengers got down from the bus.

After walking past the stranded vehicles, I saw a huge procession of people, walking with measured steps, singing songs of liberation and raising a variety of other slogans connected with Islam. Since I had to go in the very direction in which the procession was moving, I had no option but to join it. On the way, men, women, and children cheered from the windows of their homes. Some showed a V sign. The people in the procession as well as the onlookers looked very excited and their energy levels were frightening. The procession moved like a giant wave that could engulf everything that came in its way. I also heard people talking earnestly about deaths, martyrdom, and a new dispensation that would replace the current political arrangement.

Since the procession was moving at a slow pace, I reckoned that it would take me hours to reach home. So I kept on looking for opportunities to change my course. After about fifteen minutes, I found a small side road on my right. I moved into it, walked fast to reach the nearest tempo stand, and found a tempo that took me to the stop close to my home.

This was the start of my long stay in my home, for curfew was imposed soon after this. And it continued like that for many, many days.

My brother-in-law, who lived close to our home, came to tell my wife and our children to be ready to move out of the city. Next morning, they were ready, but he did not come. I faintly remember that he came on the fourth or fifth day, by which time they had lost all hope of moving out of their forced confinement. The moment my Muslim neighbours spotted his car outside our home, they rushed out to see what was happening. Hurriedly, my wife and children said goodbye to me and left.

I learnt much later that the fleeing of the Pandits caused much anxiety to the Muslims; it filled them with apprehension that something terrible would follow their exit. Some believed that it was part of a big plot that was being hatched against them, because the Governor of the state had told the leaders of the community to direct their people to leave at once.

I told my neighbour that Pandits were leaving only because they were scared. The atmosphere was charged with threat and menace. They were being told repeatedly by the leaders of the movement to leave the place; some even set time-limits of twenty-four or forty-eight hours for their exit. In spite of this, and in spite of having seen such directives in the local newspapers, they still felt that some kind of scheming was going on to cause harm to the Muslim population. One of the wild rumours was that all the Muslim localities would be bombed. The propaganda machinery of the militants was so effective that it did not leave any room for doubt in the minds of people. Even seasoned politicians from different political parties spread the theory that the Governor was responsible for the running away of the Pandits, which I found intriguing. So I am not sure if my staying back gave my neighbour any hope that what he feared would not happen.

When the car left, I went inside my home. I was happy for my wife and children. They had suffered too much during my absence and deserved to be out of the hellish world the Valley had turned into. Within minutes, I felt sad and experienced a strong bout of emptiness, but only for a short while. For soon after, I got busy in the kitchen to take care of my empty stomach.

Curfew became a part of the daily existence of people. They hardly left their homes, except to do their shopping during the brief while it was relaxed. During these little trips to the market I got to know that many Pandit families that I knew were still in their homes. The situation was not all that hopeless, I thought. Without a phone in my home, I had no way of knowing what was happening in other parts of the city.

From that time to the time I finally left the city in the month of May, I was all alone in my home, and could go to the University only two or three times, for the curfew relaxation was not long enough to allow me to make a round-trip from my home to the University and back. Besides, curfew relaxation times did not always coincide with the availability of public or private transport. Curfew was announced either by the government or any organisation almost every day and transport would disappear from the roads within minutes. So, most of the people stayed home. Being away from places of work did not invite any punishment.

Things took a difficult turn when the Vice Chancellor of the University and his personal secretary were kidnapped by the militants outside its main gate. They demanded the exchange of some captured militants for their release. Since the government had discarded the policy of exchanging kidnapped officials for captured militants, their demand was turned down. The result was their brutal killing by their kidnappers. Their lifeless bodies were found on an open road. The government announced that there would be non-stop curfew till the murderers were apprehended. And that was truly a terrible time.

I remember some significant moments during my long stay at home. One was when I had to open my door to soldiers. When they guessed from my name that I was a Pandit, they were surprised and asked me why I was still there, braving it all alone. When I told them that I was in my home, they did not say anything, but I could see that it set them thinking. They looked inside all the rooms and left. From the main window of my first floor, I saw that several other groups of soldiers were in the compounds of my Muslim neighbours. I learnt later that it was a search operation. The soldiers wanted to make sure that there were no militants and firearms in any of the homes. I wondered if they would ever be able to find anything through these searches!

Another moment was much more interesting. There was an announcement that all the people of the locality had to come out in an open space, for questioning by the army. I hurriedly locked my home and moved out. I saw a huge gathering of people: men, women, children, of all communities. A large majority of them were Muslims, but there was a fair sprinkling of Pandit men and women, too. In one part of the field sat an army officer, who called people one by one for questioning.

Although people had not gathered for any pleasurable activity, it was quite pleasant to see everyone after so long. Everybody was busy talking to somebody else. Some women had brought food items with them to feed their young children.

While looking around for familiar faces, I spotted a couple of senior Pandits who lived in houses across the main road that was right in front of my home. I went to speak to one of them. He and his wife looked cheerful and smiled all the time. He told me that I looked a bit weak, and advised me to move out during relaxation hours and see them as often as possible. That would keep me in good shape. I thanked them for their solicitude and envied their optimism, for they told me that things would be normal soon, for people cannot live abnormal lives for long.

While I was talking to them, I spotted an old friend, who lived nearby. He invited me to his home. Inside, it was unbelievably bare. Seeing my puzzled look, he told me that his parents and his wife had already left for Jammu with all their belongings, and he would join them in a day or two.

He told me things that depressed me. He said that conditions in the Valley were already bad, and they would deteriorate further. From the window of his room, he showed me some houses that had guns in them, which were hidden in places that nobody could find easily. He was certain that the exercise of searches and interrogations would not yield anything. Almost abruptly, he asked me about my plans. I told him that I was staying on because I had a job that involved responsibility, and my wife had told me that she would be back soon. He told me that this was no time for coming back. The militants were in total command of the situation in the Valley, and there was absolutely no chance of things improving, and so I should think about leaving. The administration had collapsed and the politicians had either left the place or were just not interested in doing anything.

He felt irritated that I was not reading the situation correctly. He drew my attention to the fact that every day one or two Pandits were killed in this or that part of the Valley, and they were being told openly that their time in their homes was over.

When I left his home, I felt tired and confused, and sat near a group of Muslims, who were busy talking about the current situation. I overheard bits of what they were saying. Some said things were moving in the right direction. Young leaders, who had taken to the path of violent confrontation with the government, were doing the right thing. They would certainly help in starting a new phase in the life of Kashmiris. Some were not so hopeful. They felt that the path chosen by them would only add to their suffering, for it was difficult to change things.

And then I was called by the man in the chair, who asked some questions. I gave very short answers, and went back to my home.

This outing only added to my tension, for till now, I had not seriously thought about leaving. I had stuck to the optimism of my wife who had told me to wait for her return. I had absolutely no idea about where she was and whether she still believed that she could make it.

The only other non-Muslim in my area was a Sikh; he too had sent his wife and children to Jammu. He was fond of moving around and he carried a bag-full of interesting stories, collected from people he met and talked to from some of the inner lanes of the area, where curfew was not administered with the same strictness as it was on the main roads.

He often came to my home and I too would go to his. A couple of times we ate together at each other's place. I guess he wanted to avoid being alone. He had a flourishing kitchen garden that proved useful. He belonged to a village about forty miles away from the city.

I remember one day he told me that he had to go to his village to attend to work on his land, but would be back in a day or two. He stayed away for many days, because he was caught in the non-stop curfew trap. When he returned from there, he told me unbelievable stories about what he had seen and heard in his village.

He told me that many young Muslims from his village and many other nearby villages had left their homes and crossed the border to take training in the use of firearms. It had been happening for several weeks and looked like it would continue for some more time. That is why there was acute shortage of rubber boots in the Valley, for these were a primary requirement for crossing the border. I was shocked by what he told me and asked him how so many people could cross the border without being seen and checked by the border police. He told me that people who were involved in motivating the Muslim youth to leave their homes had their contacts and could get things done by using all kinds of means. I remember how it gave a big blow to my hope of things improving in the Valley.

I encouraged him to bring copies of local newspapers because they contained all the news related to militant activities. Every day, newspapers were full of accounts of firing by the police and militants, militant diktats, warnings to people to desist from anti-movement activities, and statements from individuals dissociating themselves from political parties.

Schools and colleges remained closed. Even offices and commercial enterprises were virtually non-functional. The worst part of the news was about the Pandits: any family that continued to stay on in any locality was targeted by the militants, to send warning signals to all other Pandits to leave at their earliest. Every now and then, some known person from their community would be kidnapped and discovered dead after some days. Even the Muslims who spoke against such acts were targeted.

Two visits during this period I remember distinctly. One was from my old Muslim friend who ran a small business from his home. He came to see me as and when he could, because he knew I was alone. He lived at the extreme edge of the locality on the opposite side of the road. He had a huge kitchen garden and cows too. So he would bring me vegetables and milk which he carried inside his pheran. These routine visits would normally be brief, but one was longer than usual, because we got involved in a serious discussion.

The discussion was related to the current situation. He was in the construction business, which had come to a standstill. His income had dried out, and that hurt him, because he had to take care of a large family. His brothers who helped him in the business were also without work. I think that had compelled him to think about his future. Small and big businesses had been hit hard by the disruption in normal life.

He wanted me to tell him the true meaning of Azadi, which was the main slogan raised by the leaders, for which they implored people to contribute in whatever way they could. I said that I could not tell him what it meant, and I encouraged him to understand it by relating it to what he did in his life, to his family obligations, to his religious duties, and to several other actions that he did on a regular basis. He found that he had complete freedom to do whatever he wished. Then I told him that maybe things would change with a change in the political arrangement within which he lived in the present. This set him thinking. After some time, he said that he could not think of any substantial change that could alter his life and his living conditions. I told him that he should speak to his leaders, and ask them what kind of Azadi they had in mind and how it could improve his life. He smiled and said that that would be risky. The leaders did not encourage people to ask questions. I told him that in that case, he would have to learn to put up with what was happening.

That cast a shadow of gloom on his face, and I felt sad for him. He had just about started making money to make his life comfortable, and was now overtaken by the uncertain present. I hugged him and told him not to worry too much; things would change for the better soon.

I was also visited by my friend who lived in a village in south Kashmir. He came occasionally on his scooter to check if I was still in my home. He told me how things had slowly changed in his village. When the panic wave of fleeing had overtaken the Pandits, the Pandits of his village stuck to their homes. But now things were different, because they saw a visible change in the attitude of the Muslims towards them.

One of his Muslim friends told him that they were not sure if the presence of the Pandits was welcome. If they left, they were unnerved; if they stayed on, they felt uneasy. This ambivalence was the main source of their puzzlement.

Their ambivalence was reflected in their growing indifference towards the Pandits, which was a clear hint to the latter that they should quit. My friend put pointed questions to his Muslim friends. Some wanted them to stay, but some were turning hostile towards them. To ensure that they did not come to harm, the entire group of Pandits was packed and ready to leave.

My friend had come to tell me that perhaps I too needed to rethink my plan. Dear brother, he said, we have now no option, but to pack up and leave. Our part in this story is over.

Soon after this, my Sikh friend told me that I was on the radar of the people who ran the show in the Valley. One of his close friends had asked him why I was still in my home and what I was up to. I told him that I had a job, and my wife was returning soon. He just laughed. He told me that my answer could satisfy him but not the others; in their eyes, I was a suspect—an agent, an informer, a dangerous spy, anything that they wished. And that was enough to get rid of me. My life, he told me plainly, was in danger. I was on the list of people to be knocked off. When they would fall short of targets, they would come for me.

I remember that this did not disturb me, for I believed that I was not capable of harming anybody, but his telling me about this led me to re-examine the behaviour of some of my Muslim neighbours, who had been avoiding me in public.

Much later, another friend of mine came all the way from a far corner of the city to tell me that I was risking my life by staying on in my home. Seeing him come all the way from virtually another end of the city to tell me about the danger to my life meant that there was some truth in what he said. As if to confirm this, my wife flew in from Delhi to take me away from Srinagar. She had been told by a close friend in Delhi that my life was truly in danger.

Within two days, after making a proper leave application, and handing over the keys to my colleague in the Department, I left with my wife in a taxi arranged by a friend. When I reached Jammu, I called him to say that we had reached safely. When, among other things, I asked my friend when I could return, he said that I should thank heaven for being safe and forget about returning!

18

The Fatal Seconds

PL Waguzari

I killed him. No, I got him murdered. Not either. I became the cause of his death. Maybe, it is nearer to what I want to confess. His death has been haunting me for the last twenty-five years. I accuse myself. Rationally speaking there were many reasons responsible for this cold-blooded murder. I will try to enumerate some of them.

The first was the unilateral ceasefire declared by our Chacha Nehru in 1947 when the Indian army was re-capturing vast areas of J&K from the clutches of the Pakistani army. For Chachaji, Sheikh Mohammad Abdullah was the first and last hope for the survival of this state. Sheikh Sahab, in order to rule the roost, wanted J&K without the festering and cancerous presence of Mirpur and Muzaffarabad Muslims whom Kashmiris called Punjabis and who could have posed a threat to his political survival in the state. Hence he persuaded Nehru to declare the ceasefire. This gave birth to the Pakistan Occupied Kashmir.

The second was the notorious declaration of Chachaji at Srinagar's Lal Chowk in which he said that there would be plebiscite in J&K and the people would be given the option either to remain with India or to join Pakistan. Of course there were conditions appended.

The third was Nehruji's knock at the doors of the United Nations Organizaton with the so-called Kashmir problem. It gave birth to the popular slogan 'we want plebiscite' with which two generations of Kashmiris grew up during the fifties, sixties and seventies of the previous century. All these causes paved the way for the 1965 war with Pakistan and then the proxy war which was unleashed on Kashmir in 1990. The last nail in the Kashmir coffin was the 'staged abduction' of Rubaiya Sayeed, the doctor daughter of the then home minister of India and her subsequent 'release' in exchange for some hardcore militants at the end of 1989. This gave the final boost and fillip to the so-called resistance and freedom movement in Kashmir.

I admit that I was the cause of his death. Let me explain. Veerji of Nagam was the son-in-law of my neighbour, Prithvi Nath Koul, whom we called Daddy. Veerji was a junior engineer posted in Shopian. Because Shopian was far away from Nagam, he used to reside at his in-laws' house at Ratnipora particularly during the early months of 1990 when all schools, colleges and offices were almost closed.

Those were the days of bomb blasts. Those were the days of daylight killings. Those were the days of large processions with anti-India slogans and V signs made with index and middle fingers. Those were the days when people wearing wrist-watches exhibited Pakistan time to show their solidarity with Pakistan. Those were the days when the general public was in a mad rush to close accounts in the nationalised banks and deposit the money in the J&K bank which they believed was out of Indian control. Those were the days when the word INDIA was erased from all the signboards in the villages and towns of Kashmir. Those were the days when government employees believed that the next salary would be paid in the Pakistani currency.

The nights were more menacing and full of turmoil. From the mosques, the loudspeakers blared out slogans about Azadi and eviction of non-Muslims. Those were the nights when the processionists hurled stones on the corrugated iron roofs of Bhatta (Pandit) houses creating a hellish din all around. Pandits shrank in their houses, especially those living in the villages.

Ours was a small mohalla of about twenty Bhatta families comprising about a hundred people. From ancient times Kashmiri Pandits were called Bhats, not Bhatta. Bhatta was a nickname given to us by the Muslims. They called us 'Daali-bhattas' which is derogatory. It means lentil-eating

Pandits. We lived along the road at the southern end of a large village called Ratnipora. Those were the days when almost all social connections with our Muslim neighbours and friends had snapped. Our own houses had turned into virtual prisons for us. We could move about only in our mohalla. I and another neighbour of mine mustered courage and started moving around the village, we would go up to the postoffice which was at the far end of the village, buy cigarettes, soap, medicines, spend a couple of minutes at different shops, try to recreate the earlier bonhomie with some people, and share jokes with Rather Sahab who was an elderly shopkeeper. All this was possible because we did not want to be alienated from our neighbours.

Days went on. We used to go down to the village daily. Earlier my old students and even their parents would stand up, wish me well and showed a lot of respect whenever I passed. But this stopped and I noticed that when they saw me they ran away and hid from me. The shopkeepers considered our presence an intrusion. They started denigrating India in our presence. Mohammad Shaban Dar's shop used to be crowded. Some people would be reading newspapers and others would be discussing politics. The local papers were full of '*Main mukhbir nahin hoon*' (I am not an informer) notices.

One day while we loitered there, Mr Dar and some others asked, 'Why are Pandits fleeing Kashmir?' They were referring to a news item published in the newspaper. It said that two Pandit families of the neighbouring village, Lelhar, had fled the previous night. I retorted: 'You are the elderly and responsible residents of this village, but you don't know what is happening just under your very nose? Recently stones were pelted at our houses by some processionists. This created a virtual din in our mohalla. Pushker Nath's widow fainted. Women and children started weeping and wailing. Three days ago, on the eve of Eid, Badri Nath's cow was stolen, slaughtered and the meat was distributed among his Muslim neighbours. Arjan Nath's hay that was stored on a tree was torched at night, burning the entire store of hay as well as the walnut tree. A fear psychosis lurks among Bhattas. And you ask why Bhattas are leaving Kashmir. Under such circumstances we also have decided to leave.'

My argument had an electrifying effect on the elderly Muslims. They seemed to have been jolted awake from a slumber. They expressed their ignorance of all these events. They decided to visit the Bhatta mohalla the next morning along with other elderly people.

Ratnipora is a large village with a unique distinction. Bhattas live at one end and the peasant class at another. In the middle live the pirs, who call themselves Andrabi. Ours is a village full of educated and literate people. In 1990 there were hundreds of graduates and post-graduates among all the three classes. Pirs and peasants had a strained relationship with one another. The main mosque of the village, the Jamia mosque, which was at the centre of the village, adjacent to Mohammad Shaban Dar's shop, was controlled by the pirs. But recently one gentleman, Aamir, who lived in this village and belonged to the farmer class, who taught Arabic in a higher secondary school and was my colleague there, pulled off a great coup and proclaimed himself as the imam of the mosque. Being the only son of his rich parents he had bought a Fiat car. Every Friday he left his school around noon and went to his village to conduct the Friday prayers. He would go to an adjacent village in the evenings where he had started a madrassa for imparting religious education to the kids there. Earlier he was a happy-go-lucky fellow but after his posting to Sopore he came under the Jamat-i-Islami influence. He returned a completely changed person—serious, taciturn, fanatic and full of Islamic zeal.

One morning, as had been agreed upon, people started coming to my house. Some of my Pandit neighbours also assembled. Aamir, the imam, arrived late. Because the room was crowded, he sat near the door. I felt embarrassed.

Jalal-ud-Din, who had taught Arabic to Aamir and who was a good orator, started his speech. He talked for nearly an hour. His speech was addressed to me. It was a political speech about secularism in Kashmir. Hindus and Muslims, he claimed, were like two brothers. No power on earth could draw a wedge between their relations. He quoted Mehjoor, the famous Kashmiri poet: *dodh choo Muslim Hyund choo shaker saaf saaf / dodh te beyi shaker ralawiew paanwani* (Muslim is milk and Hindu is sugar, both are neat and clean. Both should be mixed to make a sweet brew.)

He assured us that the present turmoil was temporary. He requested all Muslims present there to rein in their children and stop them from stoning the houses of Pandits. They decided that they would keep vigil in our mohalla in groups of four or five, just to show the youngsters that Bhattas were not alone and were not to be targetted. They promised to hold such meetings regularly. They were about to disperse when Aamir the imam sought permission from his old teacher to say a few words. Quoting an Arabic verse, he posed a question to Jalal-ud-Din, 'Sir, you have been my teacher. You know this is a verse from the holy Quran. You know I deliver sermons every Friday. Suppose a youngster accosts me with a question pertaining to this verse, what shall be my reply?' The entire audience was dumbfounded. There was an awkward silence for a couple of minutes. The Bhattas could not understand anything.

Turning his head towards me the imam said, 'Mr Waguzari, remember that whatever my respected teacher said so far is nothing but political chicanery. Political parties of different hues have been exploiting this so-called Hindu-Muslim brotherhood slogan right from 1947. Actually no non-Muslim can be a brother to a Muslim. You are infidels and idolaters. You can have absolutely no relation with us. Remember there is no space for a non-Muslim in our social or political systems. These people are deceiving you, they have deceived you and they will go on deceiving you.'

This proved to be the last nail. It was a thunderbolt for the elderly people. A graveyard-like silence ensued. Mohammad Sultan Mir, Aamir's cousin, who was seated beside me interceded, 'But Islam provides for *tahafuz* (protection) to minorities.' The imam was magnanimous enough to condescend to the suggestion. 'Yes, it is our religious duty to provide you protection on the condition that you don't do anything that can be harmful for propagating *Nizam-e-Mustafa*'.

I said that I was the last man to accept any such conditions. I wanted to live like an equal. I thanked them all and hugged Aamir. Everyone was speechless except for a couple of elders who requested us not to take any hasty step. They left and formed small groups on the road. The awestruck Bhattas were frightened. Vasudevji expressed his fears and started to curse the imam but I assured him that the imam was the only true friend of Bhattas. He had the courage to speak the truth about his community. What others said was nothing but falsehood.

In spite of this episode I kept going to the village with Nathji. We tried to maintain contact. Some of our Bhatta neighbours started sneaking out of the valley in buses and taxis. Only a few families were left in the mohalla. No office, no school, no work. Inaction was forced upon us. To kill time we started playing cards for hours together, sipping hot cups of tea. Most of my relatives and friends lived in Srinagar. I had a Bajaj scooter, a proud possession those days. Once a week I used to drive down to Srinagar to see my younger sister and her family at Sathoo or visit my friend TN Dhar, who headed the Department of English at the University of Kashmir. He was alone at his Chhanapora residence. I was worried on his account because his killing by militants would make a good piece of news for them. They had already eliminated the Vice Chancellor of the University, Mushir-ul-Hak, Director Doordarshan and my relative Lassa Kaul, Ranjoor an octogenarian Communist leader and a host of other personalities.

Hima, my sister's daughter who was married just a couple of months earlier, lived in Barzulla. We didn't have phones those days and I used to visit her once a week. I used to sneak through lanes, by-paths and by-roads to reach Sathoo, Chhanapora or Barzulla. I used to rush back before the curfew was imposed at 5:30 pm. During the remaining six days we whiled away time playing cards. Thus we spent another month or so in our mohalla after the imam episode.

Veerji was married about four years earlier in 1986. He was friendly, vivacious, genial, affable and at the same time dangerously outspoken. He had two kids—a daughter about three and an infant son. His wife, Nana, was a school teacher.

It was Saturday, 12 May 1990. I locked my house, placed the keys under a rug on the verandah, started up the scooter at about 5.30 am to go to Srinagar. Veerji's in-laws lived just a hundred metres away from my house. I was yet to decide what it was. Was it fate, which I don't believe in? Was it coincidence? Or was it divine intervention? I don't believe in that as well because I am an agnostic. When I reached Daddy's house, the main door suddenly opened and Veerji came out with his infant son in his lap. When he saw me, I gesticulated that I was going to Srinagar and would be back in the afternoon or evening. Had he not seen me he would not have marked my absence till around noon. Had he not opened the door at that moment, or had he opened it just five seconds later he would have been alive today. Hence I call those seconds fatal.

I reached Tej Nath's house in Chhanapora where we had breakfast together. We had a long chat. I, once again, implored him to leave the valley. But since he was saddled with University responsibilities he was reluctant to leave. After spending some time with him I left for Sathu to see my sister. I learnt that they had gone to my village with Hima and her husband to spend the day with me. I drove back to my home. My sister had brought some food from her home and when I reached they were having lunch. Daddy, his younger daughter Nita and his granddaughter were there to give them company. It was Daddy who had facilitated their entry to the house because he knew where the keys were kept. Daddy informed me that Veerji, after seeing me go to Srinagar, had become restive because my absence meant no card games for the day. Veerji wanted to go to his office in Shopian to know about the situation there. In spite of their opposition he had left at 9.30 am.

My sister and others prepared to go back at around 4 p.m. Some other Bhatta neighbours assembled there partly to enjoy the company of the outside Bhattas and partly to have a look at the newly-wed couple—Hima and Pappuji. They were about to board the car when Hima suggested that I accompany them to Srinagar for the night. All present, including my neighbours, took up the refrain. I went in, dropped a McDowell's whisky bottle in the bag, locked the house, deposited the keys on the verandah and got into the car. We reached Sathu at about 5.30 pm. After a fairly long interval I spent a lively evening there.

On Sunday, 13 May 1990, I returned from Srinagar. When I reached Dar's shop, his son Munna Dar, who had been my student, informed me that something terrible had happened in the Bhatta mohalla. He said that he had seen Prithvi Nath Koul along with some women going somewhere in a taxi. I rushed to my mohalla, where I found some Bhattas standing in fear in the compound of Daddy's house. My neighbour, Nathji, informed me that Veerji had been killed. Veerji had gone to his house to see his mother in Nagam. She was living alone there. Her husband, who was on the hit list of the militants, had fled to Jammu. She did not leave because she owned a cow and did not want to abandon it.

I got to know later that Veerji's mother was scared by his arrival there. She never wanted him to come home because it was under the constant surveillance of militants. On 13 May 1990, people watched the TV serial *Ramayan*. In spite of his mother's precautions, Veerji had rushed out to buy a reel of thread from the shopkeeper across the road. The shopkeeper was his friend who engaged him in a long conversation and didn't let him leave. After some time, two militants reached the place and showered bullets on Veerji. He fell down. The other shopkeepers downed the shutters of their shops. People deserted the place. Veerji bled profusely. No person came to his rescue till his mother came out wailing and weeping. Some of his Pandit neighbours rushed to the police station for hiring a police vehicle to carry him to the hospital in Srinagar. The police did not oblige immediately. Somehow a police jeep carried Veerji to the hospital. While going to the hospital, Veerji told his mother that he would survive only if he was taken to the Army hospital in Badami Bagh. But when the police vehicle reached the Exhibition crossing in Srinagar it took the left turn. The accompanying policemen told his mother and his Pandit neighbours that they had "orders" to take him to the Medical College Hospital. Veerji whispered in his mother's ear that only God could save him. These were the last words that he muttered.

Veerji was admitted to the hospital. When the doctors on duty there heard that it was a case of firing by militants, they did not attend to him. The doctors forgot everything about the Hippocratic oath.

One of Veerji's neighbours accompanying him to the hospital hired a taxi, came to Ratnipora to inform his wife, daughter and in-laws. Not a single Muslim neighbour came to share the grief. Some youngsters assembled across the road and watched our movements in the mohalla from a distance.

The next day Daddy returned. With the help of other Pandits, he cremated Veerji at Nagam. Then he set the cow free, and sent Veerji's daughter, son and mother to Jammu. We still lingered on at our houses in Ratnipora.

Two days later, on 16 May 1990, Altaf, my old student, sneaked to the house of my neighbour Nathji late in the evening and told him that I should be sent away that very night. He had learnt from some reliable sources that militants had planned to kill me. Altaf left and Nathji rushed to me with the message. He suggested that I spend the night at his place. I declined the offer. The next day this message reached the other Pandits in my neighbourhood. They assembled at my place and pleaded, argued and requested me to leave. I said that I would leave only if everyone else was leaving. Since it was the first day of *Panchak*, a cycle of five inauspicious days, some women promised that they would leave after five days. Then Daddy, in spite of his recent devastating tragedy, came and coaxed me to leave. Some of the youngsters showed their inclination to leave with me. I changed my mind. I took a Pandit neighbour with me and we booked two trucks at Awantipora. We asked the two truck drivers to bring their trucks to Ratnipora at about 9 pm. The trucks arrived on time on 17 May 1990. We loaded the trucks with some household goods including my scooter. Twenty other persons also boarded the two trucks and left around 11 pm. The next day I reached Udhampur where my younger brother, who worked in the MES department there, lived. The remaining Pandits including Daddy left Kashmir after four days.

Two days after I left Kashmir for Udhampur, I came to know that the police had interrogated the imam and held him responsible for forcing the Pandits of Ratnipora to run away. A police officer I knew narrated all the details to me. The imam had told the police that I was a *mukhbir*, an informer.

After about six months the schools reopened on 1 June 1990. I rushed to Srinagar and went to Pulwama to mark my attendance in the school. There were no students and most of the staff members were absent. I marked my attendance and went to Pampore where I waited for a bus to Udhampur at the Kadalbal crossing. I saw the iman's Fiat coming from the Pulwama road. It stopped in front of me. Aamir, the iman, was seated in the back seat. His father was sitting in the front. I greeted Aamir's father and the driver. They talked cordially. But when I greeted the imam he turned his head away and ignored me. His father offered me a ride to Srinagar but I said that I was waiting for someone else.

Later in November 1990, I shifted from Udhampur to Jammu where I was adjusted in a newly established camp school for the displaced Pandit students. The school was nothing but twenty-something tents that had been erected. The teachers took classes in these tents.

In 1992, the imam visited me. He hugged me and apologised for his rude behaviour at Kadalbal about twenty months earlier. Then he narrated the entire tale of his subsequent woes.

'When you people left, the police arrested me. They beat me and held me responsible for your migration. They even demanded money. I had suspected that you were the informer. The police released me on the condition that I report to them once every week at their interrogation centre. I was on my way there when I saw you at Kadalbal that day. After several days, when the matter settled, I got to know that it was not you but one of the Pirs who was an informer and an agent. He was the one who had shared the details of the meeting at your house with the Intelligence agencies. This is why I have come to apologise to you.'

I asked the imam if he still preached on Fridays. He said that his father had been shot dead by militants some time ago and that he had stopped giving sermons in the mosque.

19

My Home! My Home!

Maharaj Krishen Koul Naqaib

February 1990
Bal Garden, Srinagar, Kashmir
Insecurity and uncertainty prevail everywhere. Hartals and bandhs are consuming us. People are scared of one another. Nobody is frank and truthful. The father looks upon his son with suspicion and prefers silence to speech. Son hides things from his father. Close friends don't trust each other. Neighbours have turned strangers. Everybody is a suspect.

There is scarcity of everything in homes. Vegetables, rice, milk, sugar, medicines and other essential things of daily use are not seen anywhere. Conditions are abnormal. I am disgusted with all this. That is why I have shifted my family to Lucknow. I am living alone in my house now.

On 1 March 1990 I picked up my ration card, locked the house and reached the ration depot to get the ration for the month. While I was handing over the ration card to the dealer, gun shots were heard. Smoke was clearly visible. There was panic. Nobody gathered courage to move. The onlookers said that a Pandit PN Handoo had been killed. I was shocked. His house was about 200 feet away from the ration depot. Ten to twelve people were standing there. Nobody gathered the courage to go near him. We had heard that the militants had issued warnings asking the people not to go near a person whom they would kill, not to help and show sympathy towards him. This prevented the neighbours—both Muslims and Pandits—from going to Handoo's place to offer help. The dead body was left to the mercy of God. The entire area of Bal Garden was in utter panic. Everybody chose to remain indoors. All were fear-stricken.

At about five in the evening my brother-in-law, BK Wakhlu, came to my house. He looked pale. He had heard about Handoo's death in his office. He saw that I was terror-stricken. He implored me to come to his house in Bana Mohalla and stay there for some days to overcome the panic caused by Handoo's death. I was trembling due to fear. I found him shaking too. When I reached his house my legs were heavy. I was mentally exhausted. I sat down in a room not knowing what to do next. The four-storeyed house proved a prison for me. Wakhlu and his wife (my sister) asked me not to go out of the room. It was said that the militants kept a close watch on the day-to-day activities of all Pandits, their relatives and guests. A twenty-four-hour curfew was imposed by the administration. On the 5th of March it was relaxed for two hours from 5 am up to 7 am. Wakhlu accompanied me to the bus stand because I told him that I would not stay at his place now. I decided to book a ticket and leave for Jammu. I was not inclined to stay there any longer because of the terror and acute fear. We walked a distance of three kilometres in the early morning. While walking on the roads I found hundreds of old and young Pandit men, women and children marching towards the bus stand. They were carrying bags, trunks, suitcases and other things on their shoulders and heads. They were like strangers to one another. The women were terrified; the old men and women were dazed and the children were terrorised. Nobody was talking to anybody. It was a scene from the World War II movies and the Indian TV serial *Tamas*. I knew many who were walking fast. None talked to me and I also did not talk to anybody. An old woman slipped and fell on the road. Nobody came to her rescue. I also walked straight. Perhaps her son helped her get up. They were all running for their lives. They were hurrying to save their honour. Some old men were walking fast. They managed to keep pace with the others. Not for a second did I think of my brother-in-law who was accompanying me. I wanted him to leave me alone to my fate. I did not think of my wife, children, brother and his family. I was thinking of the bus that would carry me to Jammu. The journey home seemed to be endless.

When I reached the bus stand in Lal Chowk I was horrified to see hundreds of Pandits in queues in front of the ticket-booking counters of the private transport agencies. Those who had bought the tickets were carrying their luggage to the roofs of the buses. I saw women climbing the ladders at the backs of the buses. The children were silent. I saw some elderly men and even women rebuking their children without any cause. Actually they didn't want the children to say anything. They did not want the children even to piss. All were in a hurry to board the buses quickly because curfew would be imposed at 7 am. Many Pandits and their women had occupied their seats in the buses and implored the drivers to start driving. The faces of the children presented pathetic sights.

While all this was going on some militants from the lane adjacent to the Palladium Cinema Hall fired in the air. The firing did not stop. Women started screaming and children wept. The old were petrified. Perhaps the militants did so to stop us from going to Jammu. Or they wanted to take Pandits as hostages. I don't know. Nor can I say anything about their plans and intentions. The army jawans standing there fired back. This exchange of fire continued for about twenty minutes. Fear and terror gripped all Pandits. The persons at the booking counters pulled down their shutters. People in the buses took shelter below their seats. Children clung to their elders. Those on the roofs of the buses lay prostrate there. Many Pandits ran away and entered the Sanatan Dharm Sabha whose gates were thrown open by the para-military forces present there with guns. Many lay on the road like dead bodies. Women went on beating their chests and weeping. Some women fainted near the Clock Tower. Some families got segregated. Fathers lost sons; sons lost mothers; children lost mothers and I lost my brother-in-law. The drivers of some of the buses drove without bothering to check whether all the passengers were seated in them or not. I was seated in a bus. The driver was about to start the engine when I heard an old man shout: 'Shanta! Shanta!' He was beating his forehead hard. I asked him: 'What is the matter? Why are you doing this?' He replied like a lunatic: 'My daughter is not with me in this bus. She could not board the bus.' I asked him: 'Where is she?' He shouted weeping: 'She was carrying a small trunk to the roof of the bus.' Both of us got out to find his daughter. I saw a young woman lying unconscious on the road close to the wheels of the bus. Foam was coming out of her mouth. When the old man's look fell on the young woman he addressed her: 'Shanta, are you okay?' I lifted her and we dragged her into the bus. Nobody came forward to help me. Everybody was watching me do it alone. The old man did not know what to do. I opened the woman's mouth, poured some water into it. Then I massaged her feet. After some time, she regained consciousness and opened her eyes. My mouth became dry. My heart was beating very fast. I wanted a glass of water but there was none anywhere.

After the firing stopped most of the passengers, who had been left there, walked up to the Broadway Hotel where the buses were waiting for them. Ultimately the journey towards Jammu started at about 10 am. I did not know where my brother-in-law Wakhlu was. The atmosphere in the bus was grim. It was like the silence of the graveyard. Elderly men and women asked the children to keep quiet and not to demand biscuits and milk. The children obeyed. When the bus reached Pampore an old woman shouted: 'My home! My home!' A young man lost his temper and shouted at her in rage: 'Shut up. We will be killed. Damn your home. Do you think you alone have lost your bloody home?' She got frightened and kept quiet. Then he stood up and addressed all the passengers: 'I warn you. Don't utter even a single word till we reach Jammu. I did not tell you … militants must be following us. Therefore close your dirty mouths. Nobody should get off the bus. We will talk in Jammu now.'

The bus reached Qazigund at about 1:30 pm. I don't really remember the time. Some young men wanted the driver not to stop there. Old men and women said nothing. They seemed to have lost their speech. But a middle-ged man gathered courage and very meekly requested the young men in the bus to direct the driver to halt there so that the passengers could relieve themselves, have parathas and tea. The permission was granted. We got down from the bus. The tea vendors were very hospitable and respectful towards all. They served snacks and tea in a very nice manner. They were affectionate towards the children and gave them milk and biscuits. They were kind towards those men and women who did not eat the things cooked or fried by Muslims. They offered them bread and fruits. I kept on observing everything with a fearless and free mind. Then I thought: 'What contradiction is this!'

When the bus crossed Jawahar tunnel everyone heaved a sigh of relief. Passengers started talking to one another. The state of mind of all present underwent a visible change. Everybody felt comfortable. People started talking about their homes and property. I too was relieved. I was carrying gold ornaments of my sister with me. I had hidden them in the pocket of the vest that I was wearing. I got down from the bus at Udhampur, a town 55 kilometres before Jammu because my brother SK Koul worked in a bank there. He was living in a rented accommodation. After some days my family came from Lucknow. We were united. There I came to know that my brother-in-law Wakhlu had reached his home safe after we had moved from the bus stand in Srinagar. I was given a position in the Higher Secondary School for Kashmiri Migrants. I taught there till I shifted to Jammu with my family.

20

Roses Shed Fragrance

Rattan Lal Shant

I

It was not unusual for us to leave Srinagar for Delhi when the colleges closed for two months in the winter. Our son was working and living in Delhi. Mostly we would leave on the very first day of the holiday. At the onset of winter in 1989, colleges were kept open more as a formality than as a necessity. Absenteeism among students in the college where I taught had been rampant even during the previous summer. When I asked them, they would invariably say that they were busy helping their fathers in harvesting crops. But I had always suspected that this absenteeism was because of their business at farther places, across the snow-covered borders, and not in paddy fields. An ineffective, unsuspecting and above all a liberal democratic atmosphere in the country as well as the free-licence environment was fully exploited by the neighbouring country. Local Kashmiri Muslim youths had started disappearing from their homes.

On the evening of 31 December 1989, my wife Raj and I went to seek Nazir Ahmad's and his mother, Ammaji's 'ijazat' (permission) to leave for Delhi. We always met them whenever we went out of Kashmir on a holiday. They were our neighbours. Nazir's kind-hearted mother handed over to us an assortment of dry vegetables and fruits for our son. In the ensuing mirthful hours of our meeting, she threw a queer, though innocent, suggestion at me to meet Governor Jagmohan at Jammu and ask him to take the army away from Kashmir. I reciprocated with equally ostensible innocence, promising to do so positively upon my arrival there. Boisterous guffaws burst out in Nazir's house. Despite my remonstrations Nazir and Ahad, his younger brother, chided their mother for the nonsensical talk. But I knew what was going on in their minds. They were in the know of certain things related to the political situation of Kashmir. We had seen our other neighbours indulge in double talk. We had also seen the rapidly changing political situation and the killings of some prominent Pandits in the autumn months. Nazir insisted on taking my wife and me in his car to the bus stop at Tourist Reception Centre the next morning.

The morning of 1 January 1990 was cold. A strange and ominous gloom ruled everywhere. My wife and I packed a few clothes and other things, locked our house, and sat in Nazir's car. As Nazir drove us towards the Tourist Reception Centre near Lal Chowk, he said, 'You should have taken along some more clothes and household items. This winter is expected to be harsh, and you may have to extend your stay over there in Delhi or Jammu.' Then he said in a conciliatory tone, 'Shant Sahib, just remember that winters in Kashmir tend to drag on and on. This is going to be one such long and severe winter. And you must not rush to return.' For a moment I thought he was acting smart and was being unnecessarily funny, for he knew well that our son's house was our second home in Delhi and that we always carried only a small suitcase whenever we went to Delhi for a vacation. 'Why don't you keep this small bag too in the suitcase? Why carry it in your hand the whole time? Have you kept some valuables in it? I mean jewellery?' Nazir went on. A polythene bag in Raj's hand had attracted Nazir's attention. Raj blushed and looked at me. 'Nazir, these are some rose saplings from the garden of the house. Raj plans to plant them in a pot in Delhi. You know pure Kashmiri roses have a unique fragrance. So we're taking these saplings along. Just for the fragrance when they grow and flower,' I explained. Nazir smirked. 'I do not think these saplings will grow outside the valley. They simply won't grow roots and bloom in the hot weather in Delhi,' he said, sardonically. I did not say anything more.

Every morning, we would wake up to hundreds of delicate and fragrant roses blooming all over the garden of our house. My wife loved white roses. Therefore, she carried some saplings along. She wanted to plant them in flowerpots at our son's house in Delhi. Both of us knew the fragrance of the white roses.

After a while, we boarded a bus and set off for Delhi via Jammu. The bus negotiated sharp turns through the mountainous roads in Banihal. We stared blankly at the fleeting villages and fields. In my heart of hearts I was trying to decipher what Nazir had said to us. His strange advice to us to carry more things was baffling. Although I looked ahead and felt excited to be going to Delhi, I also thought of our return to our home in March or April. Springtime was the best time to be home and have plenty of things to do there. Plant new rose saplings, clean our house, clear excess snow from the courtyard, if at all there was any left in there. 'We will be back in March,' I said to my wife. I knew that my words were meant to assuage my own anxieties rather than to console her. The changing political environment and the sudden eruption of mass frenzy in Kashmir were making me anxious and worried.

An incident that had taken place earlier on an August day in 1989 is etched in my memory. I was returning to Srinagar from Anantnag. Instead of getting off the bus at Indira Nagar, I had decided to go to Lal Chowk for some shopping. As the bus reached the stop, I saw a gang of boys shouting 'Allah O Akbar'. They ordered the driver and passengers to jump off the vehicle. Everyone got off the bus and ran towards the other end of the road. Within moments, the bus burst into flames. The deafening sound of the blast and the sight of the burning bus attracted many more people from Lal Chowk. I fled the scene amid loud slogans and a constant chanting of 'Allah O Akbar, Allah O Akbar.' There wasn't a policeman in sight. The bystanders cheered as the bus turned into a mangled heap of charred steel. I felt lucky to have escaped in time. It wasn't safe for Pandits to be in the vicinity whenever such incidents took place. However, this wasn't my first encounter with violence. On another occasion, Hari Krishna Kaul, a prominent writer, and I met one afternoon at Shakti Restaurant on the Residency road in Srinagar. We had placed an order for something to eat and were waiting. Suddenly the place started shaking and part of the ceiling caved in. We were sitting at a table in a corner. There was smoke all over the place. Everybody screamed and rushed out. In the smoke, I lost sight of my friend. A while later, we couldn't believe that we were alive. The blast had ripped apart the ceiling of the restaurant. Except some bruises on our arms and faces, and dust and dirt on our bodies and clothes, we were unharmed. We were too dazed to talk about the incident. Later we got to know that militants had detonated a bomb in the restaurant to warn the owner because he was a Hindu.

With the onset of autumn in 1989, attacks on police and selected killings of prominent people were reported daily in newspapers. For us, our Muslim friends and colleagues had a simplistic explanation: 'Yeh markaz ki chal hai.' (This is a conspiracy hatched against us by the central government to discredit our peaceful struggle for the liberation of Kashmir from India.) It was a belated expression of revolt of the 'wronged people'. 'Non-Muslims are targeted only by the enemies of Kashmiris,' Muslims would say to Pandits.

In December 1990, I had another close shave with death. I was on a bus to Anantnag. I had been transferred to the Government Degree College at Bemina and was on my way to complete some paperwork associated with the transfer. The police searched the bus at several checkpoints. When the bus was about to reach Anantnag, there was an explosion. A part of the crowded bus was ripped apart. Passengers fell on one another while jumping out through the gaps. I was sitting on the bonnet over the engine just beside the driver along with two more passengers. The impact of the blast had tossed me away. I fell on my face and was hurled upon a heap of injured and bleeding people near the front door which had been thrown open. The rear of the bus burst into flames. I didn't know what to do and where to go. I was bleeding and injured. It was only when a half-burnt body was dragged out of the bus that I realised how lucky I was. Everybody was cursing the policemen for their dishonesty and for not checking the bus properly for any bombs and explosive devices. No one blamed the person who had planted the bomb. I dragged myself to the other end of the road and boarded another bus.

Little did I know that this was not all. I was to go through several such close encounters with death. Kashmir had erupted with terrorism in its deadliest form.

After these incidents, I stopped travelling in government vehicles. My colleagues and I were asked to spend more time in our college even though there was no teaching work. Therefore I had to be away from home. My wife would be worried for me all the time. She spent all her time praying for my safety. But the constant spate of bomb blasts in buses, marketplaces and government buildings had made travelling risky. Having survived two bomb blasts, my wife thought that I might not survive another one.

Earlier in October 1989 we had a frightening experience. One cloudy day Deep, the youngest brother of my wife, came running to our place. He was out of breath, bruised and battered. He told us that some belligerent youths had intercepted him while he was walking in Bana Mohalla and interrogated him and asked him questions about me. He informed me that the boys had first threatened him and demanded information about me. He had tried to explain that he knew nothing, but they didn't believe him. He had been heckled, kicked on his stomach and punched on his head so that he would share all the relevant information about me and other Pandits living in the locality. He had sensed that the boys were collecting information about Pandits working in the government, and this information would be handed over to the militant organisations. We had seen hit lists in which names of Pandits were published. Such hit lists were pasted on the doors of Pandit houses. Deep feared seeing his own name, and mine too, on one such hit list. The boys had questioned him about my connections with the government. They wanted to extract information about other Pandit writers who were my friends. They had specifically asked him about my connection with the programme officers of Radio Kashmir, the Pandit members of the Cultural Academy and my colleagues at Kashmir University. But Deep knew absolutely nothing about them. He had just joined his father and uncle in their business on Hari Singh High Street in Srinagar. After an hour's tormenting interrogation in a corner of the lane that day, the boys had let him go with a warning. Deep was shaken. Listening to Deep's details, my wife sat sobbing. We consoled him and promised to send him back home the next morning. My wife sensed that we were being singled out because we were Pandits. Moreover I was a college lecturer and a writer and wrote fearlessly about many things and taught literature. This worried her. I told my wife that the madness wouldn't last for long and that she should not worry. I comforted her by saying that we should look forward to our travel to Delhi and meeting our son. 'Is it true that mujahids are entering our Kashmir to rebel against

India and to kill Pandits?' she asked me. She had heard about the mujahids from our Muslim neighbours.

Deep's traumatic experience proved ominous for him. Days later in the beginning of November, Justice Neel Kanth Ganjoo was assassinated by militants in broad daylight at the bustling Hari Singh High Street in the heart of Srinagar. Hari Singh High Street was full of traders and shopkeepers. It used to have police presence on all days. Strangely when militants shot Justice Ganjoo, the policemen seemed to have fled. Even the shopkeepers, customers and wayfarers ran away from the crowded marketplace the moment militants shot Justice Ganjoo. The killers hovered around, forbidding anybody to touch Justice Ganjoo's bleeding body. The killing of Justice Ganjoo at Hari Singh High Street created panic and fear among the Pandit shopkeepers there. Deep's parents were forced to shut their shop permanently. The hapless boy's career in business came to an end. My father-in-law struggled to make ends meet.

In December, Advocate Prem Nath Bhat too was murdered in a similar way near his house in Anantnag. After such targeted killings of Pandits, the militants would order the bystanders to stay away from the bodies and not to offer any help to the victims or their family members. Such orders were non-negotiable. Those who defied the orders were shot dead. Such acts were more motivated and demonstrative than assertive. In all this, the local police was absent. Strangely one wouldn't see policemen around whenever Pandits were killed either in streets or near residential places. Clearly, there was a nefarious nexus between the police and the militant organisations. The police were to keep away from all places which were identified for random and targeted killings of Pandits. The police were not to carry out any investigations or arrests. The police were not to register any cases against the militants. The militants were simply not to be touched. The administration was hand in glove with the militants. They knew about the Pandits who were to be killed. Yet they chose not to do anything. On the other hand, Muslim friends and colleagues pointedly told us of indiscriminate civilian killings by the armed forces. Such events were more widely reported in the press. But the killing of Pandits was attributed to agencies planted by the central government and the security forces. 'The government is behind all the killings so that you will leave Kashmir and they get to wipe us out,' one of my Muslim neighbours had said to me.

December 1990 was marked by terrible events. More and more local Muslim boys crossed over to Pakistan through the border near Kupwara for training in armed combat. Many, who had crossed over earlier, returned to Kashmir with arms and ammunition which were used to attack the security forces. They became mercenaries and militants. Widespread infiltration of foreign mercenaries went unchecked by the authorities. The paramilitary forces could do little to arrest the infiltrators. Kashmiri Pandits became soft targets of militants and it was easy to threaten them.

The ideological differences we had with the Muslims had existed earlier too, but they were not allowed to surface boldly and vitiate the atmosphere. We trusted the Muslims and had never imagined that they would think of us as their enemy and create conditions for us to worry about our own safety and security in Kashmir. The militant organisations spread lies and canards branding us 'spies' and 'agents'. The local Muslims did nothing to counter the untruths and sided with the militants.

I would have stayed on for a week more and left after getting my salary for the month of December 1989. But the bill payments at the Government treasury had not been made on 31 December due to rampant strikes and hartals. I found no merit in waiting for the salary. Moreover my wife and I had decided to leave for Delhi to be with our son. I pretended to be brave in front of our Muslim neighbours, but my wife was not able to conceal her fear. Both of us left on 1 January 1990, after bidding adieu to our neighbours.

The story of my escape from my motherland, Kashmir, and from a large number of people who were like my brothers, sisters, well-wishers, admirers and critics did not end there. Three months later, by the month of April, all the Pandits had left. The valley had been ethnically cleansed. The government forsook them and they were condemned to an unforeseen exile in their own country and were called 'migrants' instead of 'internally displaced people'.

After spending three months with our son in Delhi, my wife and I returned to our home in Kashmir in April. We had thought that we would be safe because the army protected our locality. An army cantonment was nearby. But we could not stay there for more than twelve days. Kashmir had turned into a war zone. To escape the torment, my wife and I fled on the thirteenth day in a truck carrying sheep to Punjab. We dangled between hope and despair.

The rose saplings my wife had planted in a pot kept in a corner of the small balcony of our son's two-room flat in Delhi shed some of their leaves but the rosebuds somehow continued to emit fragrance. Raj was happy that she had proved Nazir wrong.

II

Our long and tiring journey from Srinagar to Jammu ended in Subhash Nagar in Jammu. An uncertain future loomed large before us. We didn't know what to do. Home was lost. My father had built a small three-room house in Subhash Nagar, many years earlier. The three rooms were for three of his sons but only one room was livable. The other two rooms were neither finished nor furnished. The compound was littered with rubble, sand and sods of earth. We kept thinking of the communal riots that had taken place in 1986 in Anantnag in South Kashmir. Somehow we had survived the massacre that time, but we hadn't thought that a time would come when we would be rendered homeless.

None of us had any clue of what was to happen. Listening to news reports of violence and bloodshed in Kashmir sent shivers down our spines and our hope of going back kept vanishing by the day. My grandmother, parents and my youngest brother, Ashok and his wife and daughter, joined us. Then came the eleven members of three families of our two neighbours—the Kouls and the Hakhoos. They had nowhere else to go in Jammu and we made room for them to stay in our father's unfinished house. Nineteen people stayed in the two unfinished rooms of our house. The authorities started setting up camps for the displaced Pandits. Tents were erected in the camps. The government announced relief material for the unemployed migrants. Youngsters from the community volunteered to help the aged. They got temporary shelters created in temples and dharmshalas for those who had nowhere to go. Thousands of Pandits who had fled from the remote villages in Kashmir without any household goods, had nothing to wear and eat. They had no money because they were into farming and agriculture. They narrated heartrending tales of how they faced persecution in their villages. Their neighbours had taken their cattle. They had lost the produce in their orchards and fields. I saw a lone man in his seventies offloading a cow and her newborn calf from a truck. He had no other asset and had spent all his savings to hire a truck to take his cow and him to Jammu. The cow was his only companion. The Dogras in Jammu threw open barns and cattle sheds for the displaced Pandits to rent. They looked at the new arrivers suspiciously as though they were antiques from a museum.

With great difficulty and with utmost devotion, Raj cleared a small patch in a corner of the courtyard of our house, erected a canopy over it and planted the rose saplings in the soil. 'These saplings will remind us of our home,' she said to me. 'I pray that they never shed their petals and fragrance.' In her heart of hearts she was trying to reconcile herself to the fate and the misfortune which had befallen us. We didn't have sufficient money left. Like others, we had tried our best to retrieve money from our bank in Kashmir, but the bank and post office remained shut for months. Srinagar remained under curfew for most days. However, some of my friends in Kashmir were a great help. Our guests at Subhash Nagar left our house and took refuge in a camp nearby. Five of us, including my grandma and parents, were left to live in one room. Ashok and his family took the other one. Jawahir, my other brother, rented two rooms nearby for his family.

I kept on thinking about those twelve tormenting days we spent in our house in Srinagar after our return from Delhi in April 1990. I had been in conflict with myself about whether to return to Srinagar amidst worsening conditions in Kashmir or to wait for some more time. My wife and I had decided to take a calculated risk. I will never be able to forget the conditions in which we had gone to Srinagar, stayed there for twelve days, and then on the thirteenth day fled the place.

It was 6 April 1990. My wife, father, my brother's wife and I travelled to Srinagar from Jammu. On that day militants murdered the Vice Chancellor of Kashmir University and his personal secretary. Curfew had been clamped in most areas in the city. Army crackdowns were taking place. People were being searched and frisked on the streets.

Father and Kaki went to our old house in Nai Sarak. My wife and I went to Indira Nagar where our house was located. We knocked at the house of our neighbour, Ashok. Ashok's was the only Hindu family living there. Ashok received us warmly and helped us settle down. For the next three days we stayed at Ashok's place, unable to go to our house though it was just a few yards away. We noticed strange and dubious movements of a neighbour's family members. Khadija, Atta Ullah's wife, roamed around suspiciously and kept a close watch on us. She barged into Ashok's house, chatted with members of the family, making no secret of her motive to get information about any Pandits who, she thought, had returned from Jammu. She knew that we were hiding inside, holed up in a room on the second floor of the house. She warned Ashok against giving shelter to Pandits. We knew some Pandits had returned to Srinagar after a temporary stay in Jammu but they were made to flee again by their own Muslim neighbours. My wife and I couldn't bear the ordeal. Nobody in the mohalla dared question Khadija's self-assumed role and authority of an invigilator on behalf of the militants. Slogans of Azadi and warnings to Pandits to support the ongoing stir or face consequences surged out of loudspeakers in mosques and boomed all over. Strange voices and movements of our neighbours in the night fortified our fears. Ashok told us that Atta's house was a militant-hideout and used for dumping and distributing grenades and guns. Atta's sons were running the show. Years ago, we had hired Nihal Chand, a young boy from Kishtwar, as a caretaker of our house. He also worked as a domestic help. We had learnt that he did odd jobs for a living in the city and had some contact with people in the neighbourhood. The neighbours were aware of his credentials. Unfortunately, he was away at that time. After spending three days at Ashok's place, we decided to go to our house. Late in the night Raj and I sneaked into our house as though we were thieves. Nihal Chand's clothes were hanging on a rope in the balcony. The joy of being in our house almost blurred our foresight. Without switching on the lights of our bedroom we fell asleep only to be woken up early next morning by strange sounds coming from the adjacent room. Fear gripped us. We thought militants had got to know of our arrival and entered the house to kill us. I opened the room fearfully. There was no one inside the room. I bolted the door and comforted my wife.

We sat glued next to our radio set and listened to the news. We got to know of the violent encounters between militants and the security forces. We ate whatever was stored in the house. Fortunately we had stored rice, flour and pulses in some bins. We couldn't go out. It was a travesty that we had to hide in our own house as though we were fugitives. We peeked through the chinks in a window to see Nazir's and Bashir's houses. In the past, we shared very cordial relations with them. The families had moved out and the gates of the houses were locked. The shed in the courtyard had been broken open. Some children from the neighbourhood barged into the courtyard of our house and started playing without being aware of our watchful presence. They seemed ecstatic at the prospect of being able to row a wooden toy boat in a shallow pond that was just adjacent to our house.

At a distance four middle-aged people assembled near the abandoned plinth of my brother's house. They started reading a Urdu newspaper. They lit cigarettes and discussed politics.

We prayed and hoped for Nihal to appear. On the fourth day, he came. It was a great relief for us. We felt rejuvenated and sat with him to plan our future course of action. We wanted to establish contact with my father and Kaki, my sister-in-law. The next day, Nihal went out of the house locking us in and returned in the evening with a curfew pass he had got from a friend who was a newspaper hawker. The curfew pass helped him cycle down to our ancestral home at Nai Sarak. The place was under curfew. He found my father holed up in the house. Kaki had managed to retrieve some essential household things from her house. They planned to leave for Jammu the next day. Curfew was lifted for two hours early in the mornings so that people could to go to mosques and buy groceries. After Nihal Chand returned, he informed us of a gruesome incident that had happened that day. A woman who was a teacher had been dragged out of her house and murdered because she had defied a warning to shut the windows of her house. A funeral procession mourning the death of a militant was to pass by.

Hearing about my father was a relief. However, in the prevailing situation I knew it was unsafe for us to stay at our house for long. My college was shut. I feared going out to meet my colleagues. I didn't wish to leave without meeting Nazir and his mother. Indira Nagar was not as dangerous as the old city because of the heavy deployment of the army in the vicinity. Eleven days passed, eleven sleepless nights. I hadn't stepped out of my own house.

On the twelfth day some neighbours assembled on the raised platform next to our house. They were discussing a news item published in *Al Safa*, the Urdu newspaper. One of the neighbours cried out in utter disbelief: 'Look, this is the news!' 'What? Whose diktat is this?' said another one. He read out the report. It was an ultimatum by a militant group. In the ultimatum Kashmiri Pandits had 36 hours to leave Kashmir or else face dire consequences. I shuddered out of fear and sat quietly in a corner of my room. Raj was busy cooking in the kitchen. I did not say a word to her. But the time had come for me to take a decision. Our departure was imminent.

Nihal Chand was restless too, but for a different reason. His master's shop was closed and he had no work or money. I told my wife to pack and be ready to leave the next morning. Later that day, we saw Nazir and his mother return to their house. Nazir became happy when we signalled to him that we were in our house. He made no secret of his apprehensions. 'You shouldn't have returned. It's very dangerous for Pandits to be in the Valley.' He did not elaborate and I did not insist. I told him that we were constrained to return following the death of my uncle in downtown Srinagar, and that we would be leaving for Jammu the next day. Raj was surprised at my lie about my uncle's death but she understood why I had lied. My uncle had expired a year ago. My wife sat silently. Nazir's mother, Ammaji, reprimanded me for deciding to leave Kashmir. Nazir asked her to keep quiet. He whispered into my ear, 'Take along as many things as you can. I can't offer you any help in the present circumstances. You must leave tomorrow itself and not look back.' He waved his hand and left.

Raj realised the gravity of the situation. She did not question my decision to leave. Nor did Nihal. We packed whatever we thought was going to prove very essential in Jammu. Nihal went out to arrange a truck. He knew a truck driver who ferried cattle from Srinagar to Panjab. We couldn't sleep that night. When the truck came into the lane, we loaded things into it. Soon, it was time to look at our house and say goodbye. I had spent all my savings to build the house some years ago. This is where I had wished to live for the rest of my life. My wife broke down. I went to her, held her hand and took her out of the gate. 'Did you look at the rose plants?' she said. 'The rose buds have come out. Who will water them now? Let us go back and water them.' She sobbed incessantly. I consoled her, 'Stop being childish. The rose saplings you planted in Jammu must have bloomed too,' I said. A reluctant smile flickered on her lips. 'Will those roses be as fragrant as the ones here?' she said. She looked at our house for the last time and boarded the truck.

The truck carried the luggage and household possessions of two more Pandit families. Some other Pandits who were leaving their houses boarded the truck. A woman and one elderly man sat in the driver's cabin. Nihal and I sat on steel trunks. I dozed off. The blinding rays of the sun woke me up at Qazigund. Qazigund was the last exit point of the valley. That fateful morning hundreds of trucks and buses loaded with thousands of hapless Pandits were going to Jammu. My wife stopped crying when we reached our father's house in Jammu. The roses were waiting for her.

21

Merge, Leave or Perish

Kashi Nath Pandita

On 14 September 1989, I went to the house of Tika Lal Taploo who, at that time, was the chief of the Bharatiya Janata Party (BJP) in Jammu and Kashmir. That very morning, a group of terrorists had shot him dead, just outside his residence in Habba Kadal, Srinagar. I joined his funeral procession and attended his cremation in the crematorium at Karan Nagar, Srinagar.

Tika Lal was murdered because he was the chief of BJP in the state. Before leaving his house for the court that morning, he had come across a small girl from a Muslim family living in the neighbourhood. She was crying on the roadside and her mother was trying to console her. Tika Lal had asked the woman why the girl was crying. The woman had said the girl had to pay money to her school for participation in a function, but she didn't have any money. Tika Lal had taken out a five-rupee note from his pocket, slipped it into the hand of the girl, lifted her up, kissed and stroked her hair with affection and told her to go to school and never miss a day there.

Minutes after this incident, when Tika Lal was killed by the militants, it was the same neighbouring Muslim woman who caressed the wounds of Tika Lal's body and wiped the blood with her tears.

After spending some time with the bereaved family, the mourners and I went to our homes. As I crossed Tanki Kadal, I saw a large gathering of Muslim youth dancing and celebrating. I walked silently but a miscreant placed his leg before me and I tripped. The bystanders laughed and jeered at me. I got up and walked away. It was a terrifying moment. They were mocking me for mourning the death of Tika Lal.

A few days later, I published an open letter in the *Kashmir Times* in which I asked the militant organisation which had taken responsibility for assassinating Tika Lal Taploo to tell us how they planned to behave with the Pandits. Next day, the Jammu and Kashmir Liberation Front published a response to my letter. It said that Pandits should join the separatist movement and stop supporting the Indian state, failing which they would have to bear the consequences. Pandits were shocked to read it.

On 4 November 1989, Justice Neel Kanth Ganjoo was shot dead by assailants in Maharaj Bazar, Srinagar. The assailants disappeared after killing him. The police vanished too. The bleeding body of Justice Ganjoo lay on the street and nobody touched it. Two hours later a police van picked it up. Justice Ganjoo had arrived from Delhi that very morning. His assailants had kept track of him and succeeded in killing him in the crowded and narrow street of Maharaj Bazar. No shopkeeper, passer-by or policeman came near him as he bled to death because the militants were keeping a close watch. In his capacity as the Sessions Judge, Justice Ganjoo had sentenced Maqbool Bhat, co-founder of the Jammu and Kashmir Liberation Front, to death, for murdering CID Inspector Amar Chand of Nadihal in Baramulla district, and also for murdering a bank functionary in Langet. Maqbool Bhat had escaped from the Central Jail in Srinagar. The two Muslim witnesses who had testified to Maqbool Bhat's crime were not touched at all.

The Pandits of Kashmir became fearful. We witnessed the collapse of the law and order situation. The government was paralysed. The militants targeted us, and it became increasingly impossible for us to lead a normal life in Kashmir.

I lived at Bal Garden, Srinagar. The political atmosphere in the city changed with the killing of Tika Lal. The Pandits talked about Tika Lal and surmised something very dangerous was going to happen in the days to come. But none of us had thought that an armed insurgency would soon engulf the state and cripple the law and order situation.

It was November 1989. Two years earlier, I had retired from Kashmir University. But with a UGC Fellowship, I occasionally visited the Central

Asian Studies Centre where I had worked. A former student of mine, who had done his MPhil under my supervision, came to me and started talking.

He: Sir, you are so well qualified and experienced, your services are invaluable.

Me: Yes, but I have rendered my services and now I am a retired person.

He: Sir, you can get a good assignment outside the state. Why don't you try? Why waste your talent?

Me: Oh dear, I am not made of that stuff to run from pillar to post.

He: No, sir, you should go out of Kashmir and look for a good position. I am sure.

Me: I'm not sure.

He: You must leave tomorrow, if you can, and not waste a single minute here in Kashmir. It is painful for me to see you not at a good position.

I wasn't able to infer any hidden meaning from this conversation. I took it as a routine one. But my student suddenly disappeared from the campus. No one could trace his whereabouts.

Let me link this incident with something that happened after the exodus of Pandits in early 1990. In December 1990, Panun Kashmir (the newly formed political organisation of the Kashmiri Pandits) organised the historic Marg Darshan meet at the Abhinav Theatre in Jammu. I was among its earliest activists and spoke on that day to a huge audience gathered there. Thousands of internally displaced Pandits attended that meet. During the tea break, as I sipped tea amid a large crowd, a friend of mine pulled me aside by my arm. He hugged me a number of times. He said he couldn't believe that he was seeing me alive. I asked him why he was surprised to see me. He disclosed, 'I have a close relative who works for the Indian Intelligence in Kashmir. He asked me a couple of times if I knew KN Pandita. I said I did. I asked him why. He said that he knew that you spoke Farsi. I said yes, but what is the link in all that you are saying? He told me that his group had captured a Kashmiri militant who had received training in armed combat in Meshed in Iran. During his interrogation, the militant had disclosed that his group had been ordered to kidnap KN Pandita because he was needed to work as an interpreter for their Iranian trainers and handlers. You have escaped kidnapping, so I hugged you.'

Very few people know that the activists of the Islamic Revolution of Iran supported by Ayatollah Khomeini in 1979 had exported militancy to Kashmir.

Tension was growing in Srinagar; it was an uneasy peace. Somehow, the Pandits became scared, and feared for their lives. But nobody could explain why.

The Muslims were excited at the eruption of the armed insurgency. They looked at us mockingly. I was walking in the lawns of the university. A couple of research students were walking close by. I knew one of them and overheard what she said to her friends, 'Oh, if we do not see Pakistan in Kashmir during our lifetime, our progeny will.'

Upon returning from the University, I stood in front of the BEd College premises on Maulana Azad Road in Srinagar. I crossed the street and came on to the main road. Cinema goers were coming out of Regal cinema hall. The show had ended and the crowds swelled on the street. They were silent and grim. Nobody wore the usual relaxed look. They looked revengeful. I understood the situation. In the 1980s, the film *Omar Mukhtar* had become very popular among the Muslims in Kashmir. It was the story of a Libyan nationalist fighting against the Italian occupation of Libya. Actually, Pakistani intelligence had facilitated the screening of this film in Kashmir to lessen the popularity of Sheikh Abdullah. I linked it to the events that followed. This movie had become extraordinarily popular with the anti-India youth in Kashmir and everybody wanted to be a hero like Omar Mukhtar.

Reports of sporadic gunfire and bomb blasts poured in. These occurred in the peripheries of the city. In one incident, the house of one Vatali, a senior police officer, was attacked. Assailants snatched the rifle of the guard.

At the entry of the Bal Garden locality, there were a few vendors. One of them was the distributor of milk supplies. A few influential Muslims in the locality, the privileged ones, used to buy milk from the Dairy. One morning, as I went to the vendor to fetch bottles of milk, I found one of these privileged guys beating and abusing the person in the milk van for failing to deliver milk at his home. Then in the course of hurling abuses, he said to him in very offensive language, 'If you were in Pakistan and committed a mistake like this, you would have been shot dead.' This was the concept of Pakistan among the elite Muslims in Kashmir. Perhaps they were not wrong.

During those days, we found strange writings and graffiti on the walls of houses along the road or on compound walls and even on lampposts and shopping complex spaces. These were: 'Namaz ko qaim rakho.' (Don't miss prayers.) and 'Din ki rasi pakrh ke rakho.' (Hold fast on to the chain of faith.)

Outside the mosques, blackboards were placed on stands with writings in chalk. These were the Hadith (traditions) attributed to outstanding traditionalists like Imam Bukhari, Imam Hanbali, Abu Huraira and others. These were generally axioms of morality and ethics a good Muslim was enjoined to observe. Every day, the writings on these mini boards changed.

At the mosque in Bal Garden, people assembled in hundreds to offer the Friday prayers. Even on other days as well, large crowds of people came to offer morning, mid-day and evening prayers. The imam whom I knew during those days often told me that ours was the locality of educated and well-to-do Muslims, and that they did not come out in large numbers to pray at the mosque. Now suddenly, almost everybody in the locality came to join the crowds. Khwaja Noorudin, the Director of Education at the time, a prominent member in the locality, had asked some of his subordinate teachers to donate to the mosque fund. One morning, I saw him in long kameez and shalwar as he stood in front of the mosque with a large platter in his hands distributing rice to the urchins who had assembled there. His son-in-law, Dr Allaqaband, lived in the neighbourhood too. He was a fresh visitor to the mosque in his Islamic dress and karakul cap. He also donated to the mosque. Suddenly, the mosque changed. New loudspeakers were fitted and the Friday sermons became louder and more political.

Adjoining the mosque were two vacant plots of land belonging to a Pandit. One fine morning the patch of land was fenced with barbed wire and then Friday congregations assembled in the compound to offer prayers.

In my hometown Baramulla, Muslim missionaries clad in long kameez and baggy shalwars, with long beards and skullcaps and haversacks flung across shoulders, became frequent visitors moving in groups of five to eight. The Muslims of our locality provided them accommodation and food. They were Allahwale and apparently preached saintly Islam. But actually they were galvanising the Muslim youth into a pan-Islamic movement. They travelled from village to village and groomed moles and informants wherever they went. The result of these frequent visits of the Allahwale to our locality in Baramulla was that the Muslim workers and labourers refused to be hired for any work commissioned by the Pandits. We were ostracised and isolated.

The sermons broadcast from the loudspeakers of the mosques were about not accepting hegemony or external domination, completeness of Islamic sharia as perfect law and rejection of any law outside the sharia, sacrifices for the faith and legends of historical Islamic personalities who led relentless wars against kafirs and inflicted crushing defeats on them. In these sermons, the speakers lauded the heroic deeds of great Islamic warriors and repeatedly told the audience of the ultimate victory of Islam. The audience was convinced that Islam was to prevail over all other religions. However, no direct attack on non-Muslims was recommended in these sermons. In fact, it was considered below one's dignity to say anything about the Pandits. That Islam was a battle against kufr was the refrain of these sermons.

In December 1989, grenade attacks on government buildings became a routine affair. The government maintained total silence about these incidents and the newspapers seldom made a mention. Everybody felt that something unusual was happening.

It was 19 January 1990. Days and nights were cold and winter was at its peak. However, there was no snow on the ground and roads were dry. It was around 9.30 pm. The telephone rang. My son-in-law from Rainawari spoke to me. He asked about the situation in our locality. He said, sounding quite bewildered, 'Please come out on the street and carefully look around.' I conveyed it to my wife. I came out and headed for the main street towards Batmaloo. In front of the municipality office, I found great crowds of people, young and old, yelling and raising voices with green flags in their hands, shouting, 'Pakistan ban gaya, la ila illalah.' From by-lanes, people rushed in to join the swelling crowd in a great frenzy, hugging and kissing one another, raising their voices and shouting anti-India slogans. I spent about ten minutes there. I was about a hundred steps away from the actual mob and then, sensing that some great political upheaval was in the offing, I turned around and headed towards my home. The Muslim people were coming out of their houses and assembling in the streets. The slogans were becoming louder and louder. 'Pakistan ka matlab kya/laillaha ilallah.' Then I heard people abusing India and Pandits. Some men distributed green scarves in large numbers. They waved Pakistani flags. They swore by the might of Islam and proclaimed that the era of Islam had dawned and the kafirs should run away. In each of the speeches, direct threats to the non-Muslims were conveyed. They said it was an Islamic movement and the non-Muslims should either join it or leave or perish.

With each passing minute, fear gripped me with more and more intensity. I thought of my family and children and the entire community. Hurriedly, I retraced my steps and entered my home. My wife was waiting for me at the door and the kids were all awake, huddled in a corner. By this time, loud announcements from the mosque were bleating. The speakers spewed anti-India venom and prompted the Ummah to rise in revolt. It said with God's grace Indian 'dogs' had been thrown out and the land of war (darul harb) had been turned into the land of peace (darul amn).

We huddled in a corner of the room. The telephone rang once again. Friends called and repeated the same story. Nobody could say what should be done.

The policemen had vanished. The speakers announced that the police had joined the movement and that law and order was in the hands of the leaders of the Muslims and that instructions would be announced from time to time and the future course of action would be disclosed at a proper time. This was immensely threatening. Nobody knew what the future course of action was.

We kept vigil throughout the night. Even our own Muslim neighbours branded us as spies of India. And we were caught unawares in a massive movement against Indian presence in Kashmir.

We passed the night in fear. The children fell asleep in my wife's lap. I didn't know what to do. Clearly, we were asked to join the Islamic movement or leave Kashmir.

In the morning, Srinagar city shut down. No milkman and no bakery. Shops remained closed. But people moved in large numbers towards the mosques to receive fresh instructions. Mosques had become the centre of dissemination of the diktat of the armed insurgents. I managed to get a newspaper. There were reports of a revolt against the Indian presence in Kashmir, but it did not elaborate on the events which had unfolded the previous night. The Muslims congratulated and embraced one another, saying that the days to come would bring about the downfall of the Indian establishment in Kashmir and that the land would become pure. The kafirs would leave and Islam would shine in Kashmir.

'We have nothing to do with Indian Standard Time,' one of my neighbours said to me. 'Change the time in your wrist-watch to Pakistan Time.' I immediately obeyed. A friend who lived in my neighbourhood came to my house and said, 'Professor Sahab, you have nothing to worry. You are a scholar of Islamic Studies and you will get your due place in the new educational structure which will be implemented soon by Pakistan here. We need people like you.' I could not find any English-language papers. I heard their circulation was temporarily stopped. During the day, I went to my relative's place. They were in a state of shock, and were considering leaving Kashmir.

Later on, we heard that Farooq Abdullah, the chief minister, had resigned and the Governor had taken over. It sounded strange. Though the secretariat was in Jammu, yet most of the ministers were in Srinagar. After the government fell, these ministers silently left for Jammu one by one and continued to occupy the government bungalows. Police guards were set up outside Muslim ministers' official residences (though they weren't ministers any longer). The main entrance to the ministerial residential complex on Wazarat Road, Jammu, was sealed off by a barricade. Deployment of the guards was ostensibly to provide them security against the militants but in reality they feared there could be a backlash from the Hindus of Jammu. But these former ministers never came out on the streets. Later on we came to know that militant leaders and separatists were in regular contact with them in Jammu.

Finding that law and order had completely broken down, the police abandoned their posts, Muslim bureaucrats became accomplices of the insurgents, government departments were paralysed, Pandits thought that there was no safety. The worst thing was that the neighbours had overnight become suspicious, hostile and vengeful. Leaving their homes and hearths was the only alternative left for the Pandits.

I mustered up courage. Leaving my family at our house in 15 Bal Garden, I went to see my mother and brothers in Baramulla. They narrated the happenings of the previous nights and days. My brother told me that the Jamaat-i-Islami activists in the locality had published the names of those Pandits who were to be targeted. The hit lists were pasted on the doors and the walls of Pandit houses. My mother and my brothers were in great pain. My younger brother, a school teacher, used to go to the temple early every morning. Some militants issued an open warning to him. He decided to leave his home along with our eldest brother and octogenarian mother and the kids. He didn't know where to go. But he couldn't live in Kashmir any longer. Prior to that, the militants in the locality had twice tried to set our house on fire. But on the intervention of one Muslim family, the tragedy was averted.

I returned to Srinagar the next morning. The faces of my children were swollen. My wife said they had been crying and weeping all night out of fear. All educational institutions had been closed down. All offices became dysfunctional. Pakistani flags fluttered on top of the Muslim houses. People wore green arm-bands. Everyone tuned in to the Pakistani news broadcasts and bulletins. Cinemas were closed down. The order from the militants was that all cinema halls would be shut down indefinitely. They remain closed to this day.

All we heard were the slogans:

'Pakistan ka matlab kya? Lailaha ilallah. Kashmir bana hai Pakistan.' (Kashmir has become Pakistan.)

'Asih getseh Kashmir, batav begair batehnew san.' (We want our Kashmir; without Pandits, but with their women.)

Al Safa, the Urdu newspaper of Srinagar, published the first ultimatum issued by a militant organisation. The headline read: Pandits should leave Kashmir in 36 hours. One by one, the Pandits shut their shops in Amira Kadal and other places in the city. Then the most dreadful and awful incidents began to take place. Each day a Pandit was shot dead by the militants. Lassa Kaul, the Doordarshan Director, was gunned down outside his house. People said he was allowing the broadcast of news from India. But his counterpart, Farooq Nazki of Radio Kashmir, was not touched. Rattan Lal Kaul, Deputy Director of Food and Supplies, was killed in his office on the allegation that he had not allowed a truckload of rice to be diverted to the underground headquarter of the insurgents. Bushan Lal Razdan, my next-door neighbour, was gunned down in his home because he happened to be the stenographer of the Governor. I came to know that his assailants were hiding in the balcony of the house of a Muslim, just opposite his house and were closely watching his movements. As he stepped out of his house, they fired at him and killed him. He lay in a pool of blood. The killers disappeared.

Then the Pandits started to leave. They hired whatever means of transport they could, packed a few clothes and left. They headed towards Jammu in the hope that the Hindus would give them shelter.

By March 1990, the Pandits had fled, leaving behind their houses, land, orchards, shops and jobs.

My brother had four cows. One morning my brother and his family, including our octogenarian mother, came out of their home to leave for an unknown destination. My mother took a handful of grass in her hand and came to the cowshed. She stroked the cows gently, fed them the grass, and then holding the head of the oldest of the cows in her hands, she placed kisses on it, and said, 'Until this day, destiny had kept us in each other's company. We are forced to head to an unknown place and we are leaving you to an unknown destiny. Let God Almighty be our protector. Forgive me, O Mother cow, if I ever hurt you.' With her skinny fingers she untied the cows from the tether and set them free.

Wiping her tears and sobbing, my mother and my brother's family left the house. My mother took a handful of earth from the compound, kissed it and wrapped it in a piece of cloth. She never came back and, two years later, she died, pining for her homeland.

I handed over my certificates and pension papers to my wife and asked her to put them in her handbag. The next morning, we left our house. I could not carry the two thousand books I had in my private library. At dusk, we reached Jammu, broken, empty-handed, crestfallen, like culprits leaving a prison.

What happened to us in Jammu is another part of this saga. For years we lived on the fringes. We struggled to survive. We lived in wretched conditions. We felt we did the right thing by fleeing Kashmir. What choice did we have? We were made to leave. Had we not left, the militants would have killed us. They wouldn't have spared anyone. This is what they wanted. To rid Kashmir of the Pandits! The ethnic cleansing of the Pandits of Kashmir was complete. It happened at a time when India boasted of democratic and secular dispensation. The day Jawaharlal Nehru, the first Prime Minister of India, said in a public rally in Srinagar that Kashmir was the symbol of India's secular dispensation was the day the death warrant of Kashmiri Pandits was written. And we were thrown into exile.

22

The Knights of Shiva

Rajesh Dhar

22 February 1990

A village on the bank of river Vishoka (Vishav), Pulwama district, Kashmir.

A cricket match was on.

The ball was keeping low. The pitch was wet and soggy. The batsmen were trying their best to find the gaps between the fielders who, because of the cold, were loathe to chase the ball. Pandit boys were playing a hard-to-see-in-winter game of cricket in a walnut tree grove.

The walnut tree is the unsung pride of Kashmir. The place of pride belongs to the mighty Chinar. Both breathe their magic into the air of the valley, both the trees are legally protected. The Chinar will not allow anything to grow under it; the walnut tree, however, leaves some elbow space, however narrow. It was such a walnut tree grove where the game of cricket was underway.

Pandits owned very little of the vast agricultural lands that surrounded the village. They cheered for Ravi Shastri and Muslims cheered for Javed Miandad. Muslim cricket bats always had the stickers of either Imran Khan or Salim Malik. Pandit cricket bats exhibited either the manufacturer or Vivian Richards or Ian Botham. Kapil Dev or Sunil Gavaskar meant inviting censure and harassment.

Despite their patriotism in the face of a brute anti-India population the Indianness of Pandits of Kashmir and their non-Muslimness were as stark as the trunk of an elephant. Their sworn Indian patriotism was difficult to hide.

Shivratri, the night of Shiva, had just passed. The much-awaited festival had passed in a very subdued manner. A beloved Pandit social activist had been gunned down a few days earlier.

Pandit boys were not oblivious to the happenings or the atmosphere around them, but they were trying to find comfort in this innocent game. They were conscious of their curfewed existence.

Such was the dread that a few elders, trying to be as inconspicuous as possible, had mouthed into the ears of the umpire to call off the game because it was nearly time for namaaz. Besides, the mosque had warned of staying away from any form of enjoyment or leisure because the Muslims of Kashmir were fighting a jihad against India, and by playing cricket Pandit boys of the village were clearly proving their loyalty for India and enmity against Kashmiri Muslims. The boy, a graduate, who was standing as umpire was doing so because he had been promised four overs of singular bowling. The umpire could have informed the boys about the message the elders were trying to communicate to the pitch. The message was passed on, and after a huddle, it was decided to continue the match till lunch-break which was some fifteen minutes or so away.

The lunch was to go cold.

A retired Pandit government clerk Hira Lal was worried about his three daughters named Ef, En and Em (names withheld to protect the identity of the girls who're living in Jammu these days). The walnut tree grove and the cricket-playing boys were not that far from the house in which sat the father on his haunches, smoking. Throughout the previous night, he along with his eldest daughter and his sickly wife Es had bundled their essentials into gunnysacks. He had also folded some bedding. He knew he couldn't do it without some help. Asking for help from his own cousins would make his plan public, and his plan was to leave Kashmir. Because he had no notion where he was going except that it was across the Jawahar tunnel, he was trying to avoid the questions that he knew would follow once his plan crossed the door of his room. He did not know that his plan was crossing the limits of the village.

He had asked one of his relatives from his in-laws' side to arrange for a truck, which, as per his his plan, was going to be enough to carry him and his family and their belongings to Jammu—a city that was going to be the adopted home of the Pandits of the valley—a city that never made them feel unwanted. The truck driver was a Panjabi from a village in Gurdaspur. The relative had drawn the route map for the driver who had taken the map along with the advance payment. It was an assurance to the driver that he would be received by a man a kilometre away.

The truck driver saw a crowd on the road, protesting against the arrest of some school teacher who had recently crossed the border and come back after getting training in Pakistan. The truck driver slowed down. The truck had a huge P written in bold green on its side. The crowd cheered for the letter P of Pakistan.

The retired Pandit clerk saw the approaching truck and showed his hand to stop it. He panicked not to find his relative on board. He helped the driver park the truck on the margin of the un-metalled road and asked him to wait. He asked his wife to eat and offer food to the driver. The packing had kept them busy. The retired Pandit clerk's relative had done his bit. He knew a night journey would not happen. No outside truck was willing to take the hazard of driving into a village in the dead of night to fetch the household of an under-siege Pandit. So it had to be done during the daytime so that they could cross the Qazigund traffic police barrier before the stipulated time. Even the day had to be carefully chosen, as it was one-way season on the national highway. The relative had done his bit and had informed the retired Pandit clerk, the father of three daughters, about the arrival time of the truck, the day of the journey and even the name of the truck driver Jattan Singh. The retired Pandit clerk, Hira Lal, had been a favourite of his departed parents.

The retired Pandit clerk's wife was brilliant at cooking. So were her daughters. The younger one helped with the other chores. The two males were eating in a corner of the room. The girls in the kitchen were sobbing, teardrops running down their cheeks into their food. The brave woman kept serving the guest and her husband. The daughters knew well that everything was going to be different from now on.

The eldest daughter finished first. She always did for she had to serve her mother. She had kept her mother's medicines in her pheran-pocket. With ultimate gentleness she served her mother. She gave her the medicine first, and then food. She put on a very brave face for her husband and her daughters. She ate a fraction of what was served.

The walnut tree grove cricket match stopped when the truck first appeared on the village road. It stopped when the retired Pandit was helping it to reverse and park and was declared abandoned the moment the driver and the Pandit were seen moving towards the Pandit's house.

Every Pandit boy who was playing cricket, and even the umpire knew, what a truck meant at that time in Kashmir.

Pandits knew that they were being driven away.

Srinagar, a city of riches and glory, was fast becoming a city of death-to-kafir, a city of loot, plunder, pillage, rape, ransom, corruption and other ills. Pandits were leaving their towns, villages, hamlets, homes and their hearths. They were leaving because of an undeclared boycott of them and because of death threats pasted on their doors, because of the hit lists and of the danger to the honour of their mothers, wives, sisters and daughters. Pandits of the valley of Kashmir were leaving for an unknown place. But the retired Pandit clerk, the father of three daughters, threw caution to the wind. He asked his cousin for help. The cousin promptly came and together they carried the first load on their shoulders. The Pandit boys' cricket club saw the truck approaching with the load. Jattan Singh, the driver, was leading them. Soon the girls appeared carrying their share of the household load. The umpire took the lead. He rushed to help. Gingerly the others followed. They were now in the thick of things, one after the other running and carrying the stuff, someone helping the sickly mother. Soon the driver was on his seat but the truck was surrounded by the Pandit neighbours. Everyone was in tears, frightened.

Jattan Singh, the driver, saw them first. He had seen them earlier also. The orders were clear: 'Stop and unload the truck. Frighten the Pandits. If they have to leave they must leave empty-handed. The retired Pandit clerk is breaking the heart of our Amer. He is in love with the Pandit's second daughter.'

Before the retired Pandit clerk could blink in disbelief, the crowd was all over the truck. Someone pulled the driver out, kicked, punched, and beat him up. The girls were in a panic. Shrieks stuck in their throats. Their hands and feet were numb. Father was trying to lock the door on his side. Soon he realised that six or seven men were inside the driver's cabin fondling his daughters. More were trying to get into the cabin. The sickly mother braved it without a murmur. She only wanted to shield her daughters. She tried to give them cover. The daughters heard their father's name spoken loudly and angrily. He saw a new frenzy building around the truck. Some familiar voices were shouting the names of the girls. The Muslim men were being pulled out of the cabin of the truck. The walnut tree grove cricket-playing Pandit boys looked around helplessly. Some men and women of the Pandit neighbourhood were also there. They had heard the shouts. They saw the bleeding driver running towards them. They ran towards the truck as never before. The umpire cleared a passage for the mother and the daughters. The Pandit boys carried the family to the home that was nearest. Some remained behind, arguing, discussing and pleading for the release of the truck.

'Release the truck and the driver. Burn my things. Burn the old photograph of my mother and father. Mother bore me to see this,' said the Pandit in terror. His mouth was parched and his tongue seemed to cling to the roof.

And in no time bearded Muslims came from various directions and surrounded the truck. They did not threaten the Pandit. They said nothing about his daughters. They started praying in unison. Some young men were wearing sports shoes. Others looked at them as deliverers. Wristwatches showed a different time. The dreamy eyes turned towards the dull sky. They imagined a crescent there.

The bearded gentlemen waved the driver to disappear along with the truck.

Two neighbours and well-wishers of the Pandit accompanied him to his place. One said: 'My dear brother, you have no danger from us but I can't say anything to my son. My wife loves you. I don't know what else to say.' Another said: 'We love you and your family. Some strangers from another village were talking about you. You need not worry at all. We are here to protect you. Our youths are uncontrollable. I am silent when they talk. My love for you makes me suggest that you go somewhere till the conditions are normal. Now you have your time and we have our time. May God bless you and your family! I love you.'

The Pandit entered the house.

Next morning the two Muslims saw the door of the Pandit's house locked. Their eyes met and spoke. Nobody knows when and how the Pandit family had left.

Many Pandits in Jammu say that they were seen in Geeta Bhawan and then in a camp and that the girls are married and have children who are doing very well in some other state of the country.

23

The Pomegranate Tree

Namrata Wakhloo

On a cold winter day in December 1989, I was having lunch in my hostel mess in Pune and the news about the kidnapping of Rubaiya Sayeed, daughter of the then Home Minister of India Mufti Mohammad Sayeed, came in. I'd taken admission in an engineering college in Pune in 1988 after completing my schooling from Srinagar where I was born and raised.

We, Kashmiri Pandits, were aware of the psyche of the majority of the Kashmiris. Their political, religious and ideological leanings were not hidden. I knew, right from my childhood, that there were two political realities that existed in Kashmir—people who lived in Kashmir and felt Indian, and those who lived in Kashmir but identified with Pakistan, India's archrival. There was this thin line between friends at school, too, which was not to be crossed.

How can I forget the day when the window panes of our three-storeyed house were shattered by stones thrown at our house by the local Muslim youths when Pakistan lost a cricket match to India. We sat petrified inside our house, not knowing what to do. Throwing stones at the houses owned by the Pandits was always a natural thing to do for Muslim youths, especially when India won a cricket match. It was their way of telling us that we were at their mercy. We would always say in jest, 'Let Pakistan win! At least our house would be safe.' On the contrary, whenever Pakistan won, we would hear deafening sounds of fire crackers.

Ours was a joint family of more than twenty members. My grandparents, my father, four uncles and aunts, and cousins, lived together. My father's aunt also lived with us, so did our old housekeeper who had been with us since my father's childhood. His extended family lived in Anantnag but the only home he knew was ours. We had a family cook who had been with us ever since anyone could remember. He was a Hindu from Kishtwar whose forefathers had fled Kashmir during the eighteenth century to save themselves from forcible conversion to Islam. He would tell us bloodcurdling stories of how they had walked for weeks through Kokernag and crossed the mountains to reach Dachhan in Kishtwar. They had named the village where they settled Bhattapora. The village name was derived from the word 'Bhatta' which was the nickname given to Kashmiri Pandits by Muslims.

My great-grandfather was originally from downtown Narpristan, in the Fateh Kadal area of Srinagar. But we moved to the posh and uptown locality of Karan Nagar in 1960 where Pandits flourished and were in the majority. My grandfather had hired the best available architect and the best possible labourers to build a house. It was a huge plot of land of four kanals with two beautiful villas built on it. Everything was thoughtfully designed and crafted. There were two beautifully manicured lawns with a nice and long driveway separating the two. The lawns were lined with tall cypress trees and many fruit trees like apple, almond and loquat. The long circular wall surrounding the house was covered with rose shrubs, honeysuckle and snowball creepers. Beautiful flower beds of a variety of roses and flowers adorned the lawns. We also had a big patch of kitchen garden which my grandmother tended. In a corner of the kitchen garden was a beautiful pomegranate tree, the fruit of which all the children plucked before they were ripe. This would annoy our grandmother a lot, so we used to plan our heist during late afternoons when the women of the house would be sleeping. At a little distance from this tree was a strawberry creeper which produced the sweetest berries. We would compete with each other to pick the most strawberries. The house had four main gates at different corners out of which we used one and the rest were usually kept locked. Since the house was painted a beautiful white with pastel blue windows it came to be known as the White House. This was the house I was born in, a decade after the family had shifted there. I spent my childhood in this house.

As kids, we lived a very sheltered life. Our home was our world. It was self-sufficient. We divided our time between school and home. We didn't go to restaurants or movie theatres. The movie would have to be very special for our parents to take us to the theatre to watch. On weekends, we would visit Matamaal, my mother's pre-marital home to meet my maternal grandparents and cousins. These were the joys of life then. At school, I had a mixed pool of friends—Pandits, Muslims and Punjabi-Hindus. At home my younger brother and cousins were full of life. We celebrated all festivals with great zeal and in a traditional way. Birthdays were celebrated with a pooja at home and festivals like Herath (Shivratri) and Diwali were always a grand affair.

Life was beautiful. We had had a family-run business from my great-grandfather's time which we operated from the heart of downtown, Maharaj Gunj. The shop had witnessed a lot of history for more than a century and was located next to the Budshah tomb. We supplied our wares to every nook and corner of the valley and even exported to Afghanistan till the 1980s. My grandfather, father and two uncles ran the family business. One of my other uncles was a doctor at Lal Ded Government Hospital, and another uncle practised law. The children went to the best schools in town and the women looked after the household. We were socially quite active and would often throw parties to entertain our extended family and distant relatives. At these parties, the best Kashmiri Pandit cuisine would be served and, quite often, we would have live music by traditional Kashmiri singers, the Bachchas. We could never have thought of leaving this house and living elsewhere in the country.

It was during the late eighties that we first started experiencing political unrest. Hartals and occasional bomb blasts started disrupting the calm of the city. I was too young to understand these events. I doubt even the elders had an inkling of the storm that was brewing.

My matamaal was in Sanat Nagar, located on the idyllic banks of Doodh Ganga, the water canal that runs through the city. They had moved from sprawling houses in Ael Kadal to this humble abode after my maternal grandfather lost everything during the land reforms of 1972. The land reform law had been anti-Pandit. Many Pandits lost their land. My mother's parents were among the first relatives who left the valley in February 1990 because of the political unrest and militancy which broke out. They never returned thereafter.

My dad even now recalls how he and his brother left home on a cold winter morning in January 1990 to see off my cousin who was on his way to Jammu. He had got admission in an engineering college in Belgaum and had to board the train at Jammu the next day. But when they reached Lal Chowk, heavy firing between the militants and the security forces was going on. People ran helter-skelter taking cover wherever they could. Nobody was clear about the exact location of the firing but there was panic all over. Many Pandit families left their houses and fled to Jammu that day. My dad saw many Pandit women, in panic, dropping their bags with all their belongings strewn all over on the road. Food and clothes were scattered everywhere. My dad, uncle and cousin hid near the staircase of a hotel named Naya Kashmir. They immediately bade farewell to my cousin. Soon, all our relatives started leaving for Jammu and Delhi. Panic was setting in. Terror spread amongst all, especially within the Pandit community. People were getting killed. Many Pandits were targeted. They were killed inside their houses or out in the open.

Back in Pune, I was miserable. I waited for a phone call from my father. I had to go to the phone booth or book a trunk call to learn about the welfare of my family. Every single day was a nightmare. My father and other family members had to work out of downtown and that's where terror thrived. That's where, in every lane and in every mosque, the militants prowled. Militants belonging to JKLF, Hizb-ul Mujahideen, Al Badr, Al Umar, and others. roamed the streets of downtown Srinagar. They would quite often visit the traders in Maharaj Gunj, where the trader community—Muslims, Pandits and Punjabi Hindus—did their business.

One summer morning in 1990, a household help came running in and informed us that Bitta Karate, a henchman of JKLF, had killed Kapoor, the neighbourhood bakery guy. Kapoor lived in Chota Bazar and ran a bakery by the name of Vikas Bakery. He was shot on his head as he had bent down to pull a loaf of bread for an unsuspecting customer. He was taken to the Soura Medical Institute where militants made sure no doctors treated him. His helpless wife was next to him, watching him die a painful death. He died without being treated. I was home at that time. The news left me numb as Vikas, as we called him, was someone whose biscuits and bread we had grown up eating. Killing a harmless guy who ran a small bakery was nothing but a message to the Hindu Punjabi community that they had no place in the Valley. These Punjabi families had been living in Kashmir for several decades.

On another day, a servant of a house had left for Habba Kadal to buy some vegetables. In less than fifteen minutes, he came back running, completely shaken. A young Pandit, son of Shambu Nath Sapru, was shot dead near the fire brigade station at Kani Kadal. They lived in Babapora, Shalteng. The young man was returning from office when he was gunned down. His family members reached the spot but did not have the courage to go close to the body fearing that the militants would still be around. He was bleeding profusely from a wound in the throat. A Muslim woman passing by could not bear the sight. She quietly pulled out a handkerchief from her bag and covered his wound. In the weeks to come, the killings of Pandits didn't stop.

Lal Ded Government Hospital in Srinagar was one of the preferred hideouts for many notorious militants. My uncle who served there would give us first-hand accounts of how dangerous criminals would make a dash to the hospital and take cover inside for days after they had killed some Pandits. The hospital authorities would give the militants food and medicines.

We thought of leaving Kashmir, but my grandfather was completely against the decision. He probably had good reasons to stay, despite the threat to our lives. To feed and educate a family of many members would not have been easy anywhere else. Nobody in the family would have qualified for a private or government job or for that matter been able to set up a new business in an unknown territory. It would have meant investing a sizeable capital. Our wholesale distribution network in the Valley ran on credit. We supplied tea to almost every village and town in the Kashmir Valley. Therefore, at any given point in time, crores of rupees would be out in the market which were collected at regular intervals. Within months, the collections from these places started dwindling. People expressed their inability to pay, and deferred the payments as the socio-political scene in the Valley was changing rapidly. We wrote off many debts as many customers fled Kashmir. After much thought, we agreed to linger on.

Very soon, we had no relatives or close friends around us. The demography of Kashmir had changed. Many of our relatives and acquaintances did not approve of our decision to stay. They probably saw us as traitors. But nobody understood our compulsion. Almost all houses around us were rendered vacant in a couple of months' time. CRPF and BSF soldiers started moving into these abandoned Pandit houses. During one of my visits home, I stood in our lawn and kept looking at the gloomy shadows that fell on these houses, which until only a few months earlier, had life inside. It was not a pleasant sight to see men in uniform all around the houses. Yet we felt safe as these men protected us and kept us secure—during the daytime when all men would be out at work, and during the nights, which were full of horror. We slept on the floor so that we did not fall in the line of fire whenever cross-firing happened. It happened quite often. On one such evening, during one of the worst cross-firing encounters, we huddled under the beds. During the day, I would peep through the grilled window of my bedroom to see what was happening in the street. Some days earlier a militant had climbed up to the first floor of a house and shot a person who hid inside.

Because we were among the few Pandit families residing in Kashmir, we feared being easily identified, especially because of how we dressed, our accent and the way we greeted the Muslims around us. My father didn't let us go out. Some Pandits grew beards, hoping not to reveal their identity when they went out in the street.

In Maharaj Gunj, many Punjabi Hindu traders continued to run their shops. My father's workplace and the locality around it were frequented by youths who had just returned from the training camps in Pakistan. They roamed around fearlessly with guns and grenades. Volunteers from tanzeems (militant organisations) like Al Umar, Allah Tigers, Al Badr, Harkat-ul-Ansar, Hizb-ul Mujahideen and JKLF roamed around freely. They would drop into the offices and ask for monetary donations to buy clothes and shoes for the boys of the tanzeems. My father was summoned a few times to militant hideouts and asked to give money for the militant organisations.

One morning, my father had just started working. My grandfather and uncles had still not reached work. There were a few workers around though. A young boy entered our office and asked my father to accompany him to meet his chief, Shabir, an Area Commander of the Al Umar group, at a mosque near the Budshah Ghat of Jhelum. My dad knew such summons were highly unpredictable. Earlier, many Pandits had been shot dead after being summoned like this. My father reached the place, not knowing what to expect. He was asked for money to buy new shoes for the 'boys'.

Some days later, a young man turned up at my father's office and asked him to accompany him to some place to meet his seniors. He was a familiar person, often seen loitering around with mujahids of that area. My father was very nervous, yet he knew there was no choice. He tried to avoid going to the hideout, but the young man was unrelenting. The neighbouring shopkeepers were alarmed and watched helplessly, but nobody had the guts to confront this youth. They knew the repercussions of interfering. All through this journey, my father was oblivious of anything around him. He was thinking of his imminent death at the hands of terrorists. He was worried for my brother and me. He avoided taking the narrow, deserted lanes and suggested that they take the main road. They reached Bohri Mandir at Bohri Kadal and he was led to a hall above the temple. On entering the hall, father saw about thirty to forty people inside. He mumbled a prayer. It was only when he turned around that he saw a group of non-Kashmiri Hindu journalists. One man walked up to my father and, very politely, asked him to give a statement in front of a camera stating that all Pandits were safe in Kashmir and they were living quite happily. But my father refused to do so. While this was going on, an acquaintance, a sixty-five-year-old Sikh trader, who was 'picked up' from Nowhatta was brought there. He was also asked to depose on behalf of the Sikh community. This person was a businessman from Amritsar who had been doing business with Kashmiri traders for decades, and made frequent visits to the Valley for collections. My father knew him as he did business with many traders downtown. The gentleman was still on the stairs of the hall when he suddenly collapsed and fell into a heap there. Everyone fled in panic.

Life was more about survival. Everybody lived in constant fear. We had no social life. Every time I came home from Pune, my mother would ask me to cover my head with my dupatta and remove the bindi from my forehead. I would never wear jeans or dresses. There was no chance of wearing such dresses unless you wanted acid to be thrown at you.

I got married in the month of October in the year 1995 at Jammu. My in-laws had left Srinagar in 1990 and never returned. In 1995, my father-in-law was posted as Principal of Government Medical College, Srinagar. He survived an attempt on his life when a bomb was placed outside his office. He resigned and joined the rest of the family at Jammu. With that ended my in-laws' dreams of living happily in their homeland. After a couple of years of my marriage, my in-laws sold their house unwillingly. I was based in Delhi but kept on visiting my family in Kashmir, despite the risks involved.

After I completed my education, I began working in Delhi and had no help, and my baby daughter spent a lot of time in Srinagar with my parents. Whenever I visited Srinagar, I stayed home all the time. We rarely went out. It was unsafe because of the political upheaval and social unrest. I would wonder how everybody at home would spend their lives holed up inside with no outings, no cinema, no picnics, no friends and relatives visiting. It felt as if we lived in a cage. We were advised to stay away from the army vehicles and bunkers as these were the targets of the militants, and one just didn't know when a grenade would be hurled at them. Only a handful of Kashmiri Pandits were left in the city. Whenever we went out to buy groceries, we were mocked. The shop owners would give us strange looks or talk to each other in a tone as if we were unwelcome entities. And Kashmir was our place, our home and our land. It had been so for centuries.

My grandmother passed away in 1996. And then after two years, my grandfather left us. While performing the tenth-day rites of my grandfather on the banks of the Jhelum at Hanuman Mandir, some militants fired shots at the temple from the Amira Kadal Bridge and the ritual had to be hastily completed.

In 2001, my parents left Kashmir forever. In 2002, the family decided to sell the business and the house. There was no point in living there in constant fear of death. The firm still runs as a flourishing business out of the same place, and the current owner has retained our name because it enjoys a strong goodwill in the Valley. We sold our house too, at a fraction of its actual cost. Srinagar's Chief Medical Officer's office functions from the house now. They have done away with the lawns, trees and flowers. It's been converted into a big parking lot for vehicles and ambulances. The outside is a pale white with brown windows. The honeysuckle bushes are all gone. It wears such a sad and tired look. CRPF bunkers surround the house. The lanes around the house are full of filth. Most of the houses, which belonged to Pandits once, have been demolished and rebuilt by the new owners. Nothing is left there which bears a trace of our existence. A part of our history has been erased. Kashmir just doesn't seem like home anymore.

The pomegranate tree still stands tall in the courtyard of my old house.

PART IV

SEASONS OF LONGING

'How often have I lain beneath rain on a strange roof, thinking of home.'
– William Faulkner, *As I Lay Dying*

24

Seasons of Longing

Prithvi Nath Kabu

The trouble started on a day when a bomb exploded at a crowded bus stop near our house in Chhanpora, Srinagar in 1990. Soon thereafter, a group of armed militants attacked a Border Security Force Camp in front of our house and killed two soldiers. When we heard about what was done to Girja Tikoo, we knew that it was the beginning of the end of our peaceful existence in Kashmir. Girja was raped by militants and sawed to death on a sawmill in April 1990. We stayed indoors for days together. Anti-India processions and anti-Pandit slogans became a routine affair in Srinagar. That April, the local Urdu daily *Al Safa* published the militants' threat and ultimatum to Pandits to leave Kashmir.

My son, Ravinder, was doing a PhD in Botany from Kashmir University. He had finished his MPhil. He insisted on staying in Kashmir, despite the threats to many Pandits, some of whom were his friends. He got a government job and was appointed as a lecturer.

As months progressed, the conditions worsened in Srinagar. Everybody from our locality was leaving. However my wife and I lingered on for some months, hoping that the situation would stabilise. But the situation deteriorated. Srinagar was put under curfew for weeks. Blasts and violent clashes between the militants and security forces wreaked havoc in the locality. It became impossible for us to lead a normal life. Then in 1991 my wife and I decided to leave too. During that time, my son was transferred to Gool Arnas. After leaving Kashmir, my wife and

I went to Jammu and took a room on rent in Parade. I had spent all my savings to construct a house in Chhanpora which was a posh locality in Srinagar. I had struggled a lot and done a lot of hard work in my youth. I was a school teacher and I loved teaching.

We were forced to leave Kashmir because the people there said they wanted Kashmir to merge with Pakistan. How could we have continued living there? We feared that if Kashmir became Pakistan, all hell would unleash upon our community. This is why we left. But my wife and I were worried for our son. We feared for his safety. He was a brave person and passionate about his higher studies and teaching.

The memory of those terrible nights in Kashmir in 1990 still instills fear in my heart. Our dignity was under threat. Many of us were persecuted just because we were Pandits. We were mocked and told that Kashmir was not for us. We lived in constant fear.

During the initial years in exile, my health was fine. But when militants killed my son, my life changed forever. My health deteriorated. I didn't know what to do. It is painful for me to remember those days.

Twenty-five years have passed since I left Kashmir. My wife and I lived as migrants in Parade for sixteen years. Now I live alone in my two-room flat in this migrant camp at Muthi. I don't visit anybody and nobody visits me. Sometimes I read. I try not to think about the past. But when I do, I have nobody to comfort me.

I grew up in Varmul (Baramulla), Kashmir. I loved watching movies. I must have watched about three hundred movies in the cinema halls in Kashmir. I was young those days and adventurous too. My favourite cinema halls were Amar Talkies, Regal and Palladium. My favourite song is: *'Yeh zindagi ke mele, duniya me kam na honge, afsoos hum na honge.'* I relate to this song. It sums up my existence in exile. It gives me solace and reminds me of the glorious years I spent in Kashmir.

I was posted at Government High School, Khoor, Pattan. My salary was eighty-five rupees a month. For me, this salary was enough to run the household. I worked very hard those days. I had also worked as a pharmacist for many years, dispensing medicines to people. I knew everything about physical ailments and treatments. In addition to teaching, I worked on salary bills in my school. I was good at accounting and billing. I was a Jack-of-all-trades but master of none.

My wife suffered a lot during her last years. She was bedridden for years. She couldn't bear the separation from her son and her homeland. She was a fantastic cook. She knew how to cook the most delectable dishes. One morning, I had an urge to eat fish and I told my wife about it. She wasn't keeping well at that time. I knew she wouldn't be able to cook.

After some moments, my wife called me and said, 'Go and bring some fresh fish from the market.' I was surprised. 'I will cook for you,' she said.

I was touched. 'For God's sake, don't take the trouble. You're not well. You can't even move,' I said to her.

She looked at me with affection and said, 'You needn't worry. Go to the market and buy some fresh fish. Don't disappoint me. The fish should be fresh or else I won't touch it.' I felt happy and rushed to the market to buy fish. I bought some fish and returned to our quarters. My wife checked the fish and found it to be fresh. I was relieved but worried how she would be able to move to the kitchen and cook. She asked me to take her to the kitchen and place a stool on the floor and light the stove. I helped her chop and wash the fish and she cooked. After an hour of cooking, she placed the cooked fish on a plate and asked me to taste it. It was the best meal of my life. I had the fish over a period of three days.

I lost my wife in 2008. She died of kidney failure. I miss her terribly. We lived together for forty-eight years.

I feel restless now and I don't roam around much. Once or twice a year, I visit my daughter for a few days. She always insists that I stay longer whenever I visit her. My daughter-in-law looked after me for two months during my illness recently. I carry sincere gratitude for her in my heart. But I don't want to be a burden on her or anyone else. I like staying in my room in this camp.

I endure a lot of pain every day. I can't walk properly. My bones are weak. But somehow I manage to look after myself. I cook and attend to my needs. I watch television and listen to devotional songs. I keep a close watch on the happenings in Kashmir. I will live my remaining life the same way I have been living during the last several years. I will limp. I will crawl. I will bear the pain. But I don't wish to be a burden for anyone. When I die it will be difficult for people to take my body on their shoulders from the fourth floor of this building. I have made arrangements for that. I will write a note so that my neighbours locate my things easily. When

I die, my neighbours shouldn't feel inconvenienced. I have kept a rope near my bedside. My neighbours can tie the rope on my legs and drag the body out. I don't care what is done to my body after I am gone. It's only a body. My well-wishers can either burn it or throw it in the river. Whenever I feel unwell, I don't bolt the door at night. Ashok Dhar, my neighbour has given me his phone number and told me to call him in case I need anything. He is the most kind-hearted person in the camp. My only saviour is the *Bhagvad Gita*. I read passages from it every day. Reading gives me strength.

I shall now tell you one of my earliest memories of growing up in Baramulla in Kashmir. In October 1947 Pakistani raiders crossed the border and marched into Baramulla. They carried guns and ammunition with them. I saw them come in groups of tens and twenties. When they entered our village, they started killing people, robbing the houses and raping women. We had not seen such devastation in our lives. The marauding raiders set fire to almost a hundred houses in Baramulla. They asked the Pandits to read the 'Kalima'. Many Muslims joined the raiders to save their lives. Fearing for their lives many Pandits read the 'Kalima' when the raiders asked them to. The terror lasted several days. Anayat Ula Kakroo was the owner of the Regina cinema hall at Baramulla. He was a wealthy man. He thought the raiders would spare him because he was a Muslim. They got information about him and went to his house and plundered it.

My father had 25 paisa in the pocket of his coat. Some raiders came to our house and searched us. They slapped my father, took his coat and the 25 paisa from its pocket. One night, Maqbool Sherwani of National Conference came to the village riding a horse, and visited all the Pandit houses and assured them nobody would be harmed. 'Pandits, don't panic,' he proclaimed confidently. 'So long as Magaz Sherwani is alive, no harm will come to you.' We felt safe. He appeared to be sincere. He had the spirit of humanity in him. We called it the spirit of Varmul. He misled some of the raiders and they lost their way. But some raiders killed him mercilessly.

To escape this persecution at the hands of the marauding raiders and save our lives, my father took us to a Pandit family in a neighbouring village in Baramulla. We stayed with them in their house for a few days.

After some days we decided to return to our house in our village. While going back to our house, we saw hordes of Muslim men and women beating their chests and wailing. 'Nothing is left of the village. The houses have been burnt. Everything has been plundered. The raiders raped our women and marched towards Srinagar,' they said. When we reached our house, we got to know that some raiders had gone to Jawahar's house. Jawahar was our neighbour. He was left-handed, doughty and tall. He had kept dried grass and wood on the top floor of his house a night before the raiders stormed our village. Jawahar had refused to read the 'Kalima' and had rushed to the loft of his house where he set fire to the wood and to his house.

After destroying our village, the raiders left Baramulla and reached Shalteng on the outskirts of Srinagar. Their mission was to take over the Secretariat. Soon, the Indian Army was sent to Kashmir to save it from ruin.

After a year, my family shifted to Srinagar to start life afresh. Little did I know that years later we would be driven out of Kashmir for good.

The most horrible day of my life was when I heard that militants had killed my son in Gool Arnas. My wife and I were living in a rented accommodation in Jammu in 1997. It was our sixth year in exile. One night in June, we heard a spiteful knocking on the door of our rented room in Parade, Jammu. I woke up frightened and opened the door. I saw policemen outside the room. 'Are you Prithvi Nath?' they asked. I nodded. 'Come with us to the police station,' they said. I sensed something was wrong. 'There has been an accident,' they said to me. They took me to the police station at Parade in Jammu city. At the police station they informed me about the killing of three Kashmiri Pandit lecturers by militants in Gool Arnas. My son was one of the lecturers. I felt numb, as if somebody had smashed my head with a stone. I waited for the whole day at the police station for the body of my son. The body reached us late next evening and the police asked us to do the cremation that very day. My son's face was not recognisable. There were wounds on his body. He seemed to have fought with his killers. My son and his colleagues had been dragged out of a bus and shot dead by militants. How am I to reconcile myself to this horror? My son was a lecturer. He was killed because he was a Pandit and a teacher. My son's guide, P Kachroo wrote a condolence letter to me sympathising with my loss and pain.

Last month, the camp-dwellers organised a trip to Kashmir. Many migrant families living in this camp volunteered to go. They asked me if I would like to go to Kashmir. It was one of the happiest days of my life since my wife died. I travelled to Srinagar in a bus. It was a strange feeling. I went to Mata Kheer Bhavani Temple at Tulmul. It is one of the holiest temples in Kashmir. I was standing in a line when I heard someone call my name. I wondered who would know me. I turned around and saw my old neighbour. We met after twenty-five years. We hugged. He worked in the telephone exchange. He enquired about my wife. I told him that she was no more. He felt sad. He showed me a piece of paper on which he had scribbled the exact month and year in which we had left our home in Srinagar. He had written all the details on it. He gave the piece of paper to me. I enquired about the other Pandits who lived in our locality. He told me he had not seen anyone in the last twenty-five years.

I have seen everything in my life—good times and bad times. I was happy even when I worked as a labourer at the Srinagar airport when it was being constructed. My family survived the tribal raid in 1947. I lost my home twice. Militants killed my son and took away everything from me. I lost my wife in exile.

What do I have now? I'm neither here, nor there. Sometimes I feel as if I am living in a cage. There is no contentment, no discontentment. When I'm depressed, I look at the image of Lord Shiva and find solace. I have two trunks full of books that belonged to my son. I read books on Lord Shiva. I don't want to be a burden on my relatives and neighbours in the camp. I have my pension. I listen to programmes on Radio Sharda.

Many years ago someone in our village had said that Kazaks (tribals from Pakistan) would invade Kashmir and plunder everything. He had also said that India would lose Kashmir.

If everybody returns to Kashmir, I will return as well. In that case, I will live my remaining life in Srinagar. But I guess it's not possible for us to return. I can't go alone.

I have only one desire now. I want to visit Varmul one last time before I die. I dream of the winters there! The summers, the autumns and the springs! I want to visit my old house there. I want to drink the water from the spring and touch the soil there. I want to see the National High School and kiss the gate of the school. I want to meet the teachers who taught me. Dina Nath Dhar, the headmaster and Janki Nath Misri were my favourites.

Even after I die, my soul will search for Kashmir and my first home in Varmul.

As narrated to and transcribed by Sushant Dhar and Siddhartha Gigoo on 25 July 2015 at Block B, Migrant Quarters for Kashmiri Pandits, Camp Muthi, Jammu.

25

The Inheritance of Memory

Varad Sharma

'Every man's memory is his private literature.'

– Aldous Huxley

Memories are traces of life which are etched in your psyche. Memories are instances, episodes, stories, tales, and experiences which get accrued every passing day. Memories can be ethereal or eerie. They are the everyday notes from life which are remembered till the very end.

I was born in the pristine valley of Kashmir in 1989 when the armed insurgency against the Indian state had just begun. Chaos and terror ruled the streets of Kashmir. Life in Kashmir was torn apart by the turmoil created by Islamic fanatics and terrorists who wanted Kashmir to secede from the Union of India.

I was born on a day when Kashmir was under siege. My father recalls the frightening events of the day when he admitted my mother for delivery in Mirza Mohammad Afzal Beg Memorial District Hospital, Anantnag. The hospital had come under severe stone-pelting by the mobs and my father and mother were horrified.

Our house was in Akura, a village near Mattan in Anantnag district of Jammu and Kashmir. *Okur*, a colloquial Kashmiri term for Akura, was our ancestral abode. It was the home where my forefathers lived. That house stood witness to the joys and sorrows in the family. Ours was a three-storeyed house.

Two and a half weeks after my birth, on 29 October 1989, our family celebrated Diwali, the festival of lights. We celebrated the festival, but not with much fervour. My father tells me that young Muslim kids from the neighbourhood also joined the festivity. That was the last Diwali which my family celebrated in Kashmir.

Right after Diwali, my father went to Jammu. He was posted as a lecturer in Government Higher Secondary School at Hiranagar, a small town in Kathua district of Jammu region. Meanwhile, the political situation in the valley was worsening every passing day. Armed insurgency was gaining a foothold. Pandits were being singled out and selectively killed. On 15 December 1989, my mother took me to Jammu. My maternal grandmother, my uncle (father's younger brother), my aunt (father's younger sister) and her daughter, who was born three weeks before me, also left Kashmir for Jammu. My uncle was given the responsibility of our safe passage to the plains of Jammu. My mother, maternal granny and I joined my father in Hiranagar. My aunt took her daughter and stayed with her in-laws who were already in Jammu. My uncle returned home to Kashmir a few days later. My maternal grandmother stayed with us a little longer and then came to Jammu where my matamaal (my mother's parents) had taken refuge after fleeing their house at Lal Chowk in Anantnag.

In 1989, the town of Anantnag in South Kashmir became the bastion of terrorist activities. Islamic fanaticism had started brewing a few years earlier. My parents would narrate how Anantnag had witnessed communal riots against Kashmiri Pandits in 1986. That time temples were desecrated and Pandits were attacked. It was a prelude to the large-scale desecration of Hindu temples and shrines which happened in the 1990s. The infamous riots happened not only in Anantnag but the adjoining towns and villages of South Kashmir—Bijebahara, Sagam, Kokernag, Akura, Pulwama, among others. It is said that Mufti Mohammad Sayeed, the then Congress leader and present-day Chief Minister of Jammu and Kashmir State, orchestrated those riots. After the riots, when Mufti Sayeed visited Akura, where a temple was damaged, a *Kangri* was thrown at him by one of the angry Pandits to express his disapproval. One of my cousins tells me that in Bijebahara, the hometown of Mufti Sayeed, a Pandit slapped him in a gathering after the riots.

January 1990 brought horror for Pandits including my family and relatives. Anti-India and anti-Pandit slogans reverberated across the entire valley. Winter was at its peak in Kashmir. Not only the mountains but also the lowlands were snow-clad. The chill in the air was as intense as the fear and trepidation that lurked in the hearts of Pandits. As the days passed, horror and disquiet among the minority Hindu community in Kashmir valley made life difficult.

Many Kashmiri Pandit families started leaving their homes for Jammu with the hope that they would return as soon as normalcy was restored in Kashmir. Some Pandit families, with hearts filled with fright, didn't leave in the beginning of 1990 hoping that everything would be brought under control by the state government. But the state government had already lost control of the valley. Armed militants and insurgents prowled the streets and had taken over several localities.

When the insurgency started in 1989, our neighbours were involved in inconspicuous activities. My grandmother would see strangers in the neighbourhood. Some of them would visit the houses next to ours and stay there. My grandmother once asked a woman in the neighbourhood about the strangers, and the woman told would that these strangers were their guests. The woman's son was working in Jammu and with Kashmir Police that time. We got to know that terrorists used to come and stay in their house at night. The house was used as an ammunition depot and a hideout for militants.

My parents couldn't go back to Kashmir for Herath (Shivratri), the most important festival of Kashmiri Pandits, which was on 22 February 1990. It was a quiet Herath back home for the Pandits. In my home in Akura, four members of my family—grandfather, grandmother, grand-uncle (grandfather's younger brother), and uncle—were the only ones left. They didn't leave in the beginning of 1990 and stayed till mid-April. On 14 April 1990, they, too, permanently bid adieu to our home.

After leaving Kashmir, they came to Hiranagar, Jammu. We lived in a rented accommodation. The small town of Hiranagar became the 'temporary' residence for my family. We were the only Pandit family in Hiranagar at the time. My relatives had taken refuge in Jammu. Jammu witnessed a huge influx of Kashmiri Pandits for which it was not prepared.

Two communities—Pandits and Dogras—came into contact with each other. The two communities were different in terms of culture, language, lifestyle, eating habits, clothing, and so on. At a societal level, there were squabbles in the beginning with the Dogras, the indigenous people of Jammu. My elders told me that there were some instances of molestation, murders, and robberies against the displaced and homeless Pandits who were living in canvas tents in camps. In the tented dwellings, there was neither safety nor privacy. Women and children suffered. Initially, the displacement of Pandits to the Jammu region was seen as an intrusion by the Dogras. With time, better sense prevailed upon the people of Jammu, and there was acceptance of the Pandits' condition.

Kashmiri Pandits were labelled 'Kashmiri migrants' by the government. Migrant refers to a person who moves from one place to another in order to find work or better living conditions. Kashmiri Pandits were no migrants but the government at that time couldn't find a better label for them. The term 'migrant' entered the political parlance of our country. The derogatory nomenclature is still used, even after twenty-five years.

Exile brought with it struggles of several kinds—of survival, of making a living, of preserving language, culture, and traditions. The old in particular got inflicted with diseases and ailments such as Alzheimer's and Parkinson's. They had neither heard of nor experienced these ailments in their lifetime in Kashmir.

Exile took a toll on my family in its very first year. I lost my grand-uncle, my grandfather's younger brother, on 4 December 1990. He died of a heart attack. He didn't marry his entire life. He would look after the gardens in our village and run a small business selling walnuts. My father recounts that *Bouji*, my grand-uncle, would cuddle me and say that he would take me to Akura. Perhaps he was hopeful that the situation in the valley would be normal sooner than later and we could go back to Kashmir.

My uncle recalls that his close friend was under the radar of terrorists in our area in the winter of 1989. His friend lived in another locality of Akura. He had been summoned to a 'terrorist court' a couple of times for 'interrogation'. The 'terrorist court' was in Numbal, one-and-a-half kilometres from Akura, in an unoccupied government bungalow which had belonged to Maharaja Hari Singh when he used to come to that side of Kashmir for trout-fishing in the Lidder river. Although my uncle's friend faced 'punishment' at the hands of terrorists, somehow he was let off after the 'trial'. One fine evening, my uncle's friend came to know that terrorists were again looking for him and this time he knew they wouldn't let him go. A dark wintry night was approaching. There was no chance of leaving Kashmir that evening. He sought refuge in our home that night. No other Pandit family was willing to provide shelter to him because of the prevailing fear of the terrorists who had warned people against helping Pandits. Running away from the village was the only way left for him to save himself from being killed by the terrorists. Early next morning, he left.

By 1991, most Pandit families had left the valley. There was no possibility of going back to their homes, at least not in the near future.

Meanwhile, struggling to make a living in Hiranagar, my uncle decided to move to Delhi. He had got a job as a teacher in Tyndale Biscoe School, Srinagar in 1989 but had to leave it because of the militancy. He found a job in Delhi and made the city his temporary residence.

We lived in Hiranagar for about seven years. I did my initial schooling from there. In 1997, we moved to Jammu. I joined a school which was run by a Kashmiri Pandit. In the school, I came to be in touch with other Kashmiri Pandit students, which was not the case in Hiranagar. I was the only Kashmiri in my school at Hiranagar. As I grew up in Jammu, I started becoming conscious of my Kashmiri Pandit identity.

In 1996, Governor's rule was lifted from Jammu and Kashmir. Elections were held in the state. National Conference came in to power with Dr Farooq Abdullah as Chief Minister.

After living in rented accommodations for years, we decided to build a house in Jammu. Our home in Kashmir was lost. There was no possibility of going back.

Our house in Jammu became a reality in October 1998 because of my father's blood, sweat and tears. My father named it *Lidder* after the river which flowed through our village Akura. The house brought some sense of settlement to the family, in comparison to the rented accommodations where we lived at the will of the landlords.

While most of the Kashmiri Pandit families left Kashmir in 1990, a few hundred families chose to stay back. The Pandits who didn't leave

Kashmir went through a different kind of struggle and endured hardships. Terrorists would extort money from them for the cause of Azadi. The fear of being persecuted always loomed over these Pandits. They had to live under the shadow of the gun. Even then, some of the Pandit families weren't spared by the gun-toting champions of Azadi.

On the night of 21 March 1997, seven Kashmiri Pandits of Sangrampora village in Budgam were killed. It was followed by another brutal massacre the following year in Wandhama village near Ganderbal. Twenty-three Kashmiri Pandits including women and children were gunned down on 25 January 1998. These massacres were a clear message to Pandits, who had left the valley, not to return to their homes. While the shock and trauma of these massacres were still fresh in the minds of the Kashmiri Pandit community, it was further jolted by another massacre in Nadimarg village of Pulwama. Twenty-four Kashmiri Pandits were shot dead by terrorists on 23 March 2003. The massacres put a lid on whatever little hope Pandits had for their return.

The health of Ammaji, my grandmother, started to deteriorate. She couldn't cope with the daily ordeals. She wasn't able to reconcile herself with the reality of being rendered homeless. She lived for eleven years after her displacement from the valley. She bid adieu to us and to her exile on 12 March 2001. I witnessed death for the first time when Ammaji died. I was there by her bedside where she lay—frozen, immovable and silent. Till then, I hadn't known what death meant. I was eleven and a half years old at that time.

Ammaji had introduced me to Kashmiri songs, especially the devotional ones. She would play them on a black-coloured cassette player every day and would hum those songs. On the other hand, Bobuji, my grandfather, would be glued to the radio set and would read the newspaper early in the morning. He kept a tab on the happenings in Kashmir and the politics in the country. He would narrate to me and my younger brother stories about our ancestral home, the family, and his own life in Kashmir. He was a Hindi teacher and had taught in several schools in South Kashmir. He would tell us how he started smoking. My grandfather's eldest uncle was the culprit. Once, he and his school friend were caught smoking by the Army personnel. They were reprimanded severely and made to rub their noses on the ground as punishment.

After Ammaji's demise, Bobuji didn't talk much. He lost interest in many things. He stopped listening to the radio, his constant companion in exile. He lost interest in the news too. Conspicuous silence would be the order of his day. He missed his wife, his companion for several decades. Sometimes I would engage him in conversations and ask him to tell me stories about him growing up in Kashmir. His eyes would light up and he would narrate stories and tell me about the times he spent in his home in Kashmir. Home was his only memory. Bobuji passed away on 23 May 2013.

The displacement in 1990 impacted three generations of Kashmiri Pandits—the old people who became disorganised and afflicted with mental disorders; the middle-aged ones who had to shoulder a lot of family and financial responsibilities; and the children who were born in camps.

In exile, we have lost touch with several attributes which define a community—the rituals, the language, the culture, the traditions. As this homelessness progresses, the sense of loss intensifies. As a community we're facing identity crises because of being thrown out of our homes.

Thousands of Pandits struggled to live while several thousands died in exile. The second page of *Daily Excelsior* is filled with several obituaries every day. We are dwindling.

When I look back at the last twenty-five years, I feel proud of my community. Pandits went through religious persecution and were branded infidels. They were called 'agents of India' and 'informants' while they were in Kashmir. The terrorists, who claimed to be the soldiers of Islam, wanted to exterminate the Pandits. But the ethnic community of Pandits survived. They have been able to build their lives despite the hardships they endured during this exile. Many were successful professionally and didn't pass on any hatred to their children.

My family and I could not visit Kashmir in the last twenty-five years. I made several attempts to visit Kashmir but none of them materialised. My parents are still apprehensive about going to Kashmir. They won't let me go alone. While talking to my mother about going to Kashmir, she told me that she would never ever forget what happened to us twenty-five years ago. She has lost all hope of going back.

Not being able to go back to Kashmir all these years, my connection with Kashmir is only through the inherited memories of my parents, grandparents and relatives. After all, an exile possesses only memories; memories of a home, and the vibrant life in homeland. The memories are the lifeline for an exile. There is hardly a day without any conversation with folks about Kashmir. We talk about Kashmir, about Akura, about our ancestors. The memory of home keeps us alive and gives us a sense of belonging to Kashmir.

In exile, each day is a yearning for home. In exile, each day brings hope of being able to go back to our lost homes in Kashmir in the future and spending the rest of our lives there. I remember the Kashmiri adage which depicts the love of home:

> *Ghar vanday ghar saasah, bar nyeber nyeray na zaanh*
> (O home! I would sacrifice a thousand houses on you and would never step out of the door.)

At present, I envisage Kashmir through two different images—one lively, the other lifeless. While the gardens, the hotels, the tourist spots are burgeoning, there are houses which are abandoned (and some are encroached upon). Some localities in the valley are lively while some are devoid of life. Some religious places and shrines are occupied by devotees while some are desecrated. Some streets are bustling while there is no hustle-bustle in others. These are the two contrasting realities in Kashmir which exist simultaneously—one depicting the relative peace and the other reflecting the toll taken by terrorism on the ethnic community of Pandits.

In my conversations with my father, I realise that there is more to Kashmir which is mysterious, yet to be explored and understood.

The longing for home, Kashmir, came out in the form of writing. Kashmir is my muse now. Remembering Kashmir through reading, discussing and writing has become an integral part of my life. I don't know when we will go back to our homes.

I have prodded my parents for a visit which has not happened yet. They never say no but defer it to the future. From their deferment, I can infer that the past comes in the way of the present. They feel betrayed. Perhaps some day we will visit the valley together—a family tour to the ancestral home, and the revered temples and shrines.

In the winter of 1999, two Kashmiri Muslims, who were shawl and carpet traders, visited us at our residence in Jammu. They were from our village Akura and one of them was our neighbour. It was our first encounter with an old neighbour after we had left the home. Their visit revived the memories of our house. The neighbour asked us whether we would return to Akura or not. They were interested in buying our ancestral house and the piece of land we owned there. My grandfather refused to sell the house and the land.

A few years later, some people from our village visited us at Jammu a couple of times on the pretext of selling shawls and carpets but with the hidden motive of buying our ancestral house. We never agreed to the selling. My ancestral house is one of the prime reasons for me to visit Kashmir now. We will never sell our house.

Whenever I remember what Pandits faced in 1989-1990, I shudder. The terrorists wanted us dead but we still exist (though in exile). I am reminded of the lines of Kashmiri saint Lalleshwari, popularly known as Lal Ded:

Asiy Aes Te Asiy Aasav
Asi Dour Kyer Patuvath
Shivas Sori Na Yun Te Gachun
Ravas Sori Na Atugath

(We have been in the past, We will be in future also
Throughout ages we have been
Forever Shiva creates, dissolves and creates again
Forever the sun rises and sets)

Justice has eluded the minority community of Kashmiri Pandits for the last two decades. Around seven hundred Pandits have been killed in the valley due to terrorism. Till date, there has neither been any judicial inquiry into the truth of the exodus of Kashmiri Pandits (to set the record straight and clear all false claims of many locals that the exodus was facilitated by the then Governor of J&K, Jagmohan) nor any convictions of those terrorists responsible for the killing of several innocent Pandits.

Both the state and central governments keep talking about the return and rehabilitation of Kashmiri Pandits without addressing the fundamental issue of ethnic cleansing. The government must address our demands by prosecuting those who were responsible for the killings of Pandits and driving the community out.

When the resettlement of Kashmiri Pandits in their homeland is talked about, the bigger question arises: where will they go? Most Pandit homes were either burned, vandalised or occupied. Many Pandits sold their land under duress. My mother's parents sold their house, which was located at Lal Chowk, Anantnag, for a very meagre amount. The resettlement of Pandits, whether in the form of townships or a separate territory, must ensure that there is no chance of any foul play. Ideally, the resettlement should be in the same houses where Pandits lived before 1990.

Apart from the return of Kashmiri Pandits, the reconciliation between Kashmiri Muslims and Kashmiri Pandits has been widely debated under the ambit of Kashmiriyat. Kashmiriyat is nothing but a charade, as if nothing happened to Kashmiri Pandits in 1989 and 1990. Kashmiriyat, if ever it existed, is a term given to the mutual and peaceful co-existence of Pandits and Muslims in Kashmir much before insurgency erupted. Kashmiriyat ceased to exist when the ethnic cleansing of Kashmiri Pandits took place.

On an individual level, Pandits and Muslims are very friendly. But at a collective level, there are differences, particularly over nationality and political affiliations. The differences manifested themselves in 1990 when most Kashmiri Muslims supported the idea of Kashmir's liberation from India. In the process, Pandits lost faith in Muslims as a community because they chose to be on the other side of the fence. Since then, there exists a trust deficit between Pandits and Muslims.

Reconciliation in its truest sense will happen when there is an acknowledgment of the wrongdoings by the majority community of Kashmiri Muslims and when separatism and Islamic fanaticism cease to exist in Kashmir.

Will Kashmir ever be the same? Will there ever be peace in the valley like it used to be before the onset of terrorism/insurgency? Will Kashmiri

Pandits ever return to their homes? Will Pandits regain what they have lost? Will Kashmiri Pandits roam around in Kashmir without any fear? These questions linger on.

As we continue to live in exile, the longing for home continues. The lines of Kashmiri poet Dina Nath 'Nadim' fill me with hope of returning to my lost home someday…

Mye chham aash pagahich, pagah sholi duniyah
(I have hope for tomorrow, tomorrow the world will glisten.)

26

Why I Established Radio Sharda

Ramesh Hangloo

I lived in a joint family consisting of my parents, my brothers, their wives, my wife and one-and-a-half-year-old child in Hangul Gund, a quiet village near the famous tourist place Kokarnag of the Anantnag district of Kashmir. We led a very peaceful life there. On the 25th of December in 1989 we sensed that something was wrong in the political and social climate of our locality. We felt uncomfortable. This discomfort gave place to fear, mistrust and even terror. We heard horrible and disturbing stories about the persecution of other Pandits who lived in the neighbourhood. This made us decide to leave Kashmir. I arranged a truck, put kitchenware, beddings and other things of daily use in it and we left for Jammu. We stayed at our relative's in Subash Nagar for some time till we took a room on rent. The joint family died like other families. Those were extremely difficult days for us.

In spite of those dark times I founded an NGO in Jammu and named it Pir Panchal. We organised and presented many cultural events in Jammu and other parts of the country. Every year in August/September we used to celebrate Kashmir Day with a view to educate the people about the cultural heritage of Pandits.

In 2007 I went to the UK with a cultural troupe. My troupe of Kashmiri boys and girls participated in the Luton Mela there. We stayed there for one and a half months. During that period I saw many community TV and radio stations, and was amazed at their excellence in spreading information and knowledge among the various ethnic communities and even entertaining them with music, songs, plays and other programmes. The English are very good at preserving their culture and heritage buildings. The various communities living in the UK are extremely proud of their cultures. They preserve and maintain them through a number of scientific ways and methods. There I met one Dr Satinder Ganjoo, who headed the Kashmir Bhawan Centre in Luton. He introduced me to a gentleman Zulfikar Ahmad who had established a community TV channel and radio station for the people belonging to his community. The functioning of these TV and radio stations inspired me so much that I made up my mind to establish a radio station for my community in Jammu. We didn't have a radio service of our own.

On 2 October 2010 eleven Pandits including some ladies wanted to cross the Line of Control to visit the Sharda temple in Pakistan Occupied Kashmir and pray there. But we were not allowed to go there. It was a disappointment.

While travelling throughout India I got a peep into the vast Indian culture, traditions and our various ways of life. In the Somnath Temple in Gujarat I thought of the vanishing Pandit culture and the Kashmiri language which was in danger. I thought: 'Let me work for my Kashmiri Pandit community so that its language and culture don't suffer.' In the meantime I heard that the government of India had opened airways for the NGOs in the country. This meant that any NGO could establish a radio station anywhere in India.

When I reached Jammu I called a meeting of the members of the NGO Pir Panchal and told them that I wanted to found a community radio station in Jammu. I requested them to let me do whatever I wanted to do about it. They agreed and I along with them started working to see our dream come true. I told them that I would name it Radio Sharda. In September 2011 permission was granted to us to establish a community radio station. We approached the relief commissioner Mr Vinod Kaul with the request to give us accommodation to house a studio for recording and an office. He was very helpful and encouraged us in this work. The government gave us two rooms at Lower Buta Nagar in Jammu for the purpose. We composed the slogan: *buziv ta khosh ruziv* (listen and be happy) because we wanted to lift the Pandits from the morass of hopelessness and despair, and give them hope and optimism. From September up to December 2011 we played CDs of Kashmiri Bhajans, Kashmiri songs and a feature called Morning Walk. We borrowed them from certain people and from Vir House at Sarwal, Jammu and Ravimech Studio at Srinagar in Kashmir. These borrowed recorded songs were broadcast from 3 to 6 pm every day. This routine continued till 5 December 2011. Then we recorded a programme in the one room which was and is our studio. On 15 December in 2011 various programmes were broadcast from 7 am till 10 in the night. We used to record the programmes in the one-room studio for seven hours each day. Then we would edit them, listen to them, satisfy ourselves and broadcast them the next day.

I was conscious that many aspects of our culture, especially the language, were on the brink of extinction. The youngsters were losing touch with our traditions and rituals. Slowly Radio Sharda evolved. This radio lays emphasis on the preservation of the Kashmiri language, identity of Pandits and the revival of age-old rituals, customs and traditions. Most of the Kashmiri Pandit youths find it below their dignity to speak Kashmiri. They speak Hindi or English to prove their 'superiority' and 'false prestige'. This applies even to the young Muslim girls and boys living in the Kashmir province and the youths living in the Jammu province. We, through Radio Sharda, try to arrest this unhealthy trend and make Pandits aware of the dangers of the death of a language. Exile should not become the cause for the erosion of culture. It should strengthen our bond with our culture, heritage and tradition. But there should be some avenues.

In Kashmir people were addicted to Radio Kashmir before the advent of TV. On 5 December 2011 Pandits switched on the radio to listen to Radio Sharda. Since then it has been entertaining its listeners and educating the young. The range of the radio is 17 kilometres. The Kashmiris living in sixty-three countries listen to it and respond. My son, Ranish Hangloo, gave us all the help he could and devised a method to connect it to the internet so that the people living in India and various countries of the world are able to listen to it.

Some of the popular programmes broadcast on Radio Sharda are:

1. Peand ta Puran: Through this programme we connect to and involve three generations of Kashmiri Pandits. The participants talk about a

5000-year-old Pandit culture, civilisation and history. We talk about humanism which is the need of the hour.

2. Vanguej Voer: It is a lively feature in which noted and established artistes among the Pandit community participate and comment on social issues. Humour, irony and wit constitute the programme. The aim is to correct the foibles and invite the attention of the authorities towards wrongdoings. It also highlights the achievements of Pandits in various fields.
3. Safar Zindagi Hund: Interviews are conducted and the listeners come to know about the lives of eminent personalities.
4. Brand-e-Kaen: It is a programme for Pandit women. Women participate in this programme and express their opinions on social, cultural and religious issues.
5. Children's Programme: Pandit children narrate stories, anecdotes, jokes, etc. in Kashmiri. They also explain Kashmiri proverbs, sayings and solve the riddles.
6. Health Awareness Programme: Doctors talk about various diseases and suggest ways and means of combating them.
7. Literary Programmes: Authors recite poems, read out short stories, reviews and discuss literary issues. Even wireless plays are enacted.
8. Interviews: Important personalities talk about their lives and work. They recreate past experiences they have been through. These interviews are informative and inspiring.
9. Kashmiri Musical Programme: Kashmiri singers entertain the listeners. Musicians play musical instruments of their choice which are recorded and broadcast.

Radio Sharda has several programmes under thirty heads. We intend to broaden its perspective and vision and improve its infrastructure. This is the best medium to inculcate good values into the minds of the young. We intend to introduce ethnic cultures of India and the world to the Pandits so that the youths rise above their personal lives and problems and digest as much as is possible. I am personally very happy about the station. It satisfies my soul and the souls of my colleagues who have worked with me.

I meet the camp dwellers every day and listen to their stories. Radio Sharda broadcasts many such stories so that people across the world get to know about what happened to us, and what we're going through even now.

27

Remembering the Unforgettable: Kashmir as She Made Me

Badri Raina

> 'The thing to do is to return home,
> And to know the place for the first time.'
>
> – TS Eliot, *Little Gidding*

The Subject that recalls an event is never the Subject that experienced that event, although they bear the same name and are thought to be the same person in public records. The making and unmaking, becoming and unravelling of the historical Subject renders us a mosaic of consciousnesses, now expressed in fragments of awareness and allegiance, now speaking from the order of a rational mind, and now rolled into one single concocted identity to combat, as it were, other subjects who take a different view of what we hold to be unequivocal. Placed among disparate and discrete contexts, we may not recall the same things in the same ways, because in a shifting world of refractions, we never know which sort of light may hit which piece of broken glass at what angle, and when.

Individual memory recall may not, therefore, be tantamount to historical writing. Such recall is rarely ever either analytic or consecutive, and its unpredictable selectivity--often beyond the control of the recalling Subject as well—does not exactly have the status of the ideological selectivity of considered case-building. It has often, in my view, been the rather simplistic presumption of subaltern historiography to make vast generalisations about historical dynamics on the basis of single-Subject accounts of vast and complex conjunctions. With one all-important caveat: the recall of Subjects who may have conjointly experienced a crisis of life-changing proportions in a moment of history are likely to be far more uniform than individual recall of shared events in normal times can or ought to be. For example, had I been a participant in the traumatic collective experience of Kashmiri Pandits in the mid-January of 1990, my recall of my own life in and relationship with Kashmir might have been shaded differently from the texture of what may follow hereunder, in the sense that I may have been persuaded to render many nuggets of memory with greater scepticism. The fact that I left the valley in normal course as far back as 1961 after receiving my MA degree from the first batch of post-graduate students at the new Hazratbal campus, and made all my many subsequent visits there as a Subject altogether removed from the immediacy of that trauma must be a factor in allowing me to recall from a vantage unburdened by the weight of what must have been a transformative experience of an all-consuming dimension and intensity. And tragedy. A fact which, however, may not falsify the verity of my own recall before or after 1961. Always assuming that the reader reposes faith in the truthfulness of the account rendered, since individual or family experiences are not available for objective scrutiny beyond some externalities of detail.

Reminiscences essentially reside in the strength of private emotion, and its truth-value has the intensity of poetic moments rather than of coldly cerebrated recapitulation. Perhaps the reason why, despite the melancholy that often accompanies the act of remembering, memory equally provides deep sustenance in the face of the brutish immediacy of times which strip our imaginative lives to suit the conformism either of the market or coercive cultural propaganda, or of both conjointly, as clearly seems to characterise our own contemporary zeitgeist. Suggestively, in many accounts of the Jewish holocaust that one has read, one has often been astonished by the gemlike moments of a transcendent humanism on behalf of the murdering oppressors recalled in these accounts by the victims—moments that are instrumental in preventing them from going over to an irretrievable, life-long bitterness of hate and loss of faith. The plural archive of memory, then, can yield healthy antidotes to fixated moments of pain and betrayal. If only, of course, we dig deep enough and with a will to look for gold among the dross. None of which may be understood as an argument to condone any past that may have left deep scars on us but as a caution not to accord a timeless and essentialist status to such an interregnum in the life of a much vaster and many-sided narrative. If I may cite what has come to be a favourite couplet of mine: *'har cheez nahi hai markaz par, ek roz iddhar, ek roz uddhar/ nafrat se na dekho dushman ko, shaayad who mohobat kar bethe.'* (Nothing is ever too long at the centre, now here and then there/ look not with hate at the enemy, who knows he may come to love.)

As I begin to recall my own life in Kashmir from a desiccated and deracinated metropolitan existence, however conducive to the 'ease of doing business,' and however ready-to-hand with instrumentalities of success, a sense of sensuous richness wells up within me, much like one of those proverbial springs that dot the valley of Kashmir. In contrast to the hard metropolitan visage, street or next door that speaks a hard language of fear born of distrust, a fruit of mellow wisdom reaches out to me from a seemingly inexhaustible storehouse of caring, stoic and gushing all at once. A storehouse that also includes the knowledge of great pain and destitution, but, as I remember, almost always defeated by the power of love. What hard and concrete histories informed those destitutions and that pain is the subject of historiography and intellectual analysis, as I have tried to say earlier, such as underscores with varying interest and emphasis the constitutive public and political forces and issues which are in many ways still with us, both as Kashmiris and inhabitants of the divided sub-continent. Since this is a book about memories, the episodes in my stream of recall must be understood in separation from those impersonal conundrums which we deal with in the cold light of reason or ideological predilection as Subjects-in-History rather than as units of life that imbibe emotionally and imaginatively the sap or poison of everyday experience.

Kargil, 1946

I see two long parallel rows of rooms on the breast of a slanting hillside (Qurba Thang I think it was called) with a long and wide compound in between, and a monstrously huge jet black Chanthan mastiff, called

Thumboo, with a maw big enough to take in one large chappati in a single go, tied to a sturdy stake with chains of mail. In one room I see two or three full-bodied dressed-up lambs hanging by strong iron hooks from an iron rod, frozen and ready to be portioned for a meal; and in two other rooms with mud floors loads of potatoes and turnips buried under the earth to keep fresh in natural cold storage as it were. Temperature, fourteen degrees Celsius below freezing, as those who came to visit father, a lordly Naib Tehsildar, would tell him. My naughty older brother sticks his tongue into a prison bar next to father's office, and cannot get it unstuck.

And I see a child of five (me) dressed in a flowery gown, riding the tireless back of a hunk of a man, Ghulam Mohammed, with a constant supply of dried apricots—my favourite to this day—and pistachios from the copious depths of a pocket in his long robe, tied typically with an impressive sash across the waistline. I recall that this gentle giant (one of the half dozen "naukars" I would imagine) was available to me without let or hindrance, and I remember, with a mystic wonder learning to release an arrow at a czaga—an artfully carved circular design in wood meant for an archery target. And, with equal wonder, I see him, and his labouring and lowly peers—all Muslims or Buddhists, it now strikes me—make a little chimney of a hole in the ground, leading into a bamboo pipe-stem from whence they drew on an incandescent lump of lit-up tobacco in the hole for a hefty drag of satisfaction. However I might strain to recall, I cannot remember any of the naukars ever complain or make a demand, or raise their voice, night or day. These were not days when one actually saw money changing hands somehow. A few years further into my life I knew that most provisions came into the house on credit, and the one payment that the naukars seemed assured of were two meals of enormous servings of rice every day. I wish I could recall whether or not Ghulam Mohammed and the others actually got any servings of meat with the rice, although I have the impression that some fatty entrails were kept for them. Fat was thought to be necessary for insulation against the freezing cold. They were used to eating some distance away from our gaze. I think I also remember my father in khaki riding breeches on a Zanskari horse with a sayees (horse-handler) walking alongside with a maarpech (an elaborate artifice of a hookah with a decorative pipe going on for a length in aesthetic coils with a wooden mouthpiece at the end—a possession that denoted class apart from being an instrument for smoking) ready-in-hand for the Naib Sahab. And flashes of horses with tied up tails and adept riders pass my sight, as me and my older brother are shown the first glimpses of a polo match in progress. I recall that my older brother was to lose two of his front teeth subsequently from the inadvertent strike of a benthu—the sturdy stick with a solid horizontal base for the striking of the polo ball. Throughout my father's tenure in Kargil, my brother and me never were sent to any school, because I imagine there were no schools there. But I do remember being given our lessons by teachers who came home.

I was to learn later in life that these delicious vignettes of privilege were indeed aspects of a feudal way of life wherein a few with ownership of land, or officers thereof, lorded it over the army of dispossessed ones as masters over serfs, if not slaves. Come 1947, and father receives transfer orders to move to the capital city of Srinagar. This is just a few months before tribals from the new dominion of Pakistan come raiding Kashmir. I wish I had asked father sometime later in life whether his transfer was a fortuitous one or whether he had actually asked for it. I am inclined to think the former, because, as we grew up, we knew father to be a cussedly incorruptible civil servant, and one whose disinterest in acquiring assets of any kind often frustrated kith and kin, and who actually not only lost a prize piece of land around Nishat Bagh because he lost the papers pertaining to it—just as he also lost, would you believe it, his service book—but, in the early sixties sold our ancestral house for a paltry pittance. This Micawberish parent, a Sufi at heart who seemed most content when seated with folded legs deep in meditation, left us thus a legacy of aversion to avarice for which I salute him and cherish his life

And thus I remember a caravan of mules strapped firmly to loads of household effects, our family on horseback with a number of sayeeses leading the convoy across the now level, now steep face of an endless mountainside en route to Srinagar. And I remember the awesome roar of a river we cross—Suru I think it was called—which literally carried in its cataclysmic flow boulders as big as little hamlets; and I remember the near-fatal event upon one of the rope bridges when my mother's horse tangled his hoof and she came falling, only to be adroitly held and rescued by, of course, the sayees on foot.

Srinagar, 1947–1961

I see a two-storeyed house topped with elegantly shingled wood, chock-a-block with a clan of a family—ours and those of my father's two sisters with some eleven cousins, among them just one preciously pampered daughter, second oldest to boot. I recall a great and persistent restiveness among the brood of parents, and snatches of testy conversation about the scarcity of provisions. India has been partitioned, and the main lifelines into the valley have been closed off. I have vivid recall of glistening slabs of pink rock salt, a commodity that was sourced in the territory now called Pakistan and now off limits to Kashmir; I cannot think whether or not there was an alternative source of salt available then, but it was clear that this beauteously pink stone seemed suddenly more valued than gold; indeed, with shortage of currency, I hear talk of paying gold ornaments for salt, if only one could procure the pink stone from whatever source possible. I remember Ali Mohammed, no longer called naukar, fretting over the calamity, and willy-nilly procuring supplies from I cannot recall where, and happy that the clan has salt.

I see crowds of people trooping down the main arterial road of the city, a hundred yards from our house, carrying colourful banners shaped into ploughshares, marching to the rousing call of '*Hayo lukav, tuliv albaen/ pagah aasev hakumat saen.*' (Raise, O people, the ploughshare raise/ Tomorrow will begin our ruling days)—historic and memorable invocation by the secular and anti-feudal political force in the state, the National Conference, that has been offering resistance to Princely Dogra rule for nearly two decades—all of that understood by the likes of me in the later years of our growing up. Just as we were to understand how the Dogra ruler had refused to declare allegiance to either Dominion between the time of the Partition and last week of October, 1947, leaving the state in a limbo of sorts in the interim; and how the National Conference, led by Sheikh Mohammed Abdullah, the Sher-e-Kashmir, had rebuffed Jinnah's insistence that a 'Muslim-majority' Kashmir join a 'Muslim' Pakistan.

And then the gunfire! I hear those bursts of sound even now as clearly as I did then. The raiders from across the dividing line between the new India and the new Pakistan were, in fact, firing away from as close to the city as the airport at Domudar Vuddar and Shaal Teng. I see disciplined rows of volunteers with wooden replicas of dummy rifles deftly slung over their shoulders marching down the road with the ploughshare banner and two alternating slogans piercing the air: *'hamla aava khabardar/ hum Kashmiri hein tayaar.'* (Beware, O enemy/ We Kashmiris are ready for you), and *'Sher e Kashmir ka kya Irshaad/ Hindu, Muslim, Sikh Ittehaad.'* (What is the call of the Lion of Kashmir/ Oneness and unity among Hindus, Muslims and Sikhs) All along the route of their rousing march, the volunteers are greeted with garlands and food items. Within our clan, my only female cousin knits away furiously, putting together a sweater a day, to be given to the volunteers against the gathering chill.

Among the traumatizing snippets of hearsay that fill the cities, towns and neighbourhoods of unconscionable brutalities perpetrated by the raiding marauders, also arrive accounts of bravery and selflessness of ordinary Kashmiris that help bind people across communities into a steely resolve to fight off the aggressor. Among these a very personal story from the village of Wadipora, three miles north of Handwara where I was born, where my nurse maid of old, a six-footer of a snuff-chewing amazon, and Nambardar of the village, all by herself dared a truckload of raiders and prevented them from abducting a young Pandit woman who happened to be the daughter-in-law of my father's guru. The only Pandits who lost their lives lost them to the raiders, and innumerable ones owed theirs to their Muslim Kashmiri compatriots. We were to learn in later days that within the Jammu Province, however, many thousands of Muslims were killed in inter-community rioting. The Dogra Maharaja, in the meanwhile, pushed to the wall with no recourse to fight the raiders, signed the Instrument of Accession towards the late hours of October 26, thus rendering Jammu & Kashmir legally a part of the new Dominion of India. Had a referendum on the issue been held then, not more than a double digit of Kashmiris may have disavowed that Accession. But that sort of thing belongs to the writing of history, and I am not writing history in this very personal reminiscence.

We shift finally to our ancestral house in Safa Kadal—a pretty three-storey structure with a compound large enough for domestic cricket, which was the rage even then, although in a civilised and knowledgeable sort of way. I am sent off to a miserable school nearby for just over a year so I can take the matriculation examination. Monsters as they seemed then, I now have memories of two of the most outstanding teachers one could ever have had the good luck to be exposed to, one a Pandit, the other a Muslim. Unbelievably blunt jokes passed between the two, testifying to a culture of humour and understanding wholly absent for long years now in the valley and everywhere else as well.

As part of the matriculation examination—I am now all of thirteen and a half years of age—I am asked to go to the Sri Pratap College for Physics Practical exams. As the tasks are handed out by a professor in an unforgettably spotless white turban of a petite size, I notice that I have not a clue to any of the tasks. The school I went to had only a broken puppet or two and a cracked titration flask in the science laboratory, and we had actually not done any experiment except in theory. So there I am, moping on a stool in a corner of the examination hall, doing nothing, when the Professor comes over and asks me what might my problem be. I remember shedding some tears; at which he checks out my name on the roster, and asks me if I knew so and so, namely, my own father. How gleefully I must have said I did. The exams ended without my moving a little finger, and I was declared to have scored some forty of fifty marks! It happens that when my father was operating as Land Settlement Officer, he had one day noticed a man with a spotless white turban pacing restively outside his office. Upon enquiry, he was told that this was Professor Yusuf who taught Physics at S.P. College, and who had been greatly harassed by some unscrupulous land sharks over long years. At which Father-Micawber called him in, looked through his papers, and signed his decree of possession. End of story! Professor Yusuf was to teach me Physics once I entered college, and I do not recall one single day when he was either absent or late to class. It was routine with him to say 'Pakistan is my birthright' but can I say I knew a more secular Kashmiri then; I cannot.

I attend college three months after formal admission on account of an attack of typhoid. The Chemistry class is with the handsomest of all men

I have ever seen, one Mir Nassarullah Khan, son-in-law of the Kashmir Prime Minister, Bakshi Ghulam Mohammed. I am also told kindly that he has one of the largest hearts in town but also a temper to match. He calls out the rolls, and finds that I am there for the first time. At which he steps down from the podium, walks over to the front row where I am, asks me whether I might be Avtar's brother, to which I say I am on shaking legs, whence I receive the gentlest of slaps, but a slap nonetheless, across my left cheek: 'How dare you be falling ill if you are the brother of the college cricket captain,' says he. Soon enough, Nasser Sahab was to come to be an admirer of mine, and when in 2004 I made an application for the grant of a Permanent Resident Certificate, he wrote for me an endorsement which for all practical purposes told the government that if I was denied the government would be an ass. I cannot tell you, and I have not told him, how I love the man.

At home, mother is often to be seen conversing avidly with Ashae Maal, a woman of sterling warmth and nobility, who, although she comes ostensibly to sift and winnow the rice over long afternoons, is actually my mother's thick-as-thieves companion. And my father finds renewed camaraderie in an old Muslim acquaintance, Qadir Dar, who is friend, guide, and helper, all in one, and whom we never tire of lampooning for saying 'any morning' instead of 'early morning.' Our evenings are devoted wholly to playing cricket with abandon in the copious Eidgah grounds which seem to hold a hundred teams all at once. I remember sweating so copiously that none of my shirts seemed to last for more than a week. At college, soon enough, I become captain of the cricket team, as of the university and state teams in the years to come, and a reign of unmitigated joyance begins—under the aegis and kind eye of teachers and mentors, chief among them the one and only Noor Mohammed Keng—a gentle giant who nurtured us like the proverbial jinn-on-call. Never once in the course of my career, either as student or sportsman, do I recall a single reference even of the most oblique kind, to anybody's communal identity, or knew of any favours or damage done to anyone on account of his or her communal identity. As I write this, I am all too conscious of how mythical an averment this must sound today among some sections of Kashmiris. I am also aware now that among some others, the whole notion of a secular Kashmiriyat has come to be discredited.

While at college, we do all the things that young people normally do or ought to do; we go to cinema houses, fight to obtain admission tickets in heroic ways, insist on seeing the most forgettable of movies; we sing popular film numbers on picnics, or riding bicycles to college or university, and in mushy college functions, we recite romantic and revolutionary snatches of poetry from impressive archives, and we lampoon Mullahs and Pandits to our heart's content, and we adore Mirza Ghalib. At the university, I am often asked to sing a Ghalib ghazal on days when the poet is commemorated—some antecedent reason, perhaps, that I will go on in later years to attempt an English transcreation of selections from the poet of poets, remembering with a glow what the late Qazi Aahab of the Mathematics Department used to say: 'If you don't know Ghalib, please do not call yourself literate.' As I recall these things, I am unbearably saddened that neither song, nor poetry of the kind I speak of, nor cinema, nor carefree camaraderie of other sorts—those healthy forms of heartbreak and dissipation without which youth must seem mere abstraction—should no longer be visible among young people who now are in educational institutions in the valley. A stern and fear-ridden pall of austerity seems to have descended on young lives who seem sunk either in books or in prayer, or in a suggestive adulation of Allama Iqbal much of the time. One is obliged to conclude that this telling relegation of Ghalib owes to his having been a secular modernist and an imbiber to boot. One rarely hears young scholars speak of such poets as Sahir Ludhianvi, Ali Sardar Jaffri, Kaifi Azmi, Majaz, or Manto, not to speak of that magnificent bevy of poets from Pakistan, such as Habib Jalib, Ahmed Faraz, Fahmida Riaz, Kishwar Naheed; only of Faiz Ahmed Faiz occasionally. This suggestive shift in cultural preference seems topped by the dropping of the habitual—habitual to Kashmiris, that is—Persian appellation for God, 'Khuda' in favour of the Arabic 'Allah'. I may add that as I write I remain engrossed in conversation over these issues with a clutch of brilliant scholars in the valley, apart from actually being there off and on to give lectures on issues pertaining to theoretical aspects of literary/cultural studies. I have indelible memories of the footfall of habitual walkers by the riverside (over the 'Bund') and of the sight of the twilight melting in streaks of gold into the Jhelum, and of the swooping swish of swallows as they take off to find nesting for the night, and of the hauntingly captivating voice of Raj Begum or of the lilting sonority of Tibat Baqal's sufiana qalam singing wafting from the other bank of the river from a distant radio set. And as I return via Bar Bar Shah, the limpid peals of bells from the Ram Mandir, and of an answering azan, as it were, in a spiritual cohabitation of utter serenity and soulfulness.

My memory of these years is also replete with our idyllic visits to Wadipora where my father's guru ji has his house by the side of a crystal stream with a village school next on a plot of green where his eldest son is a teacher. And then further we go to the shrine upon a hill in a deep forest off the village of Bhadrakal, a shrine that guru ji dreamed of one night and set out to find and establish. In a forest full of walnut and pine, with no habitation in sight, our clan is for long years the only one that visits. Logwood huts are occupied that give shape to a long stretch of green atop a stream that flow some distance beneath; elaborate hearths also of horizontal logwood are set up for mass cooking. The slaughtering of the lambs is done some distance away, and a bevy of helpers from guru ji's village are on hand to look to every need—Hindu and Muslim. The romps up and down the hill to the shrine is still so vivid that I can in my mind's eye locate the features of every section of the climb and descent. During the Durga Navmi festival pretty little stalls are set up full of trinkets for women and children, and our adorable advocate uncle from Handwara (we call him Maam) teaches us how to put up plays for the occasion with snippets of Shakespeare and the like. He rules Handwara like a proverbial hegemon, and his most trusted and intimate family relationship was with the late Abdul Ghani Lone, who worked with him as a lawyer's agent and partner. His house is a beehive of visits, of raucous conversation, and of interminable sessions of Bridge, at which we get to be adept at a very tender age. Money and meat simply flow, and Muslims or Pandits do not exist—only friends. The clan has a permanent tongawaala, Shabana, more family than most, and trusted to take us from anywhere to anywhere on the toughest of calls.

Delhi/Kashmir, 1961

Since the time I left the valley for employment at Delhi University, never more than a couple of years have passed when I have not been there again—not to do the tourist spots but to be among the people I love and from whom I continue to receive love in return. I will now recall just a few episodes that remain deeply embedded in my being as inseparable parts of a legacy that has helped to shape so much of my cultural and political life.

1966: After our marriage the previous year in Delhi, my non-Kashmiri wife, Shashi, also an English teacher, and I visit the valley. One of the first things I have to do is to take her to meet Mohammed Sultan who runs the King Boot House in Lal Chowk; an old buddy of my eldest brother, he is indisputably not just a member of the family but a rather fearsome mentor to boot. We sit for an hour over the inevitable kebab from the nearby Standard restaurant, after which I ask to take our leave. Never in my life until then have I received the hiding I receive from him—all because I have the temerity to ask to go before he has said I may, since I am meeting him for the first time accompanied by his noush (daughter-in-law).

The harangue over, he takes us to the nearby Maisuma market, buys a fully embroidered shawl for a sum of seven thousand rupees, drapes it over my wife, and speaks one word—go. I am still in tears after all those many years.

I am with my childhood friend and brother, Sikandar and my dear Bhabi, Zahida, at his university house on Campus; Zahida serves breakfast but I notice she does not have a serrated knife to cut bread with. During the day I visit the Big Boss shop on Residency road. At the end of an hour of beseeching that I be allowed to pay, I come away with the requisite knife without paying a penny. Soon after, the four of us are shopping around the polo ground market; wanting to buy some *bakir khanies*, Zahida leads me into the Gen bakery; I ask for the stuff and am told these are sold only on order. Noticing a whole lot lying around, I speak in Kashmiri to make my pitch. Result: I leave the shop with a car full for which I make no payment, although I pay for the other stuff I have bought. At lunch hour one day, I ask Zahida for curd; she says we do not have any. I offer to go down to the Hazratbal market to buy some. She dissuades me. I go nonetheless to the very dairy woman they routinely buy from. I tell her I am a Pandit come after some years wanting curd. She gives me a long look, and gets up, although the curd pot is in front of her. When I ask her where she might be headed, she says '*Balai lagai, czhe dimya ye dodh?*' (Upon your head, do you think I will give you the curd you see?) She goes in and brings back curd of a quality I have not seen in a while. Back at home, Zahida is wonderstruck, because she has never seen such curd either. Sikandar and Zahida are Muslims but not naturally Kashmiri-speaking!

Another year I am in need of a private vehicle to be able to take the kids to visit a few places they have not been to in a long time. I go to ask an old Pandit friend who has always lived and done business in the city. He claims he just gave the one he had to someone, but that I might go to Mirza to find one. Mirza happens to be Mohiuddin Mirza of Mirza Carpets, but once a young cricketing aspirant whom I had selected for the team. I visit him, and a breakfast of tabakmaaz soon ensues. He is mortally offended that I am making a request rather than an order. Soon I have a hefty van at my disposal which stays with me for the whole three weeks, and when I leave his premises the tank is first filled to capacity at the pump he has on his grounds.

Speaking of vehicles, some years later when I am at the university for a seminar, a dear one who teaches at the department of English, likewise makes available a car which I not only drive around for a few days but also manage to mildy bash one evening. This most generous of human beings I know has not forgiven me for doing the repair job without her knowledge. I am not even mentioning the meals that have been cooked for me, the gifts I have received, and the myriad other intimacies that have been bestowed upon me whenever I am in the valley.

It may be instructive to conclude this very rambling account with a telling confession made to me by two erstwhile colleagues at Delhi, both of whom are now no more. Of the two Quereshis, one taught Urdu and another Political Science at Delhi University. Not being able to manage Professorships here, they decided to accept offers from Kashmir University. Inside of a year, the two gentlemen were back. When I asked them why they chose to return, this is what they said to me: 'You never told us it was not enough to be Muslims in Kashmir; and that you also had to be Kashmiri.'

28

An Imaginary Identity

Nikhil Koul

> *This Kashmir is a veritable heaven on earth. Nowhere else in the world is such a country as this. Mountains and rivers, trees and plants, men and women, beasts and birds—all vie with one another for excellence. I feel a pang at heart not to have visited it so long*
>
> – Swami Vivekananda (in a letter to Indumati Mitra dated 1897; translated from Bengali)

The year 1989 was a year of many upheavals that changed the world forever. November of 1989 was marked by the fall of the Berlin Wall and the Shilanyas of the Ram Mandir at Ayodhya. There was also a transition of power in the country and much-needed economic reforms were on the anvil. However, there were also events that ruptured the idea that the future was going to be utopian for the coming generations. A land once called 'Paradise on Earth' was turning into hell for its indigenous people. The minority community of Kashmiri Pandits went through a genocide and exile of an unparalleled scale in their 5000-year-old history, which owing to the slant of history and diluted by concurrent events, would not qualify to be included in the hall of shame of humanity.

As a Kashmiri Pandit, the treasures I possess are memories—memories of a life that could have been lived in Kashmir forever. Fantasies of an idyllic existence in a continual tradition of what my forefathers lived through with only the small acclimatisation of that banality called 'modernity'. I have invariably tried to reconstruct in my memory what it would have been to live in 'our' Kashmir. Memories are frail and fragile. What stokes a dream also invokes a nightmare. The nightmare of an exodus—gory and irreversible! Even from the imperfect conjuring of what I recall of my childhood, I still remember that fateful night on which we left our house. So much so that I surprised my father once when I drew and described our house, almost accurately, a decade or more after the exodus, when he had assumed that I had forgotten all about it. How could I have forgotten something that was a part of my identity? I was told that our house had been reduced to rubble like almost every other house of a Kashmiri Pandit in the valley. A few years later, the last vestige of that memory was handed over when this priceless familial possession was passed over to a new keeper as the house was being sold. A few property papers, photographs and memorabilia of a generation, which was stuck in a time warp—all that one could get as a discount offer for the price of parting with that thing you once called 'home'. But the story was not over. My late grandfather owned a shop in Kashmir. It was near the Habba Kadal post office. The shop, owing to various circumstances hasn't been sold which gives me a good feeling that my ties with Kashmir are not completely severed. Whenever I meet my fellow Kashmiris and I have to locate myself as a descendant or relative of someone they know, I immediately prop up the reference to the shop near the Habba Kadal post office. This is my personal connect to Kashmir now, part of my identity of sorts, which no one can take away from me, at least not now or in the near future.

I was born in Srinagar in 1986. The three-and-a-half years of my childhood spent in my own house, among my own people is a fond memory now. The twenty-five years that have passed in exile have been witness to an incessant struggle to preserve this memory. In the summer of 1989, the house was abuzz with wedding preparations for my grandfather's only daughter—my aunt. Some time after the wedding, weeks before we were forced to migrate, my grandfather, afflicted with Parkinson's disease and confined to his bed, passed away. Retrospectively, I assume that in a way, he was fortunate enough not to witness the ravaging of his home and city. He had stopped going to the Hari Parbat ever since the disease had taken its toll on him. The devastation around would have been an unbearable sight for him. I can never forget the horrifying events of the night on which we left our home in Kashmir. There were slogans everywhere. People were screaming that Kashmir would be free from India. Pandits were being attacked. Hundreds and thousands of Pandits were leaving their homes and going away to unknown places. Many didn't even know where they were going and for how long they were going to be away. But by leaving Kashmir, they were saving their lives.

We too left for Jammu, which became the temporary unofficial congregation ground for the exiled people of Kashmir. People also landed up in other cities depending on where circumstances took them. I remember someone telling me of his exodus experience of watching a journalist interviewing an exiled Kashmiri Pandit on National TV in 1990. The person had said: 'Will the day of the apocalypse be any more horrific than this?' The *Kalyuga* for Kashmiri Pandits had begun. The slow disintegration of the culture and society of the natives of Kashmir had been set in motion. We lost everything, but we were not to be decimated so easily.

In the early 1990s, life for everyone was an ordeal. We were also overcome by a sense of denial that everything was going to be fine soon. It has been more than a quarter of a century now. We continue to live in exile. Who would have thought?

During the early days in exile, my uncle, like many others, would go to the Relief Commissioner's office to complete the necessary paperwork for our family. Soon after short stays at Jammu and Delhi, my parents and I rented a place in Panipat where we resumed our daily life. Even though I had very little elementary schooling in Srinagar and I had joined school in Jammu for some time, my formal education began in Panipat. Those were the days when India had embarked on a journey towards globalising its economy and industry. Malls and shopping complexes were to arrive a decade or so later. The popular slogan that we heard on the streets of Panipat at that time was 'Panipat ki chauthi ladayee. Anpadh sarey karein padhayee.' (The fourth battle of Panipat has arrived. All illiterates should start reading and learning now). The allusion to Panipat's history as battleground for three important wars in the history of modern India was unmissable. Here were we, the people who had witnessed seven forced exoduses from Kashmir, the final one in 1990 eventually detaching us completely from our land. How I wish to tell my old Panipat friends, that Kashmir and Panipat are almost even now on the scale of Padhayee and Ladayee, yet how very different still.

In 1994 when my parents were transferred from their offices, we bid Panipat goodbye and settled in Jammu where I joined my old school once again. The joy of meeting old friends whom I had left earlier in Jammu was a juvenile elation almost like a homecoming of sorts. It felt like I had returned from an exile, if only momentarily.

Jammu, famous for being the city of temples had its modern city-like evolution almost in tandem with the Kashmiri Pandits who lived there. The sweltering heat of Jammu was an assault on the exiles who were used to snow in winter but on the whole the attractions of the city were and still are delightful imprints of the innocence of growing up in a small place. With time, the constant pain of exile was gradually overpowered by the concerns about our future. An interesting activity that the Kashmiri Pandits have done without fail all these years is to read the obituaries in *The Daily Excelsior* to learn about the deaths of friends and relatives. Ours is a small community, a dwindling one. Almost everybody is related to one another. In the early days of exile, no one knew the whereabouts of their friends, neighbours and relatives unless they lived in the same camps. People would come to know of their relatives and acquaintances by reading obituaries. Kashmir is the land of Shaivism where Lord Shiva (the lord of destruction) was revered the most by Pandits. During the initial years in exile, death was the only topic discussed in the camps.

In Jammu, we stayed in rented houses. A common refrain my mother used to hear from our landlady was: 'Koi kaise apna ghar chhod sakta hai? Hum aapki jagah hotey toh hum apna ghar kabhi nahin chhodtey.' (How can one ever leave one's house? If we were in your place, we would never have left). This used to upset my mother very much. I used to feel bad too whenever somebody made a mockery of our condition out of plain ignorance. Later in life, this observation struck me as a template of behavioural science. Nobody can know what we went through during our last days in Kashmir. No one can feel our pain. No one can ever imagine the circumstances under which we were forced to leave our homes. We were faced with death.

In Jammu and in other places, the generation that was exiled in childhood had to struggle for an education. One positive aspect of studying in Jammu was that we interacted with students of different backgrounds and cultures. We shared varied influences which metamorphosed the Kashmiri Pandit society in a particular way. For most part of the last century, the Kashmiri Pandit community could be described as a community of teachers and clerks. After our exodus in 1990, the youth started taking up technical courses like engineering in order to find secure jobs and support their families. It was insecurity which made them go out of Jammu to study. They wanted their parents and grandparents to get out of the migrant camps and live in better conditions. Housing became the biggest challenge. In the camps, people lived miserably without basic facilities. Thus, securing degrees became a necessity. This rat race of sorts has impacted the community at a different level. We ignored the arts and humanities. The focus on other subjects declined to a great extent. No one went for higher education, as was the norm in the past when we lived in Kashmir. These days parents send their kids to tuitions in all subjects and encourage them to pursue technical education so that they can get jobs in multinational companies and eventually be able to buy their own houses elsewhere. Clearly, we have undergone a huge change as a community. Scholarship is no more valued as it used to be by our forefathers in Kashmir.

Personally, I feel that the loss of property and home is still a minor issue. The loss of ties to a land of spirituality, Sufism and scholarship is a major matter. Those who are familiar with the history and culture of Kashmir can understand this. Most of the Kashmiri Pandits sold their houses and land in prime locations at less than one-tenth of the real market price since most of them had with the passage of time, disassociated themselves from the material value of it. Some of them sold their houses to pay for their children's education and make ends meet during difficult times in exile. My elder brother and I were the only ones in our family who were against selling our ancestral house in Kashmir. That the Kashmiri Pandits would attach importance to education more than land and material assets highlights an important facet of our ethos. The tradition of intellectualism, knowledge and scholarship was rooted in our ethos for centuries. Ours is an ethos which celebrated the arrival of Adi Shankara and Swami Vivekananda to Kashmir. We would fell proud to be the descendants of Abhinavagupta and Anandavardhana and that we still follow the teachings of Gopi Krishna and Swami Laxman Joo. These influences have remained with us for years. Kashmir has also been home to the 'Sharada Peeth'—Sharada, the Goddess of learning, is associated with Saraswati. The Sharada Peeth (in Pakistan Occupied Kashmir) is in a ruinous state now, much like our own houses and temples in Kashmir. The rites of passage of Kashmir valley, across its entire span of history, transcend from its inception as being a centre of learning to becoming a playground for terrorism, militancy and Islamic fundamentalism. Kashmir, once a seat of learning is now a hotbed of Islamic fundamentalism and terrorism where Pandits, the indigenous people of Kashmir, are not welcome to live and flourish.

Almost everyone I know now visits Kashmir on special occasions. The only benefit of that is everyone gets to update the image of a Kashmir we have reconstructed in our minds with trivia and information from travellers.

I have not been to Kashmir ever since we left that fateful night. The thought occasionally crosses my mind. But how can I visit my birthplace as a tourist? How could I possibly ask someone to show me where my street or home is? How would that feel?

I see Kashmir as an image now. I find 'home' in the stories and anecdotes my parents tell me. I discover and see Kashmir in the narratives of my elders. Kashmir exists in the memory of the young people of my generation. This memory is borrowed from our elders. Kashmir also exists in old Hindi films, songs, books and documentaries. It also exists in live television debates, reportage, newspapers and blogs. It exists in the hearts and minds of Kashmiri Pandits. We carry our Kashmir within us.

Survival is important; it was necessary for us to leave Kashmir that ominous winter in 1990. Otherwise we would have been killed. We went through a terrible season of killing in 1989 and 1990. The massacres of Pandits continued even later.

My earliest memory is of my grandfather's brother telling me of his experiences in school and college. He was Principal of the Islamia High School in the eighties and quite naturally, had many stories to tell, particularly about the academic and intellectual aspect of life in

Kashmir. The overwhelming fact that most of them were funny and humorous was surprising since most involved teachers who were extraordinary disciplinarians and even fanatical hardliners. Some were men of authority while others were political leaders. Such respect for an intellectual life in an age preceding the internet era was something that was fascinating to me. My grandfather assured me that Kashmiris would not miss an opportunity to lampoon and satirise anyone, be it a teacher, a headmaster or even a vice chancellor. Attributing nicknames was an old habit for the Kashmiris.

Back in those days, exotic locations in Hindi cinema meant Kashmir. The word for a film in Kashmiri was Khel—a sport. My grandfather's brother (the eldest member of our family) remembers the films of Robert Taylor and Deborah Kerr. Watching late night shows of David Lean's *The Bridge on the River Kwai* and Anatole Litvak's *The Night of the Generals*, commuting on a bicycle, when films were to be watched in cinemas only. Even the first Hollywood heartthrob and the personification of masculinity—Rudolph Valentino excited and charmed his audiences in 1921 with a Kashmiri love song in *The Sheik*. From the early 60's *Yeh chand sa roshan chehra* in *Kashmir ki Kali* and *Pardesiyon se na ankhiyan milana* from *Jab Jab Phool Khile* to *Kitni khubsoorat yeh tasveer hai, yeh Kashmir hai* from *Bemisaal* in the 1980s—songs of love, romance and heartbreak inevitably found their muse in Kashmir. Filmstars from Bombay would line up to throng the Mughal gardens and lakes of Kashmir. My father recalls seeing Rekha hide in a shop in Srinagar to escape from pesky fans. In the ensuing chaos and frenzy, someone broke the glass panes of the shop by hurling watermelons at the windows. Years before that, Prithviraj Kapoor visited Kashmir and in a session at Kashmir University ended up mimicking some of his contemporaries to the loud applause of the students. Some of these anecdotes and images about film stars and film shootings can be seen in hotels, shops and bars in Jammu. In Srinagar, there are no cinemas now. All cinema halls were destroyed during the advent of militancy in the 90s. Muzaffar Ali's *Zooni* starring Dimple Kapadia and Vinod Khanna could not be completed. The film, which was described in *The New York Times* as a Cecil B De Mille production, was unfortunately never completed though some shooting had taken place in Kashmir in 1989. *Zooni* was the love story of Sultan Yusuf Shah Chak and the poetess Habba Khatoon, known as Zooni to her people. Interestingly, Habba Kadal, the place I identify myself with was the place Yusuf Shah Chak had constructed for Zooni. It is possible that some lovers used the Habba Kadal Post Office as a rendezvous during the eighties. But in 1989, love was the last thing on anyone's mind. The descent into darkness for Kashmir could not be prevented, not even by the Indian security forces who were brought in to curb the militancy and terrorism. Cinema and cinema halls became one of the earliest collateral casualties of the reign of terror that engulfed Kashmir in 1989-90.

After 1994-95, when the political and economic landscape of the country had changed, young Kashmiri Pandits started lapping up the opportunities that were offered to them. While most went to cities like Mumbai, Pune, Delhi and Chandigarh, many also chose to stay back.

After the exodus, Kashmiri Pandit exiles faced tremendous hardships. The old people struggled to live in camps. Children and youngsters didn't know what to do with their future. Lives of women were torn asunder. Human relationships were shattered. Over the years, people found temporary settlement in different cities. Community events, marriages, births and deaths brought the exiles together. Yet sometimes, a strange kind of disconnect seeps in, perhaps because of a realization that we could have lived and flourished in Kashmir. A woman wearing a *dejhoor* in a mall in Mumbai or a person talking in broken Kashmiri to his mother from a different country is enough to bring out that faint smile of being a Kashmiri and connected with one's roots and moorings. I would very much like to believe that even a hundred years of exile would never erase this feeling of being a Kashmiri.

I have spent almost a major part of my life in the city of Jammu. Sometimes I wonder about the losses and gains we have incurred during these years in exile. Did I lose something permanently or did I gain anything at all? Many Kashmiris have adopted a pragmatic stance towards our exile. They seek solace in the fact that we got a better deal with job opportunities, education and career. In a sense we escaped religious persecution and extermination. In Kashmir we lived in constant fear, terror and conflict. Even now we are emotionally vulnerable. Perhaps it's the effect of the twenty-five years the community has spent in exile. This state of mind can be best described by Mirza Ghalib's couplet: *'Ishrat-e-*

qatra hai dariya mein fanaa ho jaana; Dard ka hadd se guzarna hai dawa ho jaana.' (The destiny of a water-drop is to merge in the river; when pain exceeds the limits, the pain itself becomes the medicine). We made peace with our nomadic life. Exile has become our history now.

Social media has been instrumental in getting Kashmiris to interact with one another more frequently now. This is a welcome change from the status quo that existed earlier. My interactions with fellow Kashmiri Pandits, especially those with whom I share a friendly relationship has been very congenial and full of warmth. I understand that the shared sentiment of being exiled creates a bond whatever may be our worldview regarding the future of our existence. Many Kashmiris are now global citizens and netizens living in metro cities, living a life like everybody else—jobs, family and the daily grind. There are also others who live in a township for the displaced Pandits in Jagti, near Nagrota (Jammu) where even the basic amenities are not accessible to families and life is not as easy as it is for those who live in their own houses.

About a year ago, a friend of mine who is a prominent author and translator from Bengaluru and a long-time supporter of Kashmiri Pandits met a young Pandit over lunch and described him as a bright; distinguished guy with two PhDs and patents. This person had seen his sister gangraped by Islamists and his parents brutalised while he was tied to a tree. He had fled to Delhi. In the words of my friend, the Pandit youngster didn't harbour any bitterness and worked hard to get an education. His dream is to reclaim the Kashmir of his ancestors. These are stories which need to be told. Stories of atrocities committed upon us and our day-to-day battles for survival!

As I write this, the western world is commemorating the 70th anniversary of the liberation of Auschwitz death camp from the Nazis. Across the world, the horrors of Islamic State remind me of the events which took place in Kashmir in 1989-90. The Yezidis of Iraq have become the new Kashmiri Pandits unfortunately. The massacre and the atrocities are the same, only the victims are different. The deliberate silence of the usual suspects whom Martin Niemöller shamed at the time of the Third Reich has become so normal that it seems institutionalised now. This deliberate silence adds to the woes. In 1985, on the 40th anniversary of World War II, the former mayor of West Berlin and the then President of the Federal Republic of Germany Baron Richard von Weizsäcker, a member of the conservative Christian Democratic Union (CDU) said, 'There were many ways of not burdening one's conscience, of shunning responsibility, looking away, keeping silent. When the unspeakable truth of the holocaust became known at the end of the war, all too many of us claimed that they had not known anything about it, or even suspected anything. Whoever refuses to remember the inhumanity is prone to new risks of infection. Seeking to forget makes exile all the longer; the secret of redemption lies in remembrance.' These words need to be uttered more frequently than ever in India in the context of the Kashmiri Pandits. These were words spoken by a political leader to his people. The same people and country about whom Hans Frank, Governor General of Poland and Nazi Germany's Chief Jurist, just before his hanging at Nuremberg pronounced, 'A thousand years will pass and the guilt of Germany will not be erased.'

There is an eerie silence among the liberal intellectuals of India about the genocide and massacre of Kashmiri Pandits. We are a forgotten entity in our own country. There is no talk about justice and redressal. There is no attempt to address our concerns and aspirations.

There are no farewells beyond endurance. There is always a promise of return. After all, my old Habba Kadal Post Office ID is still in my possession. It will always be my identity. I survive on it, thought it may seem imaginary. But it is real. It binds me with my ancestors. It binds me with my history. It tells me who I am.

I do not know what the future holds in store for Kashmiri Pandits. Will it depend on the kindness of strangers or the mills of our Gods? But I assume optimistically that something comforting is awaiting us. Our exile will end and we will see good days.

John Adams wrote to his contemporary Thomas Jefferson almost two hundred years ago, 'You and I ought not to die before we have explained ourselves to each other.'

We forget, we perish! We remember, we survive!

29

The Day I Became a Tourist in My Own Home

Minakshi Watts

'People's memories are maybe the fuel they burn to stay alive.'

– Haruki Murakami, *After Dark*

My father was in Kashmir throughout the turbulent years, the militancy era. He was adamant that if death were to come he would rather die in Kashmir than in exile in some unknown land. We lived in constant fear of his safety. In his letters, he did not write much about what was happening in the Valley. When he came to visit us in the plains during winters, he would just sit huddled in a warm blanket. This expulsion from my homeland, Kashmir has cost me so much. What pains me the most is how it changed the lives of my elders—my parents and grandparents. The lives that once sparkled with adventure and laughter now carry unspoken stories of a gruesome past, the wounds, and the atrocities inflicted upon us by militants and their sympathisers and supporters.

I left Kashmir in 1988. The summer of 1988 was the last time I went there with a feeling of going home. After that, my father discouraged me from going there. He would send me letters to let me know that he was well but the political conditions were not. It meant waiting for the summer holidays in college and not having anywhere to go! My classmates would go to their homes and I would not. I would count the days and months. Months became years. It was unimaginable that I would ever speak those words: I haven't been home in a year/ two years/ four years ... twenty years.

My most cherished memories are of my grandmother's home in Sopore. A tall and beautiful woman with blue eyes, Tarawati, my grandmother was grace, authority and gentleness personified. The pherans she wore in winter fascinated me. The kitchen and the rooms in her house were full of treasure hidden in boxes and nooks and corners. Now all these are just memories. Everything else we once possessed in Kashmir is gone—our home, our land, our belongings, our comfort. Everything was taken away from us. Even our claim of belonging to Kashmir!

'What should I get for you from Srinagar?' said my mother. Her voice came through the telephone. Hundreds of miles separated us. She knew there weren't any easy answers to this question. For twenty-five long years, I lived in the hope of returning to my roots. My mother went to Kashmir, but as a tourist. She telephoned me and spoke of Kashmir. She asked me if I wanted anything from our own land. A memento, perhaps! Something to keep in my house in Delhi, where I live now. Something to remind me of Kashmir, and the fact that I belonged there!

What could I tell her? To bring back the very essence of the Kashmir that ran in my blood? To bring back the smiles, the happy times! The sound of tongas in Jamia Qadim, Sopore, taking me home to Dadi! Or the aroma of fresh mint and walnut chutney from the kitchen of our University Campus! Or the sound of my father's whistle, as he went about cooking for the two of us! That life could not be relived; it could not be brought back, ever.

She knew I had no answers, as she sighed and said, 'Minnie, it has changed so much, I cannot look at the old places without feeling sad.'

That year, in 2006, I felt my ties with the Valley of Kashmir would never be revived again. The strife had gone on for two decades, with no solution in sight. Initially Kashmir was a state in turmoil. When we were forced to leave in 1990, it was a battleground. Kashmir was ravaged during the long and painful years of strife between several militant groups and the Indian security forces.

I strove to forget my past, my association with my land. The land of my birth wasn't mine anymore.

In 2009 we planned a road trip to Ladakh through the Manali-Leh route. It was going to be an adventurous road trip, taking us through some of the highest mountain passes in the world. The idea was to return via Srinagar. We kept a close watch on the law and order situation in the Valley. On the fourth day of our trip, we knew we would be going to Srinagar. The road from Rohtang pass was so bad that we did not want to come back by the same route. By then, we had also mustered enough courage to go to Srinagar. The Amarnath yatra was on, and there were reports of yatris going safely, and how the tourists were going to Kashmir in huge numbers that year and that the Army had the situation in control.

My travels had taken me to the southernmost tip of mainland India, the westernmost tip, and most of the eastern side. I regretted that my kids had not been to Kashmir, the land of their mother's birth and childhood. Suspense began to build as we began our trip to Ladakh. My father never left Kashmir, and he was still there, working as the Principal of a Training College run by one of his acquaintances. He kept telling me not to come through Srinagar. The Shopian incident involving the alleged rape of two women, Asiya and Neelofar, had set the Valley on fire. There were reports of stone pelting, clashes with armed forces, hartals and curfews in the interior parts. I was scared of going there, since I wasn't sure of how volatile the situation was. My friends in the Valley kept telling me that everything was fine, and that these incidents were part and parcel of Kashmir's reality and daily life. They said, 'This is normal.'

Finally, after twenty-three years, I began to think of my lost home in real terms.

– 'I'll show you the room I grew up in.'

– 'You must show us the apple trees you climbed!'

– 'We must take the kids on a shikara ride!'

– 'I wonder if we can see my friends who are there.'

Our plan to be in Srinagar was for only a day. Any more than that wouldn't be a good idea. Despite my frustration, I had to give in. I wanted to go to many places to see all those nooks and corners that had haunted me for years. When we entered Kashmir, an incongruous signboard announced: 'Welcome to the Paradise on Earth.'

The drive through Kargil revived memories of the TV coverage of the war with Pakistan. Gun battles, the number of dead being brought back from high peaks on horseback. That year, Kargil and Kashmir were boiling flashpoints between India and Pakistan. I had read reports of villagers being asked to vacate their houses for fear of becoming casualties of the incessant shelling and firing from across the border. As we drove into Kargil, I noticed the profusion of wild pink rose bushes all along the hills bordering the road. Blue gushing streams and tributaries, blue skies, a lush green landscape. It was so difficult to imagine that a war had devastated the entire place. An Army memorial was being constructed to commemorate the lives lost in the Kargil War with Pakistan. Construction of the memorial was on in full swing. An Army officer took us back in time as he recounted the story of that war. Tiger Hill, the helicopters, officers who dared and fought, people who were heroes and martyrs at the same time.

I had never been to Kargil in my childhood. It was strange to see it now. It brought back the horrid memory of insurgency. I was shocked to see the signboards alongside the road in Kargil: 'Beware, the enemy is watching you.' It was eerie. I looked up at the peaks facing the road and wondered who was watching us. What feelings separated us from them?

It was difficult not to feel the rush of patriotism on that road dotted with pink rose bushes, gorges and memorials for the soldiers who had died during gun battles at various spots.

As we drove into the valley of Kashmir, the sight of apple orchards and poplar trees made me want to stop and take pictures. How could I explain this feeling to my children? To anyone who has not been away from home for so long? We stopped at a place near green paddy fields so I could breathe in the air, feel the breeze rustling the Chinar leaves. A small stream gurgled parallel to the road, hidden by tall grass and cut off from us by barbed wire. Armed men in camouflage uniforms stood vigilant in the shade of the Chinar trees. For a moment, I felt uneasy. Was this the Kashmir of today? Watched, armed to the teeth, cautious, wary? It felt strange to see convoys of Army trucks and jeeps escorting the Amarnath yatris to and fro from Sonmarg. It was equally strange to feel happy on seeing busloads of people shouting Jai Amarnath! Bhole Shankar ki jai ho!

Where did these feelings come from and when? I was here as an outsider. A tourist, nothing else!

My first sighting of the Hari Parbat and Shankaracharya hills in the distance broke me. I shouted in joy as I saw these two hills at a distance.

It was like meeting my parents after two decades. My children were at a loss to understand this sudden outburst of emotion. I could do nothing but cry and smile at the same time, while telling them what these hills had meant to me when I was growing up in Kashmir. My husband understood. He told them softly, 'It's mama's hometown.'

Home is a strange thought. I don't have 'my home' now. A part of my soul is lost forever. I can't call any other place 'my home'.

There is one recurring dream I have. In the dream I see familiar people in a vast cremation ground. They are wearing white-coloured robes and looking at the burning pyres of dead exiles. I see a murky lake nearby with funeral pyres along the banks. I see a boat that is sinking, unable to stay afloat.

Over the years, the yearning to relearn a lost language and culture has grown intense within me. I find myself reading about Sharda Ma, of Sharda lipi and the Sri Yantra. I realised how closely we are connected to the Sri Yantra. That is the symbol engraved on the pedestal at Sharda temple (now in Pakistan). We must reclaim the Shaivite traditions of Lakshman Joo.

My son often tells me: 'Generations from now, people will say, "Once upon a time in the valley of Kashmir there lived a set of people called the Pandits. Now only a few exist. No one knows what happened to others."'

30

The River of My Lost Village

Jai Kishan Sharma

In the 1990s, if you asked the displaced Kashmiri Pandits where they belonged, they would simply say – the lost village. Even after 27 years, I have not forgotten my village. Not a day is spent without remembering my village which is situated on the banks of a river. Ever since I named my house in Jammu 'Lidder' (the name is also inscribed on the nameplate adorning the gate of our house here), I constantly keep thinking of my village, Akura (fondly called *Okur* by Kashmiris) and the river 'Lidder' that runs through it.

With every breath I take, my memory sparkles and comes alive. It is infinite. It flashes in front of me like an application of a smartphone.

The story of Akura is part of our folklore. Once upon a time, an idler discovered a way to earn his livelihood. In a busy market in Srinagar, he pretended to be blind like the poet Surdas, and started begging. One day, a frequent visitor to the market sensed the beggar's deception. In order to find out the truth, he went near the beggar to offer him alms. When the beggar extended his hand, the visitor placed a hot copper coin upon his palm. The beggar was shocked and he dropped the hot copper coin. Then he quipped:

Chukhye bhatt te Okryuk,
Chukhye musalmaan te Hokhryuk,
Chukhye sikh te Traluk.

(If you are a Kashmiri Pandit, you must be from Akura.

If you are a Kashmiri Muslim, you must be from Hakhura.

If you are a Kashmiri Sikh, you must be from Tral.)

This tale serves as a reminder to the society to be cautious of fraudsters. Yet it also shows us the importance of giving them an opportunity to mend their ways.

Akura was called Akurath (which means Mushak) in ancient times. According to an old Hindu legend, when Shiva was going to the Amarnath cave to recount *Amar Katha* to Parvati, he asked his son Ganesha to leave his vehicle, Mushak, at this village. Gagar (Mushak in Kashmiri) is a common surname among Kashmiri Pandits.

I remember the Ganesha idol in Akura. The mice would emerge out of nowhere and partake of the offerings placed before the idol, particularly when Pandits chanted *'Vinayakaya Ekdantaya…Herambhaya Akurathaya…'* during festivals. During my childhood, I vividly remember my elders taking me to the Ganesha temple in our village and they would invoke several Gods and Goddess. My elders introduced me to the rituals which were codified by Rishi Logaksha.

The Martand temple was a glowing symbol of our area from time immemorial. The remarkable temple finds mention in historical texts ranging from ancient to medieval times like the *Mahabharata* and the *Tuzuk-e-Jahangiri*. Our ancestors preserved and protected the holy sites of the Pandits, such as the Martand temple. Our Horoscopes are also important sources of our folk culture as they not only indicate the coordinates of an individual's birthplace but also pinpoint the exact geographical location. There is a vivid description of the place of my birth in my horoscope prepared by our family's priest. It is in the Sharada script – *'Kashmir mandle, Anantnag pargane, Martand paadmule, Akura graame niwasmaan.'*

Our ancestors inscribed their rich folk history on the walls of their houses. This is a kind of recording of history which is handed over from one generation to another. Certainly, this history has fallen silent because of terror but it is definitely not dead. In the words of Gurudev Rabindranath Tagore, the barks of the trees reveal signatures and imprints of several centuries.

Lidder, the river that runs across Akura, is cited in Vedic as well as modern Kashmiri literature. *Martand Brahman*, a branch of *Krishna Yajurveda*, speaks of Lidder as follows:

Yavacchaka vahti ch,
Nadi ledri toiy poorna,
Tavat swarge vasti,
Satatam shradhkrut suryakshete.

(As long as Chaka and Lidder are filled with water and keep flowing, till then an individual, whose death rite is performed at Martand, will find place in heaven.)

In *Rajatarangini*, Kalhana describes Lidder in the eighty-sixth shloka of the first *Taranga*. He says that the king Lava donated a village named Levar (present day Liver village in Anantnag district) situated on the banks of river Lidder to Brahmins.

My river's history is older than *Rajatarangini*. The archaeologists have found signs of early man in the Lidder valley. That's why early man in Kashmir has been termed 'Lidder man'.

Kashmiri poet Arjan Dev 'Majboor' in his epic *Padya Samyik* embodies the lineage of the Lidder:

Pyov lyeder bathis pyeth thanye aadam.

(An early man emerges on the banks of Lidder.)

Majboor further describes Lidder as sister of the river Vitasta (Jhelum) which meets her at Harnag (Khanbal):

Harnag nakhe samkheyas vyeth,
Dwon byenen pooshin maye te sath.

(Lidder meets Vitasta near Harnag.
May love and faith remain between two sisters.)

Another Kashmiri poet Dina Nath 'Nadim' also mentions the river Lidder as a female character in his opera *'Vitasta'*.

Protected by the Martand temple, the mountain ranges of Bhargshikha on the east, and the trout stream on the south, Akura's boundaries are marked by the Lidder. Lidder, which is 73 kilometres in length, has two sources – one is the Kolahoi glacier in Sonamarg and another one is the Sheshnag lake which is a high altitude lake located en route to the Amarnath cave. The river flows through Akura and then traverses Nanil, Aang-matipora and finally meets Vitasta at Khanbal. Slanting downwards at the Akura bridge, the river is divided into two streams, dissecting the entire area into two parts.

Filled with natural beauty, the banks of Lidder are calm and holy. Every morning, there was much hustle-bustle on the riverside. Till the 1960s, when there was limited means of transport, people would walk along the banks of Lidder in order to reach Anantnag town.

I remember an old man treading the path along Lidder and stopping under a willow tree for rest. He was carrying an umbrella to which several things were attached such as chillum, copper pot, tumbler and many small packets of charcoal, kehwa leaves, almonds, cardamom, black pepper etc. He reminded one of Chinese travellers like Fahiyan and Hsuan Tsang. He would prepare kehwa for himself and then, proceed for his destination.

Sometimes, in the evening, the meadows adjoining Lidder would host *Bhand Pather* (traditional folk theatre of Kashmir) where artists from Akingam or Wahthore displayed their talent. I can't forget the jester's (*Bhand*) comic antics that made people laugh, when the troupe performed the sentimental and maudlin folk drama *Aknandun*.

Bhand: Toiy chiwa paye, yi wayun woul kya chu wanan?

Dholwol: Doumb buzye te doumb buzye.

Shehnaiwol: Komaan? Komaan?

Doyum Shehnaiwol: Noman. Noman.

(Jester: People, do you know what is the musician trying to tell with his instrument?

Drum beater: I will roast intestines.

Shehnai player: Whose? Whose?

Another shehnai player: Theirs, theirs as the jester points his bamboo stick towards the spectators.)

Hearing this, the spectators watching the *Bhand Pather* would start laughing.

In old times, many saints frequented the banks of Lidder for meditation and spiritual enlightenment. In the 1960s, when I was very young, my uncle would take me to a saint who lived in a small tent on the riverside. The saint's name was Swami Hiranand. He had perhaps come to our village for meditation along with his followers.

The valley of Lidder would attract filmmakers as well. *Sargam* film's 'Dafli wale dafli baja' song or *Laavaris*, starring Amitabh Bachchan and

Zeenat Aman, was shot here only. While seeing the shooting of films, young boys and girls would dream of going to Bombay and dream of becoming actors. Even I have seen those dreams.

Lidder river and Akura village have been an indelible part and parcel of my life. Forgetting this would mean forgetting my own existence.

Timeline

1389–1413: Sikandar 'Butshikan' of the Shah Miri dynasty of Kashmir destroys several Hindu and Buddhist temples, forces Hindus to embrace Islam, and levies jizya (poll tax) on those who refuse to convert. The first exodus of Hindus from Kashmir takes place. Those Pandits who don't leave or refuse conversion are tortured.

1586: Kashmir is annexed to the Mughal empire under Jalal-ud-Din Muhammad Akbar. During Aurangzeb's rule, the repression of Hindus resumes.

1753: Kashmir comes under the Afghan regime under Ahmad Shah Durrani; the religious oppression of Hindus continues.

1819: Maharaja Ranjit Singh, founder of the Sikh empire, defeats the last Afghan governor of Kashmir and annexes Kashmir. The end of the Afghan rule concludes a long dark era for the Hindus of Kashmir.

16 March 1846: Treaty of Amritsar signed between the British Government and Maharaja Gulab Singh, the ruler of Jammu and Ladakh. The British Government transfers Kashmir to Gulab Singh for an indemnity of 7.5 million rupees. The princely state of Jammu and Kashmir is formed.

13 July 1931: Uprising against the Dogra ruler Maharaja Hari Singh in Jammu and Kashmir. Muslim rioters attack Kashmiri Pandits. Their shops plundered and property destroyed. Many are killed.

14–15 August 1947: Partition takes place. India achieves independence from British rule. Pakistan is formed. Maharaja Hari Singh indecisive on Jammu and Kashmir's accession to either India or Pakistan.

October 1947: Tribal militias from Pakistan's North-West Frontier Province supported by Pakistani Army enter Kashmir in an attempt to occupy it. Hundreds of Hindus and Sikhs are killed and women raped.

26 October 1947: Maharaja Hari Singh, ruler of the princely state of Jammu and Kashmir, signs the Instrument of Accession. Jammu and Kashmir becomes part of Union of India.

27 October 1947: Indian Army enters Srinagar to counter the aggression by tribal militias.

August 1967: A Kashmiri Pandit girl named Parmeshwari Handoo abducted, forcibly converted to Islam and married off to a Muslim in Srinagar. Pandits protest.

February–March 1986: Anti-Pandit riots take place in South Kashmir (in Anantnag and adjoining villages). Kashmiri Pandits are attacked and several temples desecrated.

14 September 1989: Lawyer and Vice-President of J&K State's Bharatiya Janata Party, Tika Lal Taploo is shot dead by militants in Srinagar.

4 January 1990: *Aftab*, a local Urdu newspaper, publishes a press release issued by Hizb-ul Mujahideen, set up by the Jamaat-e-Islami in 1989, to wage jihad for Jammu and Kashmir's secession from India and accession to Pakistan.

19 January 1990: Jagmohan arrives to take charge as governor of Jammu and Kashmir. Jammu and Kashmir Liberation Front and Hizb-ul Mujahideen use public address systems at mosques to exhort people to defy curfew and take out protest marches. Anti-India and Anti-Pandit slogans are heard across Kashmir. Mass exodus of Kashmiri Pandits starts.

14 April 1990: *Al Safa*, a local Urdu daily, publishes a press release issued by Hizb-ul Mujahideen warning all non-Muslims to leave Kashmir within 36 hours or face death. (About half a million Kashmiri Pandits leave Kashmir by the year-end and take refuge in Jammu, Delhi and other parts of the country.)

21 March 1997: Militants kill seven Kashmiri Pandits of Sangrampora village, Budgam.

25 January 1998: Militants massacre twenty-three Kashmiri Pandits, including women and children, in Wandhama village, near Ganderbal.

23 March 2003: Twenty-four Kashmiri Pandits are shot dead by terrorists in Nadimarg village of Pulwama.

2015: Thousands of Kashmiri Pandits are still living in migrant settlements in and around the Jammu province of the J&K state. Many are now scattered all over India, waiting to return to their homeland, Kashmir.

Contributors

Kaul, Neeru is a Kashmir-born bio-researcher currently working in Delhi. She is an activist and writes stories and poems.

Dhar, Sushant was one-and-a-half years old when his parents were forced to leave Kashmir because of militancy and political turmoil. Currently, he is doing his PhD in Microbiology from Punjab Agricultural University, Ludhiana. He divides his time between Ludhiana where he studies and Jammu where his parents live in a camp for Kashmiri Pandit migrants at Muthi. His short stories have been published in the *Indian Short Fiction* magazine. These days, he is writing a memoir on his growing up in exile.

Raina, Meenakshi was born in Jammu but spent her childhood in Kashmir. She migrated to Jammu in 1990 and did her Masters in Management Studies from University of Mumbai. She worked as a lecturer at a college in Jammu before migrating to Canada in 2001. Her debut novel *The Divine and the Destiny* was published in 2013.

Watts, Minakshi is a Kashmir-born poet and painter. She lives in Delhi and runs a literary journal.

Hangloo, Ramesh studied Journalism from Bharatiya Vidhya Bhawan in Jammu. He was a columnist for the *Daily Excelsior* for nine years. He is the founder of Radio Sharda, a community radio service featuring programmes on Kashmiri Pandit culture and affairs.

Shant, Rattan Lal, Dr has published four short story collections in Kashmiri, two poetry books in Hindi, literary criticism in Kashmiri and Hindi, six translations and three monographs. His plays have been broadcast and telecast over All India Radio and Doordarshan. He was awarded by the Jammu and Kashmir Academy of Art, Culture and Languages, Sahitya Akademi and Central Hindi Directorate for his contribution to literature. He is also the winner of President's gold medal and Soviet Land Nehru Award. He lives in Jammu.

Wakhloo, Namrata was born and brought up in Srinagar, Kashmir. These days, she is working in a multinational company in New Delhi.

Koul, Nikhil was three-and-a-half-years old when his parents migrated from Kashmir because of militancy and political turmoil. He is interested in literature and cinema. These days he lives in Noida, Uttar Pradesh.

Pajnu, Susheel works as a video analyst for the Board of Control for Cricket in India (BCCI) in Jammu and Kashmir. He represented J&K in cricket at various junior levels. He did his Masters in Computers from Pune. He lives in downtown Srinagar, Kashmir.

Chowdhury, Kundan Lal, Dr was born in Srinagar, Kashmir. He is a physician, poet and writer. He did his fellowship in Neurology from London. He is the author of four books, *Of Gods, Men and Militants*, *A Thousand-Petalled Garland and Other Poems*, *Enchanting World of Infants*, *Faith and Frenzy* and *Why Don't You Convert?* His book *Enchanting World of Infants* was conferred the Best Book Award for Excellence in Literature by the J&K Academy of Arts, Culture and Languages. These days, he lives in Jammu where he practises medicine.

Gigoo, Arvind taught English Literature in various government degree colleges of the Jammu and Kashmir state till 2003. He is the author of *The Ugly Kashmiri (Cameos in Exile)* and the co-editor of *From Home to House: Writings of Kashmiri Pandits in Exile* (HarperCollins India, 2015). He translates Kashmiri poems and short stories into English. His book reviews and articles on various issues are published in newspapers and literary journals. At present, he lives in Jammu.

Waguzari, PL is a translator and reviewer. He lives in Jammu.

Ajit, Adarsh is an author, a columnist, reviewer and translator. He lives in Jammu.

Kishore, Pran is an award-winning writer, playwright, theatre director, painter and filmmaker. He has written several plays, documentaries, serials, telefilms, movies and other programmes for radio and television. His creations for television include *Gul Gulshan Gulfam*, *Saye Deodar Ke*, *Noor Jehan*, *Manzil*, *Ghuttan*, *Safar Wapsi Ka*, *Razahonz (Swan of the Swamps)*, *Junoon*, *Baaz*, *Mashal*, *Patjhar*, *Baghi* and *Sapnon Ka Saudagar*. He received the Sahitya Akademi award for his Kashmiri novel *Sheen Ta Vatapod*. He also received several awards from Jammu and Kashmir Academy of Art, Culture and Languages for outstanding contribution to drama and theatre. He received the National Award for Broadcasting for his radio play *Ta Vyeth Rooz Pakan*.

Pandita, Kashi Nath, Dr is the former Director of Central Asian Studies, University of Kashmir. His book *My Tajik Friends* was translated into Russian. He has translated the Persian books *Baharistan-i-Shahi* and *Tofatul-Ahbab* into English. His writings have appeared in *The Pioneer*, *The Tribune* and *The Economic Times*. He was a human rights activist at the UN Human Rights Commission at Geneva and European Parliament in Brussels. He has travelled throughout Europe, US, Central and Southeast Asia. He is the recipient of the Soviet Land Nehru and Saadi Awards.

Saraf, Bushan Lal retired as the Principal District and Sessions Judge. He was forced to leave Kashmir because of militancy and now lives in Jammu.

Koul, Maharaj Krishen Koul Naqaib is an occasional writer. He lives in Jammu.

Pandit, Ashok is a wildlife photographer who lives in Shalimar Garden, Uttar Pradesh.

Kaul, Pradeep worked for two leading newspapers published in Jammu. He is known for his work on the two Kashmiri philosophers, Kshmendra and Abhinavgupta. He is interested in Sanskrit literature and Indian philosophy. He lives in Jammu.

Dhar, Rajesh is an occasional writer, and runs his own higher secondary school in Jammu where he teaches English.

Zutshi, BL is an MPhil from the School of International Studies, JNU, New Delhi, and taught Political Science at various government degree colleges of the J&K State. He retired from the M A M (Camp) College, Jammu. From 2008 to 2012, he was Senior Consultant to the University of Kashmir. He is a social activist and the president of an NGO named Sabzar. He lives in Jammu.

Zutshi, Indu Bhushan is a post-graduate in journalism and writes for various newspapers and journals. He lives in Jammu.

Raina, Badri, Dr taught English Literature at the University of Delhi for over four decades. He was a Fulbright Scholar and Fulbright Fellow in 1972 and 1984. He is the author of *Dickens and the Dialectic of Growth* (University of Wisconsin Press, 1986), *The Underside of Things: India and the Word/A Citizens's Miscellany* (Three Essays Collective, 2012) and *Raina's Ghalib* (Writers Workshop, Calcutta, 1984). His poetry, translations and other writings have appeared in several magazines and newspapers in India. He lives in New Delhi.

Dhar, Tej N, Dr was Professor of English at Kashmir University and Himachal Pradesh University, Shimla. He was also Professor and Dean Faculty of Arts, Asmara University, Fulbright Postdoctoral Fellow, University of Southern California at Los Angeles, and Fellow, Indian Institute of Advanced Study, Shimla. Currently, he is Senior Fellow of the Ministry of Human Resource and Development, Government of India. He has authored *History-Fiction Interface in Indian English Novel* and *Under the Shadow of Militancy: The Diary of an Unknown Kashmiri*. He has edited fifteen books. His critical essays have been published in various journals in India and abroad. He lives in Faridabad.

Kabu, Prithvi Nath was born in 1934 in Baramulla, Kashmir. He worked as a teacher in Kashmir. He left Kashmir because of militancy. These days he lives in the migrant camp for Kashmiri Pandits at Muthi, Jammu.

Pandita, Sagar lives in the migrant camp for Kashmiri Pandits at Muthi, Jammu. He is twenty years old and is pursuing a degree in Computer Applications. He wishes to go abroad.

Dhar, Vishali lives in the migrant camp for Kashmiri Pandits at Muthi, Jammu. She is pursuing a degree in Information Technology from L.E College, Gujarat.

Sani, Santosh Kumar is a PhD in Economics from the University of Jammu. He has carried out extensive research on the exodus and exile of Kashmiri Pandits, including the economic impact of their migration. He teaches at a college in Jammu and lives in Jagti, a township where hundreds of displaced Kashmiri Pandits have been rehabilitated.

Gigoo, Siddhartha left Kashmir in 1990 due to militancy and political turmoil. He studied English Literature at Jawaharlal Nehru University, New Delhi. He is the author of two books of fiction, *The Garden of Solitude* (2011) and *A Fistful of Earth and Other Stories* (2015), which was longlisted for the Frank O'Connor International Short Story Award 2015. His short story *The Umbrella Man* won the Commonwealth Short Story Prize 2015 for Asia. He has also written and directed two short films, *The Last Day* (2012) and *Goodbye, Mayfly* (2015), which were selected for several international film festivals. Two books of his poems, *Fall and Other Poems* and *Reflections*—written as a student—were published by Writer's Workshop, Kolkata. His writings have appeared in several literary journals. He lives in New Delhi.

Sharma, Varad was born in Anantnag, Kashmir and grew up in Jammu. His family was forced to leave Kashmir in 1990 due to terrorism. He holds a Post Graduate Diploma in Management from Institute of Management Technology, Hyderabad and a degree in Mechanical Engineering from University of Pune. He writes on society, politics, books and films. His writings have appeared in several newspapers and websites including *The Hindu, Mid Day, DNA, The Pioneer, Hindustan Times, The New Indian Express, Newslaundry, The News Minute, Daily O, Niti Central* and *Rediff.*

Sharma, Jai Kishan, Dr was born in Akura, Anantnag, Kashmir. He holds Master of Arts (M.A.) in Sanskrit and Doctor of Philosophy (Ph.D.) in Kashmir Shaivism from University of Jammu. He retired as Principal from Jammu and Kashmir Government's Education Department. His writings have been published in several literary journals.

About the editors

Siddhartha Gigoo left Kashmir in 1990 due to militancy and political turmoil. He studied English Literature at Jawaharlal Nehru University, New Delhi, India. He is the author of two books of fiction, *The Garden of Solitude* (2011) and *A Fistful of Earth and Other Stories* (2015), which was longlisted for the Frank O'Connor International Short Story Award 2015. His short story *The Umbrella Man* won the Commonwealth Short Story Prize 2015 for Asia. He has also written and directed two short films, *The Last Day* (2012) and *Goodbye, Mayfly* (2015), which were selected for several international film festivals. Two books of his poems, *Fall and Other Poems* and *Reflections*—written as a student—were published by Writer's Workshop, Kolkata. His writings have appeared in several literary journals. He lives in New Delhi.

Varad Sharma was born in Anantnag, Kashmir and grew up in Jammu. His family was forced to leave Kashmir in 1990 due to terrorism. He holds a Post Graduate Diploma in Management from Institute of Management Technology, Hyderabad and a degree in Mechanical Engineering from University of Pune. He writes on society, politics, books and films. His writings have appeared in several newspapers and websites including *The Hindu, Mid Day, DNA, The Pioneer, Hindustan Times, The New Indian Express, Newslaundry, The News Minute, Daily O, Niti Central* and *Rediff*.

Acknowledgements

Siddhartha Gigoo thanks:

Chander Aima, Anil Mattoo, Henna Amin, Neetu Razdan, Bhavna Gupta, Deepak Tiku, Seema Bhat, Jaspreet Raina, Manisha Prakash, Sanjay Kumar, Hari Nair, Saon Bhattacharya, Devarati Banerjee, Amrita Ghosh, Indrojit Chaudhuri, Vinod Veerakumar, Muhabit ul Haq, Sajeev Pillai, Tabassum Sheikh, Naila Inayet, Monika Kaul, Khalid Mir and Vivek Raina, for their friendship.

Pandit Bushan Lal Kaul and Pandit Anil Raina, for the music.

The Pillais (Ashok, Reenu, Arvind, Kaavya, Jaidev, Puja, Mahika and Khenesha), for support.

The Kouls (Henna, Rakesh and Aashray), for unbounded affection.

Sarla Gigoo (mother), Uma Shori Gigoo (grandma) and Omkar Nath Gigoo (grandpa) for prevailing during the 'darkest' of times and for the unfading and everlasting dreams and memories.

Sheba, for her presence.

Aishwarya Pillai (wife and fellow traveller), and Amia Gigoo (daughter), for everything that matters.

Varad Sharma thanks:

Deepak Bhat, Charan Kamal Singh, Anirudh Injeti, Mohit Jhawar, Mayank Chaturvedi, Akshay Bhandari, Kanika Sharma, Madhulika Appasani, and Mehmal Sarfraz, for their friendship.

Jagan Nath Sharma and Pushkar Nath Sharma, for their grandfatherly love. They are missed dearly.

Surinder, Ramesh, Rakesh, and the entire Pandita family, for their support.

Richa Sharma, Girja Sharma, and Veer Krishan Sharma, for their affection.

Sharad Sharma, for sharing the dreams and enthusiasm, and for being the best brother.

Santosh Sharma (mother) and Dr Jai Kishan Sharma (father), for their eternal love, unwavering faith, and for being the pillars of strength.

The editors thank Neeru Kaul, for her insights.

Special thanks to Muhabit ul Haq, Seema Bhat, Sanjay Tickoo, Vijay Dhar and Vijay Koul for photographs, and to Arvind Booni, Anurima Roy, Faiza S Khan and everyone else at Bloomsbury India for making this book happen.

A Note on the Cover Photograph

Muhabit ul Haq

The House of Shadows

In the autumn of 2013, I went to Aharbal in South Kashmir to take pictures of its beautiful and famed waterfall. The road was dotted with blazing poplars, willows and chinars. A riot of colours lit up the surroundings. People gathered apples, cherries, pears, peaches, plums and pomegranates that had fallen off the trees in an orchard. Young girls stood by the roadside selling the produce to tourists and passers-by. Men and women sang mirthful songs of harvest while working in the paddy fields.

In the evening, I stopped by Haal, an idyllic village where once Pandits and Muslims lived in harmony. A Central Reserve Police Force (CRPF) camp fortified the road leading to a cluster of abandoned and dilapidated houses that once belonged to the Pandits who lived there. The houses were in a ruinous state. The ruins stood like mute witnesses to the tragic happenings of 1990, when Pandits fled the village in horror. The ruins were homes once. Now, they are nothing but rubble.

An accursed hamlet, I thought, as I surveyed the desolation around. At the CRPF camp, I got the Commandant's permission to take photographs of the houses.

Among the ruins stood a deserted house with a wooden door and latticed windows. The nameplate on the door bore the name: *Madhusudhan Bhat*. I wanted to go inside but the house was locked.

A strange sight caught my attention. The vestige of a mud-brick façade that once was a house. Defiantly, it stood steady upon the grassy ground. There was no sign of the rest of the structure. As if it never existed. I took a photo, thinking that even this remnant might not survive the coming winter. Nothing of it might remain. It had one last story to narrate. The story of a family that once lived in the house. The story of how they lived and how they left. No one knew the family's whereabouts. No one knew whether the family members were dead or alive. I wished they were alive somewhere and dreaming of their home. I wished they would return to their house to save it from complete annihilation. The remnants of the house stood mute and bore a testament to the history of a forgotten clan. Not without reason did this fragile structure continue to exist. Year after year, the structure had summoned up all its remaining strength and might to withstand rain, hail and snow. It stood tall with dignity, waiting perhaps for its old inhabitants to return one last time.

Etched on the vestige was a fading memory of a home, of a family, and of the family's fortunes and misfortunes.

Behind this vestige was another decrepit house with no door. I went inside through the dingy corridor leading to what was once a kitchen. The floor, paved with debris, was uneven and cracked. A vision flashed past: *Women washing utensils and preparing dinner. Smell of cooking. Children playing pranks on their grandparents. Sound of laughter. A beautiful girl with dark lustrous tresses holding her brother's arm and leading him to her room full of treasure. They climb the stairs. As they climb, the stairs collapse one by one. They fall through a crack and crash against a floor full of glass and potsherd. A shriek.*

The half-broken staircase led to nowhere. A large wooden slab that once supported an entire floor stood on three wobbly columns of decaying wood. An earthen oven was strewn with broken bricks and clumps of hay. A shrub peeked through a crevice. A streak of sunlight entered through the ventilator and lit up a portion of the wall. On the wall, faint impressions concealed other stories.

I counted eleven such decrepit houses in the hamlet. The locals had spread cow dung and vegetables for drying around the houses. I tried asking them about the abandoned houses and their owners. Two Muslim families claimed to have been close to the Pandit families prior to 1990.

They sighed and reminisced about the times gone by. 'The Pandits were our brethren. We celebrated and rejoiced during their festivals. They did the same on Eid. After their exodus from this village, we lost a part of our lives,' said one person. Has anyone returned? I asked. 'Many sold their houses. Some came to see what's left behind. They hugged the trees in their courtyards and left teary-eyed,' said another man.

Pointing to some houses, the two men told me the names of the Pandits who lived there. 'Some Pandits returned to either search for their lost existence or to give it all away because it seemed impossible for them to resettle here and rebuild their homes,' they lamented. Who looks after the houses now? I asked. 'The houses in a better condition were taken over by the army for some time. Now the CRPF is keeping a watch.'

Seeing me take photographs of the houses, an elderly Muslim man came out of his house and stood next to me. Sensing my curiosity, he said, 'The people who lived in these houses left but we are still living in this hell.' The man seemed to be the lone witness to the once-glorious history of this village. I asked him if he remembered the day Pandits started leaving this village. I wanted to know what all had happened in the winter of 1990. How was life here back then? 'There is nothing I have to say,' the man said somewhat morosely and walked away.

I spent some time amidst the ruins. I sat next to the mud-brick façade and looked around. The ruins looked back at me. The remorse, the loss, the wait, the lifelong earnings and dreams of a people now gone... Everything that belonged to the Pandits was on the verge of obliteration.

The sun started to set. The yellow rays of the dying sun pierced through the broken windows of the mud-brick vestige. There wasn't a shadow. What lurked around were shadows of a people who were far away from their homes, yet desirous of return. I didn't want to leave the house that once was. It screamed: *Tell my family that I'm waiting for them. Tell them I don't have much time left. Tell them to touch me one last time before the snow buries me.*

I took a last photograph of the house, hoping that some day its old inhabitants will chance upon it and retrace their journey home. I fear going back to the village now. What if the House of Shadows is not there any more?

Muhabit ul Haq is a Delhi-based photojournalist